Stop Blaming Adam and Eve

John P. Foley

WESTBOW
PRESS®
A DIVISION OF THOMAS NELSON
& ZONDERVAN

WestBow Press books may be ordered through booksellers or by contacting:

WestBow Press
A Division of Thomas Nelson & Zondervan
1663 Liberty Drive
Bloomington, IN 47403
www.westbowpress.com
1 (866) 928-1240

ISBN: 978-1-9736-1464-7 (sc)
ISBN: 978-1-9736-1463-0 (e)

Print information available on the last page.

WestBow Press rev. date: 01/25/2018

ACKNOWLEDGEMENTS

My primary acknowledgement is to Donata Ardito Foley, my bride and joy. Without her love, friendship, and support for the past fifty-nine years, I would not have finished college, taught theology and philosophy for half a century, or more importantly, would not have been the father of five children and grandfather of eight; so thanks Babe...and thank you, Lord, for leaving us enough clues to find each other. Thanks also for our parents who first opened our eyes to see the wonder of life.

Thanks to our five boys and their wives and our eight grandchildren for filling our marriage with life, laughter, hope and happiness.

Thanks to the students and colleagues of Xavier High School, NYC, and Saint Peter's University, Jersey City, NJ, for fifty years of challenges, opportunities and growth as a man of faith, hope and love. You have made the Jesuit principle of "cura personalis" – care of the whole person – a reality in my life and have helped me to "find God in all things."

Thanks (for the past forty-four years) to the community of Immaculate Heart of Mary parish in Brooklyn, NY. Your friendship and your faith have confirmed our marriage and parenthood, my teaching vocation, and life.

Thanks to the five former Xavier students who regularly pushed me to publish: Rich Nolan '83, Joe Pierce '94, Greg Casimir '95, Anthony Sapporito '97 and Hani Sarji '98.

Finally thanks to my Bride, my granddaughter Micaela, my dear friends, Sister Liz Kelly CSJ, Mary Tesoriero, and Bob Brady. Their concern, corrections, and comments helped to shape the book in the form it appears.

PREFACE

This is a book about *humanity* – the significance of humanity in a world that far too often treats humanity as a prop, or a plaything to be seen as "something" amusing or somewhat useful at times. This taken for granted view of humanity sees as its importance whatever certain individuals or groups suggest is important. This relativistic view tends to categorize or stereotype humanity by gender, race, creed, color, physical or mental capabilities, or social, political and economic situations, arbitrarily assigning levels of importance to the different man-made categories. It overlooks the reality that humanity is *primarily* a gift…of life. This gift is bestowed on everyone who embraces humanity regardless of gender, race, creed, color, physical or mental capabilities, or social, political and economic situations. Humanity is a gift that transcends labels and categories. And the Life-giver is always involved in our gift of life.

I have taught in Jesuit schools for fifty years—twenty-nine as a tenured Religious Education teacher at Xavier High School in NYC and for fifty years as an adjunct professor in Philosophy at Saint Peter's University in Jersey City, NJ. My mantra has been the insight of the ancient Greek philosopher Socrates that "the unexamined life is not *worth* living." I subscribe enthusiastically to the Jesuit educational principle of "cura personalis"—the care of the whole person—because I believe that the human person is the most significant expression of God's creation—and to the Jesuit principle of "finding God in all things"—because I believe that God is the author of *all* life and seeking Him in tradition, innovations, and surprises makes life *worth* living.

My approach to teaching is to bother students to think by drawing primarily upon what I have learned—my Christian convictions, marital adventures with my bride and best friend, Dona, my experience as son and brother, father, grandfather, friend, neighbor and NY Giant football fan. (The latter keeps me humble, but, thanks to my niece, I did attend Super Bowl XLII and we weren't the team that was humbled.) I love the classroom because in it are people seeking to grow in wisdom and knowledge, people who resist growing, people who struggle to grow, and people hoping to "skate by" with minimal effort. It's the world. It annoys me when I hear graduation speeches that tell students they are going into the "real world." That's nonsense. Their high school and college years are prime times during which their life experiences, their developing of knowledge and understanding [apart from transcript grades], and their personal interactions will tremendously influence and deeply contribute to the persons they will become in life. This is because they are building on what their family upbringing has offered them, or they are rearranging what will evolve as their priorities. Through reflection, students become aware that most learning occurs after the classes are completed. People come to realize that what was really being taught were not simply various disciplines such as math and history, or literature and psychology, but how to deal with and appreciate what life will present by prioritizing what is important. It is the process through which teenagers, later on in life, come to realize that sometimes their parents really are smart. After all, humanity is a work in process.

This book is an appreciating of my own life's journey. It is a series of essays about topics upon which I have reflected and taught for years. I invite you to see how these same topics may relate to your own life. After all, we do share life together; so we can learn from one another. Over the years students have encouraged me to write on some of the ideas of which we have spoken and studied in class. The reason I have undertaken this challenge now is because, I believe, there is an increasing number of people, throughout the world, who have lost or who ignore the significance of the gift of our shared humanity. The gift of humanity, life, is the same for each one of us who receives it. The expression of each individual's humanity reflects the appreciation or the lack of appreciation for this generous freely bestowed gift.

Each essay, or chapter, is a self contained unit, but there are connections. Chapters four, five and six are an attempt to develop the ideas originated in chapter one, two and three. [Chapter 1] Humanity is a gift with a purpose. [Chapter 2] Because we are distinctively individual while simultaneously being social by nature, it is necessary for us not only to hear but to *listen* to those messages which are supportive and to those which are disruptive in our earthly journeying. [Chapter 3] Our humanity recognizes life includes strengths and weaknesses because the world is in process. [Chapter 4] Humanity and Divinity are related. [Chapter 5] God is not only creator but also a messenger. Will we *listen*? [Chapter 6] Life has not only an origin, but a goal as well. Are we up to responding to the invitation to appreciate the beginning and pursue the goal?

I have always viewed the educational process as primarily a positive experience. Towards encouraging such an experience, in the classroom I introduced "exercises in reflection' or "invitations to be great"— challenges to students to share their understanding of what they had been offered. As a teacher you can only invite students to learn and every invitation can be accepted or rejected. Through these essays, I invite the reader to reflect upon what is presented—courtesy of many people; family, colleagues and students who have contributed to my own educational and personal process—and judge how it may, or may not, contribute to one's own appreciation of being a human person. As a Christian, I think humanity, will all its bumps and bruises, is the greatest gift we have received because it is a gift which every human person shares.

I am a teacher; so throughout this book I will be passing along what scholars and non scholars have thought about the human person, God, good and evil, necessities and possibilities…in short, about life. My back drop, or point of departure, for the initial three chapters is primarily Old Testament scriptures. I will use historical figures as well as imaginative and contemporary figures to help us understand how origins are important and what they can lead us to discover. The first essay, *Stop Blaming Adam and Eve,* begins with origins of life acknowledging both evolution and creation. Philosophers rely on reason, on thinking things through, and theologians rely on studying our link to God and trying to explain why God would want to "hang out" with us in our contemporary "Garden of Eden." The basic premise is we are guests in the land God created. In chapters two and three of the Biblical Book of Genesis, we deal with "original grace" and "original sin." Finally we will deal with the "act of faith" that is Genesis one, the preface to the Bible, which was written four hundred years later. I address two perennial excuses we use to dodge responsibility for our actions throughout life. One is the "I am only human" copout which suggests that I don't know everything; so I shouldn't be held accountable for anything. That is disingenuous because my humanity is everything. I can't use it simply as a convenience or an excuse…I am my humanity. It's all I am! The second dodge seems to have begun in the Adam and Eve story. We know it as "passing the buck" or excusing our responsibility and shifting it to someone or something else. Is human nature an incredible unsolicited and generous gift or a taken-for-granted state in the process of life? We will have insights and images, both ancient and modern to help us to appreciate that the "Garden of Eden" is still with us today.

In the second chapter, *Don't Kill the Messenger,* I deal with the messages we receive and send throughout our lives, which are shaped by traditions, new adventures and the unknown. The messengers may be persons, events, nature, or the divine. Musical shows, atheist and theist philosophers, economists, fantasy characters as well as some of my college professors will help to appreciate messaging. The "Tower of Babel" story, the last of the Genesis creation myths, highlights the importance of not simply hearing the sounds people make, but listening to what they say. If our society is to function as it ought, we have to understand the messages. "Babel" or babbling is a contemporary reminder of the political and social unrest we are currently witnessing streaming from people not willing to listen to each other. In this essay we will distinguish between free will and freedom, teaching and preaching, between faithful believers and blind followers. I share the idea of the four great "No's" in life which have been included in the classes I have taught and will emphasize the significance of the individual. The prophets were probably the first people who preached "tough love" and weren't always appreciated. We are subject to many messages in life, often conflicting, but all of them necessary for our growth, individually and socially, and it is amazing to discover where we find God in some of them.

The third selection, *Why Me, God?* focuses on the reality that "life is not [always] a bowl of cherries"—even though at times it can be. The spirit of the sport of Rugby with its motto "no pain, no gain" is a companion to the Book of Job in which there is lots of pain before eventually there is plenty of gain. (I thank our rugby playing sons for this insight.) The eye-opening scene shows God betting on Job and Satan betting against him. What are the odds? Harry Potter helps us to understand Job's "dark night of the soul." The "Chronicles of Narnia" along with the Book of Ecclesiates and Psalm 139 help us to appreciate what unfolds. Referring to [Chapter 1] which identifies life as a process, I conclude that life is incomplete, not yet finished, not yet perfected, but still perfect as created. There is hurt including the pedophilia scandal in the Church that I love. Job's three friends begin with compassion for his plight, but end with condemnation. What happened? Three movies are considered which involve suffering, and how the characters address it. There are three personal experiences involving family, society, and a friend. Finally there are three lessons to be learned from the epilog to the Book of Job and to the psalms.

For the final three chapters, I include theological observations which should help to more easily understand the implications of the infancy narratives of Jesus (in Matthew and Luke's gospels), and His public ministry and the passion accounts in each of the four gospels.

The fourth essay, *Thanks for the Gift* deals with the surprise Christmas birthday party God throws for us with the "Good News" that He loves us so much He becomes like us. He embraces our humanity giving us a significance we would never have enjoyed. The promise of a Messiah, a savior, led people to expect a "new David," a warrior king who would drive out the enemy, currently the Roman oppressors. But Jesus comes as Emmanuel, God become man. What an acknowledgement of the significance of humanity! But, for some, over the years, this is news that is "too good to be true." For others, it's an eye opener…God became man! God became like us. How can that not be wonder-filled, and to use the word correctly, *awesome*? Thanks to St. Francis of Assisi, we have the Christmas crèche, or stable, which weds the infancy narratives of Matthew and Luke. We also have artists who help us to appreciate how wonderful an event this is, as well as Grinchs and Scrooges, and Christmas movies urging us to celebrate the wonder of humanity as

God's greatest gift. Over the years, so many shepherds and magi, writers and artists and believers, have helped us to appreciate this "holy night."

There's a wonderful song from the musical show "The King and I" in which a teacher is trying to know her students from a different culture. *Getting to Know You* is the song and title of this fifth chapter. The basic premise is "to teach is to serve." However, instead of the students as the object of the learning process, we will get to know Jesus, the Teacher. I selected eight scripture passages as messages which reveal Jesus' vision of life, His storytelling ability, His range of friends and what He expects of them. There are also His ideal of a religious person and the notion that actions speak louder than words. Calling upon Saints Augustine and Paul, I will deal with how Jesus manifests the virtue of hope. Finally, I will comment upon Jesus' friendly advice. Included are some questions Jesus might have asked in order to "bother" us to think...and to act... and to appreciate our humanity.

The final essay is entitled *The Price of Love*. It begins with "There are contemporary movies and songs which claim that 'love means never having to say you're sorry!" *Au Contraire!* The greatest expression of love in human history is Calvary's Cross, and sorrow is certainly at the heart of that scene. Maybe the deeper question ought to be: if love is associated with joy, with happiness, with friendship, then how can sorrow, or hurt, or pain or suffering be related to love?"

For the balance of the chapter, I try to shed some light on this phenomenon. There are three acts in the chapter: joyful, sorrowful, and glorious. The joyful act celebrates the family, mealtimes, hospitality, table fellowship, the Last Supper, the Eucharist. The sorrowful act identifies betrayal, abandonment, cowardice, torture, injustice, [both past and present] the crucifixion, and Jesus response: prayer and forgiveness. It includes Jesus acceptance of our sins in the utterance of Psalm 22: "My God, My God, why have You forsaken me?" It includes an ignominious death and the original Pieta scene where Mary holds her Son's broken and defiled body in her arms...just as she held Him in Bethlehem. The glorious act deals with the Father's acceptance of His Son's sacrifice so that we may be saved from ever being alone and for sharing our humanity through loving and being loved. It includes how the disciples, including us, "put our acts together with and through His love." Fulton

Sheen, Lumiere and Cogsworth from "Beauty and the Beast,' Aslan from Narnia and Saint Iraneus help to appreciate how to do this.

In life there are financial, political, social and religious distractions. There are individual character flaws that we feed rather than eliminate. Some are annoying and others frightening because we don't know what will happen or how those we love will be affected. Some seem beyond our ability to change, but all distractions can be addressed and, at least, made bearable. Some offer opportunities to advance and deepen our appreciation of life. This is true of history as well. There have been times of war and peace, times of famine and plenty. I wrote in the second paragraph (above), "I believe that the human person is the most significant of God's **creation**." We enter this world with the gift of life and are called into the **covenantal** friendship with God and given the responsibility to be the world's caretakers. We are the very special guests of a life giving God. How should we respond to show the incredible significance of our humanity?

In the fourth paragraph, I wrote that "[today]...I think there is an increasing number of people who have lost the sense of how significant our humanity really is." History can teach us about distractions and attractions throughout life, but the bottom line is that our contemporary experience will lead to fulfilling or failing as individual human persons. How can we not realize the significance that **Christmas** gives our humanity? God became like us and gave Himself for us in the **Crucifixion** so that we would always know there is *nothing* that gets in the way of God's love for us...except our refusal...which is a refusal to accept the significance of our *humanity*.

The Life-giver is involved in the life-giving gift of humanity. As an "exercise in reflection" I invite you to explore this statement throughout this book. Thanks.

CHAPTER ONE

Stop Blaming Adam and Eve

Years ago, I worked in the import-export business. All shipped products had to be marked with the "Country of Origin." The origin of any product offers information for the recipient. Products from certain countries or areas were considered to be of higher value than similar ones from other regions. Some countries or areas would be on restrictive lists, and therefore subject to closer legal and consumer inspection. The label served as both an evaluation as well as a warning about the product. Origins are important, primarily because they are informational.

When I was growing up, one of the initial questions upon meeting someone was: so, where are you from? You would answer with the city, or the neighborhood, or, in cases of Catholic or Christian people, the parish, which was located in a particular area. I grew up in Saint Rose of Lima parish in Washington Heights in New York City. Most parishioners would be blue collar families, of primarily Irish or Italian immigrants. Then the other person knows something about you. Your origins may reveal religious, economic, social, political, or even ancestral insights. It may be misleading or it might be insightful and useful information. We are cautioned about allowing first impressions to be lasting impressions. This is true because all our human judgments are subject to change based on further knowledge. This more developed, or new knowledge may result in changing your mind from being "turned off" by the person to gradually coming to see his or her attraction and accepting that person. That change will eventually result in either a closer bonding or an eventual rejecting of the other person.

If I were raised in a religious or social environment that viewed abortion or capital punishment as immoral, then I have been influenced by a particular moral viewpoint. If I study the issue by reading about it and speaking to others and become more firmly convinced that abortion or capital punishment are immoral, then my moral viewpoint has changed. It has deepened. Or further study may cast doubts on the influences of my upbringing and I may become convinced that abortion or capital punishment might be acceptable decisions in some instances. My moral perspectives have changed. Change, whether we are speaking about persons or issues may involve a deepening of past viewpoints, or substituting previous viewpoints with opposing ones.

Change is a staple in life and changing one's outlook on issues, or about people, influences how we come to view and value life. And yet, there are first impressions of both people and ideas and those impressions are shaped by our background and our upbringing. After all, we are social by nature. We can't really ignore them; so we should explore them. By the way, first impressions may be correct or may not be correct. Only time and the developing of knowledge will tell. You may really be the offensive person I thought you were when we first met. Or you may be the decent person I thought you were when we first encountered each other. I eventually learn that what I had thought, positively or negatively, can change over time. In any event, introductions to people or to issues are interesting whether or not they change as time passes. Human knowledge, like the human person, is always in process, and this process can lead to an ever deepening certainty about what is important in life. It can help to adjust our understanding; so that we are able to appreciate more fully the wonders we can discover on life's journey.

Both the theory of evolution and the Genesis Creation myths are stories about beginnings, our beginnings as human persons. Both seek to appreciate the significance of our origins. Darwin's work is found in his "Origin of Species." The Bible begins with the words, "In the beginning..." The authors of each theory or story claim that trying to understand beginnings are important, and yet there were neither scientists nor theologians present at the beginning. The scientific theory of evolution eventually formulated by Darwin speaks of the developing of plant and animal life by hereditary transmission with slight variation from generation to generation. The surviving forms become those that are best adapted to the environment; hence, the idea of "survival of the fittest." This phrase was originally coined by the Sociologist, Herbert Spencer, and eventually wed to Darwin's notion of natural selection. The scientific theory of evolution looks backwards to our roots as animal life adapting to the earth's environment. It identifies human expression as following from biological forms of life which preceded us. The religious story of Genesis looks at the source of all creation, including human life, involving a pre-existing God, a Divine Being, Who freely willed all other beings, human, animal, plant, and mineral into existence. Adapting to the environment in which we live and having a purpose to living life are both necessary and real concerns for anyone on life's journey. I think that "purpose" is the more important consideration.

Philosophically or reasonably we think of some life forms having a greater significance than others. Initially there is mineral life, inert life, which requires whatever happens to it to be done from outside; a source other than itself. We see this happening in our back yards. Rocks are simply rocks. We might move them or chisel away at them, or paint them, but they need an external agent to move them. Plant or vegetable life includes not only existence, but also the power, or potential, to grow and to reproduce. We plant seeds and look forward to reaping the benefits of what we have planted and what we have nurtured with our care and concern. Some plants survive and others don't, because after all, "Mother Nature" is involved and she doesn't always seem to be on our side, or to be very consistent from year to year. In this sense, I believe that plant life is "higher" on a scale of existence than is mineral life and yet both are life forms, whether one is a scientist or a theologian, or a gardener who is removing rocks in order to dig the soil and allow for plants to take root and grow.

The evolutionary process progresses from the plant to the animal kingdom in which the animal inhabitants not only grow and reproduce, but also are instinctive. They "know" how to respond to surroundings by accepting or rejecting what is offered. They respond to commands and acknowledge affection and react towards fear and danger. They adapt to their environment. They allow themselves to be exercised and fed, to be pampered and to develop a sense of belonging. I think that dogs and cats are among the more intelligent of the animal kingdom, and yet, I would not go out on a date with them, or go to a ballgame with them, or engage them in discussions about origins. Yet for many of us, as pets, they are of very special concern in our lives, far more than either minerals or plants. Whether looking at the evolutionary process or the religious understanding, humanity stands atop the pyramid of created beings. Dogs are not our best friends, other people are and that's why we differentiate between pets and friends.

Being able to think, to choose, to laugh, to decide, are among the qualities which characterize human being as distinct from other earthly life forms. These are among the reasons I believe that humanity is the most significant of the forms of life in our world. We have the greatest gifts, and with these come the greatest obligations, or responsibilities, not only for our human life but for *all* life. The consequences of using or misusing our gifts will change mineral, plant, animal, and our own human life, either for better or for worse. We are responsible for using as well as abusing nature's resources, and how all other created beings are affected. Man's responsibility for all created life is an ongoing challenge. Scientific application to nature's growing processes, for example, genetically modified plants, have clearly given rise to meaningful increases in world food production. Long term effects of genetically modified organisms, which are currently unknown, have also raised questions regarding how safe they might be. There are some concerns regarding human experimentation in nature's role in the food chain arena. Technological advancements have revolutionized the manufacturing of goods and services for all people. At the same time, they have produced worldwide economic difficulties which must be addressed. Then there are the dramatic shifts in weather patterns, brought about by manufacturing activities, which create climate changes affecting the quality of life for many people in many areas. Pope Francis' encyclical, "Laudato Si," is about our responsibility for taking care of our "common home," the earth and her resources. Humanity is clearly the most important of created beings because we can create, alternate, and eradicate aspects of the world [-] mineral resources, plant life, the animal kingdom, the human condition and the temporal and spatial boundaries which constitute the universe into which we have been invited.

To look at where we might have come from offers insights into life. I do not see the theory of evolution, which I reasonably accept, being the *more* significant of the human explanations of origins. If my significance is that I evolved from a lower form of life and that is my claim to fame, then I am not sure if I can claim much more than I "lucked out" when distinguished from the form which preceded me. And there still remains the difficulty of the origin. How did the beginning begin? If life as we know it began with the "Big Bang" then who is responsible for the "original" particle that was present for the expansion of the universe as we know it? It doesn't make sense that some-thing, the universe as we know it, comes from no-thing.

On the other hand, if my origin stems from a creating Being, from God, Whose concern is that I embrace the creation that has been made for me, then, I think, there is a greater significance for humanity. I have a value that stems from who I am and in what I do and eventually in who I choose to become, not simply into what I evolved. I contribute to shaping my evolving as a person. The Genesis Creation stories begin with the theological or religious explanation of the origin of life and looks forward to what unfolds. There are two distinct biblical creation accounts of creation and we will explore both which speak of our purpose and our special relationship with the Creator of all life. Both tend to look forward to what the human relationship to God could become.

This is certainly a simplistic description, but it is not incorrect. A simple explanation can sometimes be the best explanation. It is looking at the same object, *humanity*, from different perspectives, which don't cancel each other out, but together offer a broader understanding and appreciation of the nature of the human person. Is the significance of the human person dependent upon how well we adapt to nature or in how deeply we care for nature? For me the initial question is whether or not it makes sense to speak of some kind of being that is not simply natural; that is, a "being" which is not mineral, vegetable, animal or human? Both the scientist and the theologian must begin with human reason, with one's ability to think, to engage the world with the intention of developing understanding and drawing conclusions. I do not believe that the ability of the human mind is limited by what we can simply see and touch or what is immediately present to us. I do believe that the human mind is capable of appreciating and understanding, in varying degrees, what lies beyond or behind our sensory experiences. I think that human mind is capable of reasoning to the existence of a supreme being, distinct from nature and who, or what, exists as the source of all that belongs to what we call nature.

Having taught philosophy for many years. I value the gift of reason. To be able to think is our access to meaning. I believe that reason, or consciousness, or the mind allows us to understand and appreciate what we see, hear, smell, taste and touch. A philosophic argument, or proof, for the existence of a being beyond the existence of worldly beings is an exercise in reason. It tries to grasp the idea that time and space are not simply limitations but boundaries…and there is a beyond and a being responsible for what is, for what exists. One such traditional philosophic approach is called the cosmological argument. This argument or proof or evidence for the existence of a Supreme Being looks at the elements of our cosmos, or universe, and intelligently concludes that there is a source for our universe, which, or who, is distinct from the universe. This reasonable exercise, or proof for the beginnings of the world formally originates with Aristotle (384-322 BC.) Others developed and used this argument for understanding cosmic beginnings. Saint Thomas Aquinas (1225–1274) is acknowledged as the philosopher-theologian who formulated the argument as we know it today. The "Five Ways of Aquinas" are essentially reasonable attempts to understand, as far as possible, the existence of a distinct Being, apart from created beings, who is also the Creating God of the Old and New Testaments Whom we meet through divine revelation. Is the existence of a "Supreme Being" reasonable? Does the existence of God make sense? If reasonably, the answer is "yes" (and I think it is), then we begin the quest to figure out what humanity's relation to divinity is.

Briefly, Aquinas acknowledges five arguments, or reasonable ways, beginning with the idea that we can distinguish movement from the source of movement. The world is in motion, not simply local motion from one place to another, but growth in society as it deals with its citizens, or building up relationships in the world, or changing one's outlook regarding individual habits and values; in other words, all the varying kinds of external and internal movements there are in life. Trains or buses may be the source of local motion as we journey from one town to another. Employment opportunities may be the cause for a particular society to grow or to move forward economically and socially. Family and friends as well as specific talents many be the source of one's own personal growth. We recognize intellectually, that the source of movement or growth is distinguishable from the actual movement or growth. We experience a world in motion and intellectually distinguish a source responsible for all movement. Aristotle calls this source the *unmoved mover*. The moving world happens *because* of the unmoved mover who, or which, is itself not moved by any other thing.

The second argument is based on the idea that for every effect we experience in life, there is a cause which the intellect recognizes as different from the effect. The universe is an effect which reasonably suggests a cause distinct from the effect. This cause which is itself not the effect of anything else is named the *uncaused cause*. It is the cause of the world, but is not itself an effect of any other cause; hence, *uncaused cause*. The world in time and space happens *because* of a being both different and distinct from the world. The world as an effect exists courtesy of a cause distinct from the world – a cause which itself is not the effect of anything – an uncaused cause. We don't know, at this point, whether the unmoved mover, or uncaused cause, is personal or not.

All of the beings in the world, mineral, plant, animal, as well as mankind, come into and go out of existence. They depend on some being other than themselves for their very existence. We humans are contingent or dependent beings. All earthly beings depend on "something else" to exist. This third proof reasonably argues that there must be a being who, or which, *necessarily* exists in order to keep everything else in existence, and it must be distinct from any other being. The universe is contingent, always in motion, changing, dependent on some being which necessarily exists, a being which has always existed and always will exist. This *necessary* being does not owe its existence to "anything" outside of itself. I think these are the major reasonable or philosophic concerns in identifying our cosmos and a being responsible for its existence.

Just to "round out" the traditional approach, or Thomistic expressions, the fourth argument seeks to identify the *perfect being,* as distinct from all other life expressions in the great chain of being. We are not the source, or cause, of our own existence; therefore, we are imperfect. The "perfect" being necessarily exists and does not owe his, her, or its existence to any other being. The last proof, or fifth way, is referred to as a *teleological, or goal oriented, or purposeful* universe. The universe has purpose, which reasonably suggests the designer, the cause, the necessary being is intelligent. It is up to us to identify and appreciate the work of the designer by how the design is accepted. It is similar to viewing the world, the universe, as a work of art which is the result of the artist who is distinct from his work, just as Vincent Van Gogh is distinct from any and all of his paintings, and the sculptor Auguste Rodin is distinguished from any of his works.

I would like to comment on the philosophical arguments from causality (*uncaused cause*) and from necessity (*necessary being.*) These make the most sense to me. For every effect, there is a cause distinct from the effect. If reasonably, I view the natural world as an effect, I understand there is a cause for this effect which is distinct from the world. As a religious person, I believe God is the cause for the existence of the world in which I live, but I am also a reasonable person. I have identified what is reasonable to me (there is a cause for the world's existence) with what I believe (there is a God Who created, or caused, the world.) When I view the natural world as constantly changing, as coming into existence and going out of existence, as living and dying, I acknowledge that the world is contingent, that it and everyone and everything in it, is dependent on something or someone distinct from this changing universe. There must be something or someone whose existence is necessary in order for nature and the universe to remain in existence. Minerals, vegetables, animals and humans cannot guarantee their own existence from one moment to the next; so there must be some kind of being that does. This (other) being must be able to guarantee his/her/its own existence; so that our natural universe can continue to exist in time and space. It makes sense that something, anything (human existence, the natural world or universe) cannot come from nothing, but rather depends upon the existence of a *necessary being*, which doesn't depend on anything outside of itself. He or She or It always existed and always will. This *cause* of nature, or *necessary being* for natural life to come into existence and go out of existence to be replaced by other natural beings, is claimed by the human mind as a reasonable explanation for the existence of everything, including us. I believe that Aristotle's "uncaused cause" and "necessary being" are philosophic terms for the source of this natural world and the life found within its boundaries. Reason certainly suggests there is more to existence than what we can experience and demonstrate. I think that reason confirms the great chain of being [-] from mineral to vegetable or plant, to animal, to human, and ultimately to a Supreme Being, known as God in most of our cultures.

The next question, for me, is: what is the nature of this primary cause, or uncaused cause, or necessary being? Is it personal or impersonal? If impersonal, can there be any significance in the different levels of natural existence? I think it is reasonable to say that humankind, with our ability to think, is more significant than animal, vegetable and mineral life. The ability to understand and create, to develop and protect is greater in humankind than other forms of natural life. I am aware we don't always act as we should, but that is not the fault of our nature, rather it is the refusal of some of us to appreciate our human nature by not exercising our responsibilities to other natural beings and to the world. My conclusion is that this primary or uncaused cause, this necessary being is a person, a divine person, a person we have come to call God. I think it is reasonable to say that a personal God is the cause of our natural world and is the being necessary for the world to exist from day to day. I have come to believe that this God is the creating God of the Old Testament Who becomes the Redeeming God of the New Testament. In what follows I will attempt to support and share this conviction as reasonably and passionately as possible.

The above does raise the question of the relationship between faith and reason. I do not think that faith and reason are the same. I can understand a situation without being reasonably convinced one way or the other about its value. I can hear two political candidates arguing for different approaches to a social or economic issue and not be sure that either has the correct approach. Each might have a reasonable understanding of some points, or they may have "missed the boat" on the entire issue. I can understand people deciding to live in this neighborhood rather than another one, based on economics. I may agree or disagree, but my own final decision has to *convince* me rather than simply offering debatable reasons. As a teacher, I might choose one approach to a course over another one, but once I choose, I must believe in its effectiveness to make a difference in students' lives. I do not think that faith and reason are simply opposed to one another. It is reasonable to believe in a particular political, environmental, or a religious movement. It makes sense to trust some people and to commit oneself to a cause. I wouldn't have this conviction or make this commitment without it first making sense, or being reasonable and thus allowing me to understand what is involved in my decision making. However, once I make a commitment or become convinced then I have moved beyond simply understanding and beyond the reasoning process. I now agree with a movement or a person and this is a judgment which will result in further action on my part. Faith builds on reason and goes beyond it by free choice and through committing oneself by action. Reason leads me to understand that there is a source for all life which is distinct from life itself. Philosophically, I am comfortable with the idea of an uncaused cause or necessary being. Theologically and religiously, my conviction is that the God of the Old and New Testament meets the reasonable criteria of "uncaused cause" and "necessary being" and is the personal creator of Genesis and the personal Redeemer proclaimed in the New Testament. God makes sense to me and I believe in God revealed through the historical Jesus, Who becomes the Risen Christ! Reason opens us to wonder, to speculate, to reflect. Faith calls us to act, to bond, to commit.

Before one begins any project, it is a good idea to understand some ground rules, or procedures to follow. The purpose of rules is essentially to have some guidance; so that we may be able to understand more clearly what it is we are studying. Before one goes to visit a foreign country, it makes sense to have some useful phrases available so that one can more easily maneuver through different customs and experiences. This can make the experience of exploring a new country or a new culture more rewarding. The same can be said for trying to understand and appreciate the Genesis Creation accounts, which is our focus. My background is not as a scientist, but as a teacher of religious and philosophic knowledge. I don't ignore the scientific, but I do consciously embrace the religious. This is not a bias on my part, but a choice based on what is more reasonably attractive to me. Bias has the connotation of a prejudice and prejudice involves judging without adequate knowledge of what or who is being judged. I acknowledge there are both scientific and theological approaches to the beginning of life. They are not identical, and I do not think they contradict each other. I admit that I am not as concerned about the age of the world or the universe as I am about the people whom I encounter in my own life's journey, which by definition is both temporal and limited. In what follows, I have chosen to focus on the theological, or religious, approach, without ignoring that the evolutionary approach exhibits valid scientific knowledge. After all, I hope to evolve as a more caring and spiritually concerned person as I journey through life.

In trying to appreciate the Genesis creation stories, the ground rules point to a single content to the Bible with many forms through which this content is expressed. The content of the Bible, the Old and the New Testaments, is theology. Theology is described as *the study of God, revealed in time and/or history, and the human response which eventually is "yes" or "no" to God, acceptance or rejection of God, or faith or disbelief in God.* Any "ology" involves studying. Biology involves studying living things and psychology involves studying the "psyche" or mind, or consciousness. Sociology involves studying the individual as a unit of society. Anthropology involves the study of man, "anthropos," in Greek, and so on. The biblical content of theology is expressed through various forms in the Bible. There is myth in Genesis, legend in Genesis, legality in Numbers, poetry and prayer in the Psalms, history in the Deuteronomist's and the Chronicler's stories, and other forms of literature, such as the letters of Saint Paul to different communities, the four gospels and the apocalyptic literature of the Book of Revelation. Throughout all these forms or ways of expressing, the content is theology.

11

The first form of writing we encounter is *myth*. A *myth* is an imaginative, dramatic, poetic story that tells us something about the human condition. In contemporary times, the word myth suggests some kind of fantasy of unknown origin which is a fabrication about life. This is not true. A myth is a literary form. When the Bible was first put into writing, there were no short stories, or novels, or twitter, or Youtube, or any other form of expression with which we are currently familiar. In order for the audience to appreciate the stories, they were often told in colorful language which would help people to "get the point" of the story. Most people could not read and there weren't any resource libraries as we know them. The audience remembered the stories which were dramatically and poetically told about life, and passed them along from generation to generation. This is how any people or culture developed: there are the stories or experiences which take place in historical time and real space. Then these stories are handed down to following generations by word of mouth (the oral tradition) and finally put into writing (the written tradition.) And so it is with the Genesis creation myths or stories which make up the first eleven chapters of the first book of the Bible. While there are specifically two accounts or descriptions of creation, there are other stories which flow from the Adam and Eve myth, and together they constitute what we refer to as the Genesis Creation Stories or myths.

The initial Genesis creation story, the "anthropological account of creation" is more familiarly known as the "Adam and Eve" story. It is a story of mankind's beginning, chapters two and three, and is followed by the "Cain and Abel" myth, the "Noah" myth, and ends with the "Tower of Babel" myth in chapter eleven. These stories include the creating of humankind and our evolution, our friendship with the Creator God and then a "falling out" through what theologically is called sin and its consequences. The second written creation story is found in Genesis one, written four hundred years later. It deals with the cosmological creation of the world by God. It is the story of the world's origin. Genesis one is the preface to the Old Testament.

Most people can recite the details of the Adam and Eve story. Genesis two depicts God creating mankind, represented by Adam and Eve, while Genesis three tells the story of mankind's fall from grace, with humankind's break from companionship with God. With an assist from the serpent, Adam and Eve are banished from the Garden of Eden. Now let's take a closer look not only at what the author wrote, but the meaning of the story for us today. My bride, Dona, and I married in 1958, in a Catholic Church, and the Adam and Eve story means something to us because our marriage is meant to be a reflection of this "covenant story." The author is a theologian, not an historian, not a novelist. He (or she) is writing about the relationship between us and God. He (or she) is not an eyewitness, but rather is trying in a very imaginative way to describe the original relationship that existed between mankind and God and how that relationship continues today. It is looking at the past reasonably and faithfully in order to appreciate more fully the present. This suggests that we rely on those who preceded us for understanding relationships, but we can go beyond them by how we fulfill, or live out, our own interpersonal relationships. These are biblical first impressions, and without them, we couldn't have gone much further. The covenant into which Dona and I entered should be a reflection of the Adam and Eve story, because, after all, our marriage should have some of the elements of the Garden of Eden, and hopefully, we will not succumb to being less than our relationship calls for and will not, as Adam and Eve did, move "East of Eden" in our own relationship with God.

In Genesis two, God creates the human person in the form of Adam, who is placed in the Garden of Eden, previously created by God. God takes the clay of the earth and breathes into it, forming the first man. This is the basis of the duality of the human person. Each of us is material, or natural in being with the earth, but simultaneously distinctive because we are the only created beings who are also spiritual in nature [-] the breath of God is within us. We are both a part of the world (material or physical) and apart from the world (spiritual.) As physical beings, we are capable of being scientifically understood, and as spiritual beings we are capable of religious appreciation. The mystery of the human person is that we are embodied spirit, not just body and not just spirit. We are truly material beings, part of the matter of time and space, but we are also spiritual beings who are gifted with the breath of God in us. How wonderful is that?

I acknowledge that we can speak of a "spirit" or life force in plants and animals, but I do not think they are comparable to human spirituality. The difference is that we are conscious and capable of developing our spirituality in a manner that plants and animals cannot. Hopefully, I will develop this clearly in the chapters that follow.

Adam is given a task or a purpose which is to take care of the garden and to name the different species. It turns out that Adam is less than thrilled to be the only human being, (my conjecture, of course) and this brings us to a wonderful insight into this creation story. Each one of us is incomplete by himself or herself. Psychologically, this means that each of us needs others in order to be fully developed human beings. The key word is "need." By myself I am incomplete as a human person. The reality that I need others in order to be myself implies that, by nature, I am meant, designed, and purposely created to be "social" by nature. Yes, I am as individual a person as Adam is in this creation account, but our individual humanity is not meant to claim separateness from everyone else. Our individuality is distinctively our own, but that does not mean each of us is isolated from others. Rather it means that I am incomplete and need to be completed in and through various relationships with others. Even the hermit needs other people in order to try to separate himself from them as much as that is possible.

Without parents, I would not be a son and a brother. Without my bride, Dona, I would not be the husband, father, and grandfather that I am. Our psychological and social dimensions of existence involve all the occasions in life which shape and reshape the persons we eventually become, no matter how many years an individual journeys in this life. Among other considerations, to be human means to be incomplete, to be not yet finished, not yet perfected, and to be in some kind of process which will eventually complete me or not. This incompleteness is not a negative aspect of the human condition because it offers the possibility of achieving varying degrees of personal fulfilling through our relationships with others. This is part of the meaning of this biblical theologian's story. We are called to complete each other through the developing and sustaining of our personal interrelationships. That is why Dona and I married. We were called to complement each other as clearly as Eve was called to complete Adam. Without Eve, Adam is incomplete and therefore not as fully human as possible, and vice-versa.

While the author of Genesis two through eleven is unknown by name, he or she is referred to by scholars as the Yahwist author. The primary reason for this is that he refers to God as Yahweh. And Yahweh, Who brought Adam into his human existence, now involves Himself in Adam's seeming dilemma: his incompleteness, his imperfection. The story unfolds with God taking a rib from Adam's side and using it to create Eve. The theologian author is very insightful. Eve is not formed from Adam's head, which mythically or poetically might suggest that woman is meant to dominate man. Nor is she taken from Adam's foot, which mythically or poetically might suggest man is meant to dominate woman. She is taken from his side meaning that side by side man and woman are meant to walk through life as companions, to complement each other, to complete each other as humanly as possible. We need others in order to be ourselves means that the ones with whom we walk through life are the ones who will most contribute to our completing ourselves as human persons. To put it another way, we need others in order to fulfill ourselves as individuals. Without Eve, Adam would never have been able to address his incompleteness as a human person, or fulfill himself as an individual. He needs her in order to become the individual he can be, and Eve needs Adam for the same purpose. And they complete each other, and fulfill God's purpose by the generous passing on of the gift of life to the generations who follow.

It is important to note that religious language is more like poetry than science. Religious language points beyond itself; it is not supposed to capture life in any kind of a precise situation, which is the nature of mathematical and scientific language. When I send a Valentine's Day card to my bride, I speak in poetic language. I speak the truth, but it is much more romantic to describe her as a blossoming flower than someone who is quantitatively measurable by a specific physical height, weight, and density. If I do, then I had better be ready to run and hide. The flowery language is not only true, but appropriate and yet my bride is not a plant either. If, as a ballplayer, I am pulled out of a football game because I could not block the opposing team's defensive end, what is my excuse? I tell the coach that the guy wearing number 97, on the other team, is as strong as an ox and as fast as a cheetah. My coach is not going to imagine an opponent leaping faster than some animals and devouring the quarterback before he can pass or run. But I will have made my point and probably resigned myself to sitting on the bench for the rest of the game as the coach tries to figure out how to protect our team's quarterback. Religious language tries to capture the meaning of the transcendent in earthly terms. Like poetry, it aims at making the sublime an immediate reality.

God is also an "other" person to us. The human person comes into existence, into time and space, but he or she can only do that thanks to the power of another being who already exists, who is eternal. We refer to this personal being as God. Mankind does not have to exist. You and I do not have to exist. Each of our lives is a gift. For the eternal being, existence is necessary, not contingent or dependent on any other being. That certainly distinguishes an eternal person from temporal persons; namely, ourselves. But if each one of our lives is a gift, it suggests that God is not only eternal and creatively powerful, but also a giver of gifts. One who gives a gift to another does so out of generosity, out of care or concern. That is the nature of gift-giving. I care for you and I want you to have this present or gift. If a gift is not given out of generosity or concern or care for the other person, then the meaning of the gift is distorted. It is no longer a gift, but a perversion or a trick. The gift of life is given to each of us by Someone Who cares. I believe that rather than having a right to life, I am privileged to be alive. My life is a gift which is to be God's guest in this journey of life. Whatever rights I possess come with the gift and the most significant rights are the powers to think, to choose, and to share life.

In Genesis two, it is clear that God's concern for Adam and Eve goes beyond the gift of life. They are companions in the garden. It is not as if God created Adam and Eve and then left them to figure everything out for themselves. He is available to them. He is familiar with them, He is family. (The roots of "family" and "familiar" are the same in Latin.) Yahweh walks in the garden with them. There is a relationship between God and humanity, a friendship. The theological term is *covenant* which is the relationship between God and us and is based on unconditional love between each other. Unconditional means no conditions, no "buts", no "ifs", no "untils", no "as long as". These are all words which imply conditions. I will be your friend "as long as" you drive me to work. I will support you "if" you continue to say I am the best person you have ever met. I will work with you "until" I no longer need you. God lovingly created Adam and Eve as surely as Dona and I created the love relationship of our marriage and confirmed it at the altar of Regina Pacis Parish in Brooklyn, New York. The two great insights we find in Genesis two are that we are called to *complement each other* in our earthly journeying because each of us is incomplete by himself or herself, and that from the beginning we are meant to *live in familiarity* with God. This is the essence of the covenant, of friendship. The original covenant begins with the friendship between God and man and woman. Marriage is the covenant between husband and wife and God. The purpose is the same. Contemporary marriage is a reflection of the original covenant.

When Dona and I married, we entered into a covenant, not a contract. A contract involves conditions. I will do this, *as long as*, or *if*, you will do that. I will work for you and you will satisfy this contract by giving me a certain amount of money. As long as you fulfill your work requirements, then as your employer, I will compensate you with salary and with benefits. A contract is conditional with the conditions being satisfied by both parties to the contract. Marriage is not a contract. Marriage is a covenant, because it aims at an unconditional attempt by each party to care for the other, no matter what. That is the hard part [-] *no matter what*. It essentially says that you are more important, or significant, than what you do, and I will honor that. Even if our careful planning does not unfold as we had hoped, your lover's care should be the primary purpose in any relationship. That is as true in Genesis two as it is in marriage, whether the marriage takes place in Church, in a synagogue, in a mosque, or in a municipal building.

There is another element in Genesis two, the "tree of the knowledge of good and evil." God tells Adam that everything in the garden is for his nourishment except this particular tree. To eat from this tree is to bring death. This could present a difficulty. Why would God Who has freely given the gift of life to humanity, who has addressed Adam's "aloneness," and who is their companion, would create "something" that is dangerous, or, at least, potentially dangerous? This seems to be "something" that could interrupt or break the friendship that exists between them. Let's see how this plays out, especially after we take a look at the second part of this story, Genesis three.

I think that one of the very sad misunderstandings of the Adam and Eve story is that most people identify it primarily with their fall and their banishment from the garden. Too many people focus on Genesis three and overlook Genesis two. They resonate with "original sin." I can certainly understand this dwelling upon "sin" and "sinfulness" and "evil" and "temptation." I have lived through World War II, the "cold war", the Korean and Vietnam wars, the assassinations of Martin Luther King and the Kennedy's, the scandal of Nixon, the horrendous destruction and deaths related to the events of September 11th 2001, the Iraq and Afghanistan wars, as well as the immoral actions leading to the recession of 2008 for which there has been almost no responsibility demanded of those financial and political people who caused it; so I can appreciate those who are angry or disillusioned or even negative towards life. I don't live in a third world country with its added poverty and more terrible injustices which further unfairly burden so very many human persons. And yet, as a Christian husband and father, and as a teacher, I know that it is very important at times to take a step back, to "retreat", to take a closer look at what we might have overlooked or taken for granted and see if there might be something more substantial in our roots, in our past, that might help us today to see greater possibilities for life in the future. After all, we should learn from the past in order to appreciate the present and plan more hopefully for the future. Beginnings are important. Without appreciating beginnings, the rest of the story might not be fulfilling.

Most of us are familiar with the story as it unfolds in Genesis three. Evil, in the mythical form of the serpent, tempts Eve to eat of the fruit of the Tree of the knowledge of Good and Evil. The tempter claims that this will enable her to be as knowledgeable as God. Adam joins Eve and then there is a realization (pangs of conscience?) that they have done "something" to damage their relationship with God, and they hide themselves. God looks for them and finds them. They admit what they have done (and here is where "passing the buck" began.) Adam blames Eve who blames the serpent and the "blame game" is instituted. Unfortunately, the "blame" game thrives today when so many people excuse themselves from responsibility for actions done or for actions which should have been done but were not. By the way, it is not simply Eve who sinned, which is why we have the unjust subjugation of women in so many times and areas of history. In Genesis two, we saw that the complementing of Adam with Eve acknowledged not only their individuality, but also the reality that they, and we, are social by nature. Being social by nature and being familiar with God identified both their and our significance. In Genesis three they complemented each other in turning away from their friend, God, and asserting their own interests, which didn't involve their *necessary* friendship with Yahweh. They blamed each other and walked away from God.

There probably hasn't been a war declared in human history, or a negative social or political situation which did not include blaming the other side for starting it. Think of our recent financial crisis, which is blamed on people who lacked credit but bought houses, and on people who invested in the various money and commodity markets with monies they did not own in order to make more money they did not deserve. Adam and Eve are banished from the Garden of Eden and seemingly tossed out on their own. Traditionally, this "original" sin has been identified a sin of disobedience, and among others things, it is, but it also certainly involves betrayal of friendship, and that leads to terrible consequences, no matter what the situation is. They betrayed what it means to complement one another by rejecting their familiarity with God. They denied who they were called to be, which is what we do when we sin, when we break the relationship with God by breaking the relationship with each other. We deny the significance of the person we reject, whether that person is God or a spouse, a parent or a child, a sibling or a friend, a teacher or a student, a neighbor or a stranger. This happens in war, in social, economic and political situations, as well as in interpersonal relationships.

There are a number of fascinating aspects to the Adam and Eve myth, which really is our story as well. I would like to focus on three related questions. The first deals with the nature of sin. What is the "danger" of sin in our lives? I have previously stated that throughout history we have tended to focus on "original sin", the Genesis three part of the story. What is sin? Essentially it is the theological or religious term for the breaking of our relationship with God by how we harmfully treat ourselves and others. The human person has the power to help or to hurt by what one says and does, or by what one chooses not to say or not to do. We can build up ourselves and others by our words and our deeds, or we can use them to tear down ourselves and others. Sin is essentially the tearing down of a relationship which previously existed. This is what we are missing when we reflect upon the Adam and Eve story. There could be no sin in Genesis 3 if it weren't for the relationship (the covenant) created in Genesis 2, which is really the story of *"Original Grace."* The theological term "grace" refers to the lived friendship between God and us. This is what is damaged, broken by the actions of Adam and Eve, by our actions in today's world. Does God care? Well, in freely creating mankind, in responding to Adam's and to our "aloneness", in "hanging out" with Adam and Eve in the garden, Yahweh made clear his love, His care, His concern for all of us, for all mankind, for all womankind, for all created persons.

The refusal to accept God's love, the rejection of God by man is mythically, poetically, dramatically expressed by the "eating of the apple." The sin is not the actual "eating of the apple", rather it is what this action represents, or symbolizes. The leading characteristics of Genesis two are that God created us so that we could complement our fellow man (complete our fellow man or woman by how we interact with them) and live in familiarity with God (from the beginning God made us so that we could enjoy His love by the choices we make in life.) This is what Adam and Eve, what we, reject by our freely chosen attempts to tear down a relationship instead of gracing it or accepting it. The "danger" of sin in our lives is that we choose to reject God's original offer of love by substituting what we *desire* rather than what we *need* or how we *ought* to act. It is a refusal to complement our fellow man and a rejection of God's familiar companionship. When I reject your love, the consequences are going to differ from my accepting your love. It is clear that Adam and Eve rejected God's love [-] then [-] but what about now? How do we reject, or accept, God's love today? Let's stop blaming Adam and Eve for what we fail to do today! Adam and Eve knowingly and freely rejected God's companionship and so do we through our choice to sin. We refuse our invitation to be welcomed guests in the garden of life. Although we have had more opportunity to understand and appreciate what this entails, it excuses neither Adam and Eve nor us.

The idea of being social by nature involves interrelating with others. We influence others and they influence us. I am sure most us have been advised at some point not to associate with certain persons because they may be a bad influence on us. We are cautioned to avoid certain risks in life which could lead to being hurt. We know what the warning means, whether we listen or not. To reject God's influence, to sin, means that we are turning away from God being part of our lives. Who then replaces God in our lives? The influence people have on us and likewise, the influence we have on other people involves the development of attitudes and habits that might very well differ from what we should view as important. This should also bring about different behavior patterns in our lives. To sin means more than simply breaking a commandment at a particular point in time; I stole someone's wallet; I lied to the principal; I disrespected my parents. Sin is *not only* about a particular action, *but also* about the developing of particular attitudes, and given Genesis two, the attitudes will result in not complementing my fellow man and woman and in not wanting to be friends with God. In other words, to sin means to act contrary to our nature, the purpose of which is to complement each other and live in familiarity with our Creator God. It is the absence of love which should naturally exist between people. Instead of reflecting God's love, it is a deflecting of God's love.

To get a glimpse of how a sinful attitude results in more terrible and destructive actions, we need only look at what happens as the result of a sinful attitude escalating in the remaining stories of the creation myths, Genesis four through eleven. Cain murders Abel (Genesis 4). This particular action is more terrible than Adam and Eve's. Murder is more damaging because it unjustly ends another's earthly journey, taking away any possibility for that person to love, to grow, to forgive and be forgiven. The significance of the individual always stems from his ability to understand and to choose, and choices have varying consequences. We may understand Cain's jealousy, but we should not agree with it, and clearly we should not condone the action Cain took. Would Cain have developed this bitter attitude unless Adam and Eve had failed to complement God's friendship? In the Noah story, (Genesis 6) the basis for God's call to Noah is the general or public immorality rampant at the time. Sin has damaged the human condition not only by its more terrible actions, but also by how it has publicly spread. We are not simply speaking of sinful individuals but of a sinful society. We remember the sinfulness of the Nazi party prior to and during World War II which resulted in the horror we know as the "Holocaust." Or we might consider the hatred and bigotry of one group of people against another group, whites and blacks, Jews and Christians, northerners and southerners, Irish and English, Sunnis and Shiites, rich and poor. You get the idea.

Sin involves some people trying to hurt others because they don't agree on what is important. They might claim a false superiority over others, or an equally false inferiority before others and seek to lash out and make them suffer. We are social by nature and that means that our attitudes and choices can become malignant causes of reaching out to hurt rather than to heal. Would the Cain and Abel story and the Noah story have happened unless Adam and Eve denied their relationship with God? The short answer is "no." The longer answer involves choices that put more and more people at odds with themselves and push more and more people into saying "what's the use" of reaching out to others because they may hurt instead of help you? When we withdraw from others, they become people with whom we are less concerned. What happens when there is as much, or more, hurt in the world than there is healing? No matter how much we may try to hide from the hurting world, there will be newspaper and newscasts and social media accounts which will continually remind us: God's people are hurting. What should I do?

The Genesis myth of the Tower of Babel story (Genesis 11) has a dual purpose. On the one hand, it shows how sinful attitudes lead people to refuse to listen to each other. They become unwilling to communicate with one another and hence unable to work with others for the common goals and the common good sought by each society. Why didn't the Catholic hierarchy, or at least some of them, hear the cries of those who were abused by pedophile priests? Why didn't American politicians hear the cry of immigrants trying to better their family life? Why didn't political leaders in Third World countries share with the poor what international businesses brought to their countries? Why do so many rich people hoard their possessions instead of sharing with the disenfranchised, with the outcasts of society? Why are so many of us bitter about what others have rather than being more appreciative of what we have? Life becomes meaningless. There is nothing we can share, nor is there any hope for what we could possibly accomplish together because we refuse to listen to each other. We cannot even begin to relate without communicating meaning between ourselves, but because God refuses to give up on us, there is hope. The myth also serves as a transition to the next section of the Bible, the patriarchal history of the Jewish people (Genesis 12 – 50) beginning with the call of Abraham. This will lead to the enslavement of the Israelites, the Exodus and the Sinai covenant between God and Moses and His people. The Old Testament story reflects the story of so many different peoples throughout history.

God continues to reach out to us. He simply renews the covenant with the people who have rejected Him, by bonding with a particular group, the Israelites, in the hopes they will lead all of us back to the God Who made all of us. The sin of Adam and Eve became the groundwork for the sinful condition that permeates the world. However, the sinful condition in our world is not the only condition. Just as Adam and Eve, in the mythical story, could have rejected the serpent's temptation, so can we. Sin involves choice, and that means we are not helpless in the face of sin. Sin has become part of the human condition, a part which does not determine who we become, but which does hinder us in our growth process, and in our evolving as persons capable of loving one another. If we choose to let a sinful attitude, such as greed, or envy, or malice, become a priority in the choices we make in life, then complementing our fellow human beings and living in familiarity with God doesn't happen.

This is what is expressed in the Cain and Abel, Noah, and Tower of Babel stories in the opening eleven chapters of the Book of Genesis. This is what goes on today in our contemporary societies, and only the names have changed. If love becomes the possibility for hope, for growth, and for friendship; then fear and hatred become the possibility for hurt, for dominance, and for destroying the other person. If fear and hatred wins out, then the purpose of Genesis two (Original Grace) is lost, or, at least, temporarily broken. If love triumphs, then the covenant established between God and us is alive and well [-] as it should be.

A second interesting, and somewhat worrisome aspect of the Adam and Eve myth is that " The Lord God made various trees grow that were delightful to look at and good for food, with the tree of life in the middle of the garden and the tree of the knowledge of good and evil." (Gn 2: 9) Why was the Tree of the knowledge of good and evil in the Garden? If there were no tree, then does that mean there would have been no temptation, and if there had been no temptation, would we have lived happily ever after? No. This tree mythically represents the power of choice, and good and evil are the consequences of choices made by people who are both blessed and burdened with free will, the power to choose between alternative courses of action. The tree represents possibilities. What this suggests is the world created by a loving God is a world in process. Ours is a world that is not yet completed, not yet perfected. It is a world in which God has called us into a relationship that deals with His created world. We are created to be caretakers of this world. Adam and Eve were meant of take care of the "garden" while complementing each other and "hanging out" with God. God created the world, the "garden" and Adam and Eve, His friends, were called to take care of things. Just like us! It is a *perfect* world as created with us in it as caretakers. Another term for care or caring is love. A loving God creates us to love each other and to return His love by caring for whom and what he created. This gives us a purpose. If the world were created as *perfected*, meaning that it is without possible blemish, without any need for concern, then there is no need for our caretaking. There is no purpose for us. We would have no significance if there were nothing for us to do. There would be no subjective value to us. And yet there is.

We make choices and this leads to consequences. The consequences are that our choices help or hurt others. Adam and Eve choose to reject God's concern for them by "eating of the fruit" of this particular tree. The question for us is did God put this tree in the garden to "set up" Adam and Eve for a fall, or did He try to counsel them, advise them, that this tree represents potential harm for them? Was God trying to entrap Adam and Eve and if He were, then where is the love? If God were trying to advise them, warn them, to counsel them that this is a situation in life that can be harmful to them then He is doing this out of love for them and for us. This is entirely consistent with everything that goes on in Genesis two, God's concern for all of us. This is an interpretation of the "Tree" that is consistent with Original Grace, with the covenant between God and us.

Why do we give advice to people in life, especially the kind of advice that warns them to avoid certain courses of action? Is it because we believe that it will be harmful to them? The world is not yet perfected; that is, the world is not without the possibility of harm. Yet the world, like our humanity, is what we have, and where we are, and that is good. With goodness in life, we should appreciate and develop it. We are not meant simply to be spectators in life, but caring guests. Unfortunately, the possibility exists that we may not help. Whatever our advice might be, it doesn't guarantee it will be the best action to pursue or the possibility exists that our advice may be refused. We offer this for people we love. They may or may not accept our advice, and whether they do or they don't, there will be consequences. The Tree of Knowledge deals with the moral decisions people make which have consequences for themselves and for others. It symbolizes the challenge each of us faces in our life's journey; will I be *care-full* in tending to God's creation, or will I be *care-less* in the way I treat myself and others?

Why did Adam and Eve stop listening to God? It's a good question and one that can only be answered if we reflect upon why we stop listening to God. After all, we live in our own Garden of Eden in the sense that, just like our first parents, this is all there is.

Oh, our Garden of Eden is probably not as pristine as the Genesis authors imagined; ours is complicated and busy and filled with much more diversity and many more distractions than the original myths depict. Our Garden of Eden has urban and rural, national and international boundaries. They are the cities and countries in which we live. Our contemporary garden is where all of our earthly actions and activities happen, both those that are wonderful and fulfilling and those which are destructive and lead to failing relationships with others, including God. Sometimes, through ignorance or malice, we let our Garden of Eden rot and decay, and we abandon it. At other times, we have to clear the weeds which threaten the possibilities for growth, and begin again to work at the developing of all that is fruitful in life. We all know how persistent weeds can be; so nourishing and cultivating our garden is an ongoing activity. Sometimes, there is simply a need for pruning, for trimming unnecessary hindrances to our harvesting and sharing more generously our abundance with others. Or maybe, mistakenly or hopefully, we look for a different Garden of Eden. No matter where our garden in this life is, it will still require our complementing our fellow man and living in familiarity with God if we are to express our purpose in life, which is to love one another as God loves us.

The author of Genesis two and three, the Yahwist author, is writing about beginnings well into the history of the world. Scholars place the writing of Genesis two through eleven around 950 BC, during the reign of King Solomon. Israel as a nation was prospering at the time and the Yahwist theologian was putting into written form what had orally been handed down by their Jewish ancestors. It was after the Egyptian captivity (circa 1500 – 1300 BC), the exodus (circa 1275 BC), and the settling into the Promised Land (circa 1200 – 1000 BC). The Yahwist reminds people that beginnings, or origins, are important and is presenting beginnings to emphasize the significance of their roots. They are meant to be with God from the beginning of life, they need others in order to become themselves, they sinned and turned their backs on God, and they were saved by the God Who has always loved them. The influences on my life include my Catholic upbringing, my marriage to my best friend, my being a father and a grandfather, my being a teacher in the twentieth and twenty-first centuries, but the basics of creation are similar; I have been meant to be with God from my birth, I need others in order to be able to become as fully a human person as I can. I have sinned, and I have been redeemed by the God Who wants to be with me and wants me to be with Him. Genesis speaks to us in the same way it addressed the people of the Yahwist author's audience. We live in the Garden of Eden today and the tree of the knowledge, of Good and Evil, is still with us. What we do about it leads to a grace-filled life or a sin-filled life, just like Adam and Eve, except we are contemporary. We choose through our actions to complement our fellow men and women and to live in familiarity with God in our own Garden of Eden, or we sin, and (to use the title of John Steinbeck's book,) choose to go

"East of Eden." We leave the Garden because we reject it, by rejecting God's friendship.

Given that I believe God did not "set up" Adam and Eve with the Tree of Knowledge, then the third question arises: what did He do for them, when, through their choice, they were mythically exiled from living in the Garden of Eden? This was the consequence of their action. Let's look more closely at what God did *for* Adam and Eve after they sinned, rather than what God did *to* Adam and Eve. Viewing the events of Genesis three, we can identify a sequence, or a process. The relationship was broken, there were consequences, and there was a response by the injured party. The theological approach is to identify the sequence as: *sin - punishment - forgiveness*. I agree with this; however, we run into a difficulty with the punishment aspect. The initial interpretation would seem to be that Adam and Eve (mankind) sinned by disobeying what God told them regarding the "forbidden" fruit. They didn't listen to God, whose concern was that they wouldn't be hurt. Then God punished them by banishing them from the garden because they didn't listen to Him. And then God forgives them. Why?

Let's explore this. God punishes…then…God forgives. It certainly fits **IF** the Tree of the Knowledge of Good and Evil were put into the Garden of Eden to set up Adam and Eve. **IF** they don't eat of the fruit of this tree, they pass the test and God is okay with them. There is nothing broken; so there is no need for forgiveness. **IF** they do eat of the fruit of this tree, then they fail and God can "sock it to them." If I test those whom I love to see if their love is genuine, then my love is not genuine. I understand that punishment is a valid aspect of the quest for justice in the world when its purpose is not simply to hold someone responsible for actions, but also to encourage rehabilitation…to offer the "defendant" an opportunity to change his or her lifestyle for the better. Usually we can distinguish the punisher, the punishment, and the punished.

As a teacher, it is necessary that I express the virtue or value of justice in the classroom. Do I treat all the students as fairly as possible? Do I have favorites? Do I let some students slide by while holding the rest of the class to all the requirements identified in the syllabus? Certainly there are some students whose needs and abilities and, in some cases, circumstances differ from others. Am I aware as a teacher of these needs and do I address them in such a way that I am not unfair to the class as a whole? I have ministered in Jesuit education (high school and college) for half a century. The Jesuit (Society of Jesus) approach to education includes the notion of "cura personalis", which is, the care of each individual student. I acknowledge this approach with no reservations, but putting it into practice with consistency is no easy feat. To what extent do I try to get to know my students; so that I can appreciate their strengths and their weaknesses as much as is humanly possible? If a student fails to do what is required then as teacher I administer the punishment, a failing grade. I can be seen as the one who punishes, and yet that was, and is, never my intention. My intention in the classroom is clearly to bother the students, but to bother them to think, because thinking is necessary for making the decisions in life that ought to be made. I can't live their lives for them, but I can and I ought to influence them in varying degrees. They make choices in life. I have the responsibility of informing them of possible consequences to the choices they can make. The value of each of my students depends on how they *form* themselves, using in part the *information* which I and other teachers, including parents, family and friends, offer to them. Their significance (or lack of significance) as persons emerge through their responses to life throughout their individual journeys. Education is not "value-free" because of the responsibilities each teacher has to contribute to students' recognition of their own values and talents in life. And yet, there is no guarantee that either I, as teacher, or they, as students, will always be successful. This is as true for the thousands of students whom I invited to learn, as it was for Adam and Eve in the Garden of Eden, as it continues to be for me and for my family.

I do not think that the Tree of the Knowledge of Good Evil was set up in the Garden as a test. In the same way, I do not think that Judas was set up in the Garden of Gethsemane to betray Jesus with a kiss. I do not think I was set up by God at the times in my life when I failed as a husband or father or teacher, to be as loving a person as I could and should have been. For this reason I do not see God as punishing Adam and Eve. Sin – punishment –forgiveness is the theological terminology for what happened in the Garden of Eden. The sin part is clear. Adam and Eve did not accept what God offered and that constitutes a rejection of the other person, God. They broke the relationship. They sinned. The mythical expression of the sin is the "eating of the apple" which involves them freely succumbing to the temptation of Satan, the snake, the animate expression of evil. You can be equal to God is the temptation offered. This means that you don't accept who you are and in not accepting who you are (created by God), you reject the relationships formed. I refuse being made "in the image and likeness of God" because I want to be "equal to God." In deluding myself that I can be God, I refuse my own humanity, my own individual being. I don't want your love, I want your power. I don't want to be who I can become because I want to be who you are.

If I don't accept who I am, how can I ever meaningfully reflect on my strengths and weaknesses? How can I ever grow, if my primary concern is to be who I am not? The mythical expression of the "eating of the apple" is Adam's and Eve's, and our rejection of God's companionship. This aspect seems clear. The mythical expression of the "punishment" part needs a little study. Punishment connotes pain and suffering. Who brought this hurt into the covenant relationship between God and Adam and Eve? Adam and Eve did by choice. They brought pain and suffering into the relationship through their actions. The banishing from the Garden is not so much the result of God's choice, but the consequences of their breaking the relationship with God. They, like us when we reject God, bring pain and hurt [-] punishment [-] into the relationship. When I lie, when I cheat, when I mock and ridicule, when I steal physical things or ruin someone's reputation or livelihood, when I rape or murder, I am the one breaking the relationship with another person. I am the one who is the cause of the hurt and the pain which the relationship suffers. The degree of hurt and pain reflects the horror of the sin (which is why Cain's sin is more terrible than Adam and Eve's sin.)

God is not the punisher here; God is the injured or innocent party. The consequences of our original parent's sin, of humanity's sin, is the breaking of the covenant and the hurt they introduced is the punishment mythically expressed by losing their place in the garden. You can't break a relationship unless it already exists. Genesis two is Original Grace, the living out of a love relationship between God and man. The ones who choose to break the relationship are the ones who bring hurt and pain, the punishment, into the relationship. If I offend you by my actions, then I am the one who hurts you. If I fail to support you, then I am the one who disowns you. I am not only the offender, the sinner, but I am also the source of the punishment in the relationship.

What occurs next is: what will be the response of the injured party? If you are my friend and you hurt me by word or deed, then I have choices. I can seek revenge through some overt action or perhaps by never speaking with you again (ignoring you) [-] or [-] I could forgive you. Adam and Eve broke the relationship and they brought the pain and suffering into the relationship, which is mythically expressed by the banishment from the Garden. The response of God, the injured party, was to forgive them, which is mythically expressed by clothing them in preparation for their journey. In addition, God makes a promise to Adam and Eve and through them to us. He promises that good will triumph over evil. Life as created is good and no amount of human evil will overcome or destroy the goodness of God's love which is the cause of, and the hope for, all human existence. God didn't give up on Adam and Eve, and He doesn't give up on us. But the covenant is a relationship and relationships require both parties to contribute or it isn't as alive as it could and should be. Our own human experiences confirm that it is possible to love another person without that love being returned. It is painful, but possible. However, since love, by nature, is a relationship, a "one-sided" love affair will always fail to become what it could be. Throughout the rest of the Bible we come to see that God's promise to Adam and Eve, to humanity, is fulfilled in God's own time, (and we will deal with that in the final chapter of the book.)

Sometimes I think that we would like God to be the "heavy handed" person in this creation account. After all, what can I do? God is in charge. He creates, He judges, He punishes, and here we bring an element that is so important in the "pass the buck" blame game. After all, *I am only human.* This can be one of the all-time self pitying statements when it is designed exclusively to excuse me from responsibility. I'm only human. What can I do? God is in charge and there's not much I can do. He punishes me and I have to take it. I think this follows from concentrating on Genesis three, our fall from grace, and completely and conveniently, and unfairly overlooks the significance of Genesis two, the story of

Original Grace. The primary concern of the Yahwist author is on the establishing of the covenant between God and us. From the beginning we are called into unconditional friendship with the God who freely created us and loves us so much that He wants us to take care of the world He has created, not as slaves but as people He loves. Do I really believe that or don't I? Maybe the only sin in life is the refusal to accept who I am: someone who continues to be loved by the God who fashioned me and gave me the purpose of complementing my fellow companions on this earthly journey.

But, I am only human. Instead of using this phrase as an excuse, we should explore it. My humanity IS who I am. My humanity IS all I can offer anyone. Instead of excusing myself from my obligations in life, maybe my primary responsibility is to discover who I can become, to identify my strengths and my weaknesses, to recognize that I am never alone because the God who made me is always concerned about me. Maybe this is why the words of Socrates and Plato, the ancient Greek philosophers, are so important: *The unexamined life is not WORTH living!*" The key word is WORTH. My significance, my worth, my value in life ultimately flows from how I respond to others throughout my life's journey, whether the journey has lots of speed bumps and potholes, or is as smooth as a newly paved roadway. I can never begin to appreciate any value to myself unless I reflect; and it is in my reflecting that I can become aware of what is worth-while as well as of what is use-less. (" Flecto," " flectare," in Latin means to bend..."re" means back...so reflection involves the bending back of the mind in order to understand "something.") Reflection allows us to think again about persons we have met and experiences we have had and do something positive about them now, even if I failed to see their value in the past.

Looking back, or reflecting involves not only who I am, but also who I could become. If sin involves the refusal to accept who I am, then the primary temptation in life is be "less than I could be" as a human person. I am only human becomes an excuse not to reflect, not to care. There is no "magic fruit" in life from which we could take a bite and be someone other than we are called to be. All the self-help books in the world are useless if I do not put into practice the kind of person I have been created to be. Self reflection, choice, care and concern are meant to be characteristics of the human person. This is no different for Adam and Eve, or for Socrates and Plato, than it is for us. Original Grace means that I recognize and appreciate that by myself I am incomplete and therefore need others to complement, or complete me, and that I am meant, from the beginning, to be familiar with God Who gives me life. Perhaps this is why we ask God, in the "Our Father" or Lord's Prayer to "lead us not into temptation, but deliver us from evil…" The temptation is to "sell ourselves short," to think that we are less than what God thinks we are. In creating us, God never intended that we journey through life alone, or without support. That is why love is first and foremost a relationship.

For years, Dona and I worked in our parish Pre-Cana program. Its purpose is to help engaged couples prepare not for the wedding, but for their life long committing in marriage. The program begins with viewing marriage as a covenant, an unconditional friendship between husband and wife, rooted in the significance of Genesis two, the story of Original Grace. The program further explores *communication*, coming together as one in understanding (if not always in agreement); *sexuality* which involves the complementing of man and woman not only physically, but psychologically and emotionally as much as that is possible; and then *spirituality*, which raises the question of how alive (spirited meaning aliveness) I am to the presence of God in my life. We know what a spirited game or a spirited party is: they are ones in which we are involved through rooting for teams or enjoying the company of others. We are with others "in spirited" connections or involvement. We complete the program by exploring marriage as a *sacrament*. A sacrament identifies a human expression or pursuit as holy by consciously bringing the presence of God into its exercise.

The initial sacrament of Baptism involves welcoming someone new. It is not only a human welcoming, but God is involved in welcoming the person into the community we call the Church, the community of God's people. The welcoming is made holy by consciously acknowledging God's presence. The Eucharist involves nourishing and it is God who nourishes us. This nourishing takes on a holy or sacramental aspect by consciously being aware it is God's presence we receive in Communion. The sacraments of Penance and Anointing of the Sick involve our personal need for healing both spiritual and physical frailties, as well as acknowledging God's willingness to redeem us. God is involved in the healing. The sacraments of Confirmation, Holy Orders and Matrimony relate to our willingness as followers of Christ to witness to His love and life by how we live ours. We know that actions speak louder than words and these sacraments are opportunities for us to express our Christian lives; so that others can be touched by the presence of God. Marriage involves friendship and the married couple at the altar call upon God to witness to and be a part of their married friendship. The sacramental experience is ultimately a personal interrelating with God. Sacramental people are those who are aware that God is intimately involved in their lives. Genesis two which deals with original grace is a foreshadowing of the sacramental relationship we have today with Our Lord.

To return to the Pre-Cana program, one of the more important communication questions we asked the engaged couple involves their reflecting on their own worth as human persons. We ask them: what does it mean for you, now, to be a man...to be a woman? The questions are clearly related to the idea that I am only human, and it is my humanity that I am offering my spouse for the rest of our lives. After all, marriages are made on earth, not in heaven. If I don't understand or appreciate what it means to be a man or a woman at this time in my life, then what am I really offering my spouse? Marriage is the most intimate of human friendships. Without self-reflection, without choice, or awareness of a personal value system, what am I really offering the most significant person whom I will complement and expect to be completed by throughout life? Vows are serious messages.

Adam and Eve overlooked this. They sought something "magical" to fulfill themselves by ignoring their own friendship with God. Many married couples also seek something "magical" to get them through life without acknowledging the author of all life, God, their creator. By the way, very few couples could answer the question of what it means to be a man or a woman, because they hadn't given it much thought. That was the purpose of the question. To get each of them to reflect upon their own meaning; so that when they called upon God to witness to their marriage, they had consciously started their complementing of each other. The great thing about the question is that it accompanies us all through life and is never fully answered until death, when there is no more time to reflect. At death, there are only the consequences of how I lived my life and whether the life I lived expressed some meaningful reflection. Death acknowledges whether or not I came to appreciate my humanity as the wonderful gift God intended.

If we can understand friendship, I think we can understand the covenant and marriage. To become friends with another person involves the A, B, C's of life. It involves in the course of time, *acceptance* of the other person for who he or she is. Unfortunately, in our contemporary society, acceptance is usually identified with agreement. And here we begin to see the connection with Genesis two. Agreement is connected to conditions. As long as you agree with me, I will be your friend. Agreements are the basis for contracts, but neither friendship nor the covenant is based on the conditions which must apply to any contracts. Friendship is meant to be unconditional, just like the covenant as it is described in Genesis two. Acceptance goes beyond agreement. The significant challenge in any friendship involves whether or not I accept you, even when I don't agree with you in certain situations, or on certain decisions. We are not talking here about each other's interest in sports or movies or food, but in what is crucial to holding our relationships together and encouraging us to grow. What should be the values we share in life? How should we express what we claim is valuable? How do these practices affect our relationship? How am I complementing you?

Benevolence is the second characteristic of friendship, marriage, and the covenant. *Bene volo* means to will the best for the other person even at my own expense, whether the expense is in time, effort, worry, concern, or appreciation. Do I put you and your considerations before any of mine, no matter how important my individual concerns happen to be (and my concerns are most important to me because ultimately I am responsible for who I become)? How much am I willing to surrender of my own interests in order to address yours? To will the best for the other person is more than wishing the best for another. I wish you well, which doesn't involve any further particular action. If I wish that we would win the lottery, I buy a ticket. There is nothing else to do. Then it is a question of chance or luck. To wish is not the same as to will. To will the best for the other means I decide to act in such a way that your concerns, fears, or hurts are more important than any of mine. This includes whether mine are more or less important. You take center stage. Perhaps the issue of compromise enters into this characteristic of friendship. I will the best for you as long as this does not compromise my integrity as a human person. This means that I will not prostitute my own values simply to please you, but I will call upon my value system to help, to counsel, to support and to love you.

The third aspect of friendship, marriage, and the covenant involves *committing*, since life is an ongoing process. To commit myself to the other person in the face of an unknown future is either the most incredible act of personal involvement because it is based on trust and hope and love, or it is completely stupid because I do not know what will happen tomorrow. Committing to another person highlights the vulnerability of love, and the mystery of the human person. It is certainly heroic and honorable. It is the stuff of which martyrdom is made. Without knowing the circumstances of tomorrow, you are claiming that the person to whom you commit yourself is more important than whatever may happen in life. That is what happened in the Adam and Eve story. God committed Himself to mankind, to us, freely and without reservation. This is the covenant [-] God's friendship with all of us [-] the unconditional committing of God to us [-] through the story of Adam and Eve. There was no committing by God to us as long as we don't eat of the "fruit of the Tree of Good and Evil." There were no conditions on God's love, God's friendship. The Old Testament and the New Testament witness to God's ongoing forgiveness and concern for His people when we are faithful and when we are not so faithful. This is why the covenant has always been the basis for Christian marriage and for human friendships. Marriage should always be more important than the wedding just as friendship should always be more important than any particular experience which might challenge the relationship or which might enhance or develop the relationship. Marriage is simply the most intimate of human friendships. This is the nature of "Original Grace", of the Adam and Eve myth in Genesis two, the covenant model.

This covenant concern is not limited to the creation accounts, but we'll explore it further through prophetic messages, through Job's "conversion", through Jesus' birth, His public ministry and His suffering and death on the Cross. God's love for us is not a one shot deal that began and ended with Adam and Eve. To sum up the first written account of creation in Genesis two and three: God freely creates us to complement, to complete each other in our shared earthly journeys and from the beginning commits Himself to be with us always, whether we are with Him or not. This anthropological account of creation shows that we have the possibility of accepting or rejecting God, and, of course, this is done through accepting or rejecting ourselves and others. God is a familiar part of our temporal journeying in life. This is as true for every person born today as it is for the author of these words, as it is for my contemporaries, as it was for the Yahwist author and for all who preceded him or her. Today's Garden of Eden is similar to the one in which Adam and Eve made their decisions. They didn't make our decisions. We make them. We are certainly like them insofar as God made us and calls us to the covenant friendships. We are responsible for the decisions we make and for the consequences which follow. We can learn from Adam and Eve but we cannot hold them responsible for what we do and why we do it. As the saying goes, "The buck stops with us!"

What I would like to do now is to reflect upon the "other" creation story. Genesis one is the cosmological account of creation. This is the preface to the Pentateuch. The author provides a preface once the story has been written, because it is the overview of what follows: a general introduction to what has been written, or to what will develop or occur. The author of Genesis one is called the Priestly author. We don't know who he is, but we do know he is responsible for editing these first five books, namely Genesis, Exodus, Leviticus, Numbers, and Deuteronomy. It is significant to note that Genesis one was written around 550 BC, some four hundred years later than the Yahwist author's writing of Genesis two through eleven. Some will point out similarity of themes in both accounts, especially the goodness of God's creation and the establishing of the covenant relationship. However, the historical developing of the Israelites during these four hundred years point, I think, to the Priestly author's creation description being a wonderful *act of faith* in the God Who called them out of slavery in the land of Egypt. Genesis two and three were written, based on the oral tradition handed down over the generations, around the time of King Solomon while the Israelite nation was growing in economic and political strength and prosperity reigned throughout the land. In the ensuing four hundred years, because of political infighting, the earthly kingdom split into two separate kingdoms. Eventually the northern kingdom was destroyed by the Assyrians who in turn were conquered by the Babylonians. A century later, the Babylonians crushed the southern kingdom and the Israelites were enslaved in Babylon.

This time period included the rise of the prophets who preached the message that turning away from God involves dire consequences while fidelity to God will bring the rewards of the covenant friendship. We will hear more about them in the next chapter. Eventually, the Persians lead by Cyrus the Great, conquered Babylon and set the Israelites free. It is around this time (600 to 500 BC) that the Priestly author edited the Pentateuch and introduced the "cosmological" account of creation, Genesis I, a declaration of faith in the God who never abandoned them, even after the people had turned their backs on Him and tried to live as if they didn't need Him. The author writes around the ending of the Babylonian captivity and the return of the remnant of Israelites to Jerusalem to begin the onerous and terribly sad and challenging task of rebuilding their home, Jerusalem, which had been destroyed and leveled years before. It is not written in the glory days of King Solomon, but amidst the woes and burdens of a remnant of the people recently released from captivity and without much hope, or resources, for the future. Their primary desire was to rebuild the Temple, their place of worship.

The creation themes are the same: the world is created by God and it is good as created; God calls the human person into the most significant of relationships, a love relation; and the human person is the only being of all God's creation who is given a specific purpose: each of us is called to be a caretaker. The story of Original Grace as part of the Adam and Eve story contained identical themes, but what makes Genesis one so significant is that everything has changed for the Israelites. They are neither economically prosperous nor politically powerful and yet the faith conviction of the ones who returned to Jerusalem is still unshaken in the God Who made all [-] and what God has created is good! When life is going well, to praise God highlights our thanksgiving and joy. When life is not going well, to praise God underscores our fidelity and hope.

I think that Genesis one is an act of faith because the author, in the face of the few historical accomplishments and many disasters reiterates and emphasizes the love of God for His creation. The people of God have long since persevered throughout the Egyptian enslavement, endured the Exodus experience, and more recently had risen to some political and economic achievement. However, their secular prizes jeopardized their relation with Yahweh, sacrificed their unity as a people by dividing their earthly kingdom, succumbed to earthly foes, and now they have returned to their desolate and destroyed land in the hopes of rebuilding both their earthly and their heavenly relations. They could only undertake this task if they truly believed that God loves them, no matter what the current social situation happens to be.

I think it is wonderful that the Bible begins with an act of faith in Genesis One and concludes with an act of faith in the Book of Revelation. This last book is an apocalyptic expression which contends that despite the trials and tribulations of the first century Christians at the hands not only of their Roman persecutors, but also of the Jewish leaders, who ostracized them from their places of worship God is with them in their hour of need. God does not abandon those whom He brought into creation, no matter what the particular contemporary times present. After all, God's love for us, His most significant creation, is unconditional and therefore, timeless.

Unlike the very earth-focused story of Adam and Eve, the Genesis one story is the writing not only of a scholarly person, but one with great imagination. It begins with God depicted as Spirit, or wind, or breath, creating form out of what is formless, creating an orderly universe (the meaning of cosmos) out of chaos (disorder or formlessness), giving life to what is void of life. It is this universal life giving form which is as creative as when we create friendships. The creation is unique, intimate, and life giving. In the creating process, God begins to form this universe, separating light from darkness, and land from sea. He adorns this material universe with plants and animals while saving the best for last [-] the human person [-] us. It is like watching an artist designing a magnificent work of art, or a maestro conducting a beautifully moving symphony. From works of division to works of embellishment, the world takes on its wonderful forms and shapes. The sun and the moon and the stars decorate the skies overhead, while the fish fill the seas with life and plants grow to nourish and to adorn. Animal life fills the hills and the valleys. God's artistry is at work, and it is His final masterful stroke [-] the creation of the human person [-] who gives the cosmological canvas its most spectacular and awesome beauty.

Whenever I reflect on Genesis one, especially on the creation itself, I like to think of places and scenes which remind me of how wonderful this world is meant to be. I can remember the first time we visited Muir Woods on the western side of the Golden Gate Bridge in San Francisco. We drove up a winding road early in the morning with our friend, Father Bill Wood SJ. Parking the car, we walked a distance into the woods and stood transfixed. The sunlight, filtered by the majestic heights of the redwood trees, revealed the true meaning of "awesome." (I cringe whenever I hear this wonderful word abused by so many people in ordinary conversation. Most of the events in life are not awesome but ordinary, which in and of themselves can be amazing; but there are some sights and events which allow the human person to pause and be awed by the majesty of creation.) Muir Woods was like standing in a cathedral illuminated by some kind of angelic light. There was a quiet reverence to the scene that made us realize what God has created is good. There was a blending of power, the redwoods, and beauty, the sunlight, which needed no comment from us. It simply called us to appreciate where we were standing and what we were seeing. This was one of the few times in life where I felt small, but not insignificant. After all, I am part of the magnificence of creation.

On another occasion, we were cruising in the south Atlantic. The ship's captain announced that he was turning off the running lights for a minute; so that we could gaze at the night sky without distraction. It was a visual miracle. Looking up at the stars and constellation soaked sky was a wonderful invitation to accept the power and majesty of God's artistic gift to us. We couldn't name the constellations or the configurations; we could only look and admire. We venerated God's creation without a word. When visiting friends in Callicoon, in upstate

New York, we would walk to the top of a hill around midnight and stand in awe of the magnificent work that God created in decorating the night sky with thousands of twinkling stars. Uninhibited by the distraction of large city lights, we could only imagine that we were viewing the very same creation scene that our ancestors viewed a long time ago. We felt a kinship with those who had gone before us.

We have been privileged to see what people have created in cooperation with nature. Visiting Taormina in Sicily, especially on the feast day of Corpus Christi, leaves you shaking your head in admiration. The decorated family shrines line the streets advertising the covenant between God and us. The illumination tour of Paris at night is another unforgettable visual memory. It shows the best of what humankind can accomplish working with God's materials. The darkness of the night is enlightened by the brilliance and the architecture of man-made buildings and monuments, like the Eiffel Tower, the Arch de Triumph and Notre Dame Cathedral. These sights reveal the hand of God's caretakers at work. The Brooklyn Bridge, which spans the East River in New York City, Michelangelo's "David" in the Academia in Florence, the Cathedral of Our Lady at Chartres in France, with its magnificent Rose Window, the Sistine Chapel in the Vatican, and the wineries, castles and towns of Tuscany are some of the wonderful man-made additions to nature that we have been privileged to see in our lives. But nothing compares with Muir Woods or the nighttime view from the ship in the south Atlantic, or the Cliffs of Mohr in Ireland as you look out to sea, or the Atlantic waves pounding the rocks along the coastal village of Nazare in Portugal, or sunrise and sunset at the Grand Canyon. These reveal hints of the power and the majesty of God's creation. These are scenes which help me to appreciate the cosmological account of creation in Genesis. For me, it offers a wonderful appreciation for His creation of the world. Why do so many of us lose our sense of wonder? What God has created is good! The fashioning of nature is a gift which too few of us take the time to gaze upon and simply appreciate in all its glory.

But, of all the creatures to whom and to what God has created, only the human person is made in His image or likeness. While this is a beautifully poetic statement, it is the most important insight into life because it partners us with God in a way no other creature is bonded.

We are "imago dei" [-] made in the image of God! God is freely creating all that comes into existence. For the human person to be created "imago dei" means there is a unique relationship between God and us that does not exist between God and any other creature. We are saddened when earthly relationships fail. They are usually created by us in the hope of a fruitful and long life experienced together. But we do know that some relationships fail, however unexpectedly...and yet, what Genesis one tells us is that we are created out of love and for loving. This means that even if some human relationships fail to blossom as they could, we are still loved by the God Who will always consider us His *special* creation. Isn't this the first principle of Social Justice? The first principle listed is the principle of "Human Dignity." Every person deserves dignity because we are made in the image and likeness of God. While this is not always practiced in life, it is what we can expect from our Creating God.

Our purpose in life is to take care of all He has created... "*have dominion over the fish of the sea, the birds of the air, and all living things that move on the earth...*" God created us to take care of His wonderful creation. This is probably the first ecological statement ever made. Dominion is entrusted to us not for the purpose of enslaving creation, or misusing creation, or raping natural resources as has happened in the name of economic and political development, but rather for the purpose of caring for what God has generously bestowed upon every man, woman, and child ever to be brought into life. It bothers me when I hear of corporations trying to patent plant and animal life, and even the human genome, as if, what God has created can be claimed by man and business to become products for profit. Patenting life as a business practice is misusing the creation offered to all of us to enjoy and explore. When we create, whether something useful, or a work of art, or a friendship, we entrust it to those we love, whom we hope will care for it as much as we do. It is the same in this creation account. God freely created the universe and called the human person, made in the image of God, to be His caretaker. He created us, humanity, to care for the world, to use it wisely and never to abuse it.

For mankind to be caretaker, the human person must possess *reason* to understand what could be done, *free will* which is the power to choose from different possibilities what should be practiced, and to be *social*

41

by nature so that we can interact with each other to exercise the shared responsibility of taking care of creation. To have a purpose or a goal means that there is "more" to life, to each one of our lives, than simply existing. Another meaning for being a caretaker is to be a lover. Taking care means to love. When I look at the cosmological account of creation, I understand that being made in the image and likeness of God means to have the power to freely create love relationships. What is God doing throughout Genesis one? He is freely and lovingly creating a world, a single unity or universe for all of us to appreciate, and we can only fully appreciate life by caring for what has been entrusted to us [-] the physical world from the valley to the mountain [-] plant life which nourishes us and beautifies our surroundings [-] animal life whether on the land or in the sea or in the air [-] and finally all human life, including friends and strangers [-] in short, with all of God's carefully crafted creations. We share God's universe and image God by the width and depth of our care for all He has created.

I am a Christian. For me, the New Testament builds on the Old Testament, the foundation or the covenant. Later on, Jesus will tell us to love one another as He (the Son of God) has loved us. The love story begins with Genesis one and continues throughout all the biblical stories to the Book of Revelation. But it starts here, with the creation accounts in Genesis one and two. The cosmological and anthropological accounts of creation are two ways of viewing the importance of beginnings and for us the importance of beginnings means that God has always loved us and entrusted us with caring for and being concerned about everything and everyone who exists. This is what it means to be in the image and likeness of God. We are not identical to God. An image is a reflection. We look in the mirror to check our appearance before we go out to dinner, or to work, or to serve. What I see in the mirror is not me, but rather a reflection. Does this reflection show an appearance that has been paid attention to, or does it reflect an appearance that doesn't take care of itself? Am I care-full about the image I project or am I care-less? Is the way I act in life a reflection that I am an image and likeness of a caring God, or is the reflection blurry or shadowy or distorted because I am not reflecting God's love in my relationships with others and with the world? Am I an appreciative guest who acknowledges the gracious Host Who has invited me to His home to celebrate?

In a sense, the sin of Adam and Eve is not being willing to reflect God's care for His creation. They refused to accept who they were. They did not want to be in God's image and likeness, and be caretakers of His creation. They wanted to be God, but that position is already filled. To be human means to be in process, to be incomplete, to be social by nature and to need others in order to become oneself. To be divine, to be God, to be the Creator means to eternally exist, not to be dependent upon others for existence, to be necessary being, to be the uncaused cause. The nature of being divine and the nature of being human are not identical. What God and we do share in common is that we are both *persons* and therefore capable of interrelating even given our different natures. To relate intimately with God means to appreciate our differences and share our similarities. This relationship is mythically and theologically expressed in Genesis two, when Adam is formed from the earth (material, natural, physical, human) and breathed into by Yahweh (spiritual) and thus differs from every other creature. Hence, we are called into a relationship with God, not into equality with God. In Genesis one, this is poetically, imaginatively, and theologically expressed by the Priestly author describing the human person, and only the human person, being made in the *image and likeness* of God and characterized by having a purpose, which is to be responsible for what God has created; in other words, God's caretaker. What could possibly be more important than that?

But here we are in 2018. What has changed? The geography, the history, the political scene, the literature, the religious and philosophic considerations, scientific understanding and achievements; and these can be mind boggling as we attempt to evaluate their meaning. The internet has exploded with information that our ancestors were never capable of gathering. Perhaps the bombarding of information has given us less time to reflect, less understanding of what is happening, less willingness to listen to the other person, and less time to appreciate what he or she is saying. We see television commercials that boast of how fast information can be acquired but when it comes down to what is important, we don't seem to have the time to prioritize it. A televised newscast of what is happening in the world today takes thirty minutes and covers events that can be life threatening or frivolous, local events that are tragic or silly, and extended weather reports that can be learned by looking out the window. There are no priorities given to what is affecting us, to what should bother us, to what we should celebrate. Every news event has a thirty second window and that's it. Our celebrity adoration, whether figures in sports or entertainment, or more recently on the political (burlesque?) stage, whether their behavior is normal or obscene, takes center stage over the written and visual media, and steals our responsibility to understand what is serious and what is inane. Too many of us live our lives vicariously through other people. But isn't this what Adam and Eve were trying to do? They were trying to live their lives through "being God." How far have we come? We are certainly more sophisticated, but I am not sure if we are any wiser.

As a teacher in high school, I was in charge of the senior year retreat program. Having a religious purpose, it offers students the opportunity to "retreat" for a few days from the routines of daily schedules in order to prioritize what is or should be most important in one's life at this time. While I was at Xavier High School in New York City, I directed and assisted in many retreats at Manresa Retreat House in Staten Island. I did this because it was not far from home and by the end of a retreat with seniors, I was always exhausted because the experience of trying to make sense of life and God's presence in their lives will always be demanding, as long as one is serious about what is important. I was trying to share this with teenagers because I think they are great people. Obviously their greatness does not always come simply from agreeing with them, but in sharing with them. I always told students to have older persons with whom they could relate. Parents were preferable, but that didn't always work. Older people should always have youngsters with whom they could converse and from whom they could learn. Children and grandchildren are preferable, but it doesn't always happen. So find someone.

I still believe that wisdom comes with age. Wisdom does not emerge because of the number of years lived, but rather through what one continues to learn about himself or herself and others, and to the extent that one is willing to share that with others on life's journey. In the Garden of Eden, the youngsters, Adam and Eve, had Yahweh as their companion, and Yahweh had them. What happened? Maybe the simple answer is that the young people didn't listen to Yahweh's wisdom, and maybe part of the "backlash" from the Garden of Eden is that today many young people still lack the tolerance, or wisdom, to listen to their elders. There is always a flip side. How many older people listen to the youngsters? I know that in church services, some people are annoyed by the crying or voices of little children. I always think children are God's voice reminding us that we should take care of people, because all of us are dependent on others. We are all children. If that means speaking louder in the homily, then speak louder [-] or shorten the homily.

When we sort through everything, are we the caretakers of the world that God has created, or we are part of countless cosmic eruptions that make us accidental contributors to the ongoing process of evolutionary life? I don't think that we are simply one species among many species in existence. I believe that we are responsible for what happens to all the species in the world. I think that the human person is the most significant of God's creation and that significance includes his and her responsibility, his and her obligation, his and her commandment to take care of everyone and everything that God has brought into existence. I do not think that one's significance is in possessions, or titles, or power, but in the generosity and the strength necessary to love one another. One's purpose is not measured by what he or she accumulates, but by how he and she care-fully shares life. In short, our human meaning arises from how we live out our covenant relationship.

Maybe the Genesis Creation accounts and the theory of evolution are not simply about beginnings, about origins. Life is a process and all of us are in the process. We are here and now. Beginnings are important. I believe that, but maybe more important than the issue of origins is the issue of goals, or purposes. In the midst of the Babylonian Captivity, the Old Testament prophet Isaiah writes:

> "Listen to me Jacob/ Israel, whom I named/ I, it is I Who am the first/ and also the last am I/ Yes, my hand laid the foundations of the earth;/ my right hand spread out the heavens./When I call them/they stand forth at once."

Four times in the Book of Revelation, the last book of the Bible, Jesus states that"

> "I am the Alpha and the Omega, the Beginning and
> the End."

The Jesuit priest/paleontologist Pierre Teilhard de Chardin spoke and wrote about the relation between science and religion. His focus was on our evolving towards the Omega, Christ, our goal and purpose in life. When Jesus is referred to as Alpha and Omega, the beginning is necessary, the end is fulfillment. In my life I must be as conscious as possible in appreciating my meaning in life, my purpose. Perhaps the best way to put this into perspective is to appreciate the gift of life and how each one of us is called to contribute to the purposeful ending, or in theological terms, salvation.

What did Adam and Eve "lose" for humanity when they sinned in the Garden of Eden? I think they lost our sense of *holiness*. By refusing God's companionship, they brought pain and suffering into the human condition [-] the pain and suffering of not wanting to accept God's love. That's what we do when we sin, when we reject God's hand in friendship. Holiness involves consciously recognizing God's creative presence in our daily lives. Holiness involves being aware that God's involvement in humanity's concerns is that of one who cares, not one who seeks to control. This is God's creation and we become holy people to the extent we willingly enter into the co-creating of this world by being caretakers of ourselves, of others, of the universe in which we find ourselves. One cannot be a holy person without being alive to God's presence in his or her life. We have a saying that there is a time and place for everything, but in speaking of our relationship with God, the time is always now and the place is always His. The great thing is that, like Adam and Eve, we are always welcomed.

To try to put this into the perspective of the New Testament, there is a story in the New Testament synoptic gospels that I think relates to what Adam and Eve "lost." In Mark (chapter 10), Matthew (chapter 19), and Luke (chapter 18), there is a story which focuses on Jesus teaching the crowds. Little children are present and the disciples and some of the alleged grownups are trying to keep them quiet and out of the way. Jesus tells them to bring the children to him and He says to the crowds that unless they become like little children they shall not enter into the Kingdom of God. Now we know that Jesus is not talking about regressing back in time. What are the characteristics of little children? Two come to mind immediately. They have a *sense of wonder* and they have a *sense of belonging.* How many parents could count the number of times they have heard their children say, "Why Mommy?" and "How come, Daddy?" The questions stem from their sense of wonder or awe at what they see in life. It is marvelous to behold even when parental patience is challenged. They truly see life as an adventure which keeps them thirsting for more. It is such a shame that, as so many of us age we lose that sense of wonder and often become jaded or cynical. It is so sad when people are told stories and their response is "What did you expect...he's a politician...or a doctor...or a lawyer...or a teacher...or black...or white...or rich...or homeless...or a Jew...or a Christian?" There is no wondering about the story, only a stereotyping which occurs without any knowledge of who is involved or why they are involved. Would that we could develop our sense of wonder instead of choosing to retire into our own uncomfortably molded prison cells. There is "nothing" to see when we choose to be blind.

Little children also have a sense of belonging to a family. They know they can go to Mommy or Daddy or other family members when they are hurt, or when they need a hug, or need to be fed or clothed. Or, at least they should know this. Family life has always fostered the sense of belonging, even if there are situations in which this doesn't happen. The nature of belonging to family should always be understood and appreciated even when, unfortunately, there are exceptions to be found in our world. Children epitomize the beauty of what it means to be "social by nature." It is why child abuse is so heinous a crime. Maybe that is what Adam and Eve, and we, have lost. God's world is no longer awe-some or wonder-filled. We take life for granted. We lose a sense of belonging to God and with God. We are seriously deluded if we think we don't need God in our lives, in the very lives He gave each of us as an individual gift. Adam and Eve lost their sense of belonging with God.

They didn't want to wonder about life and what they could do. They looked for the "quick fix" and in so doing, rejected God's friendship and His gift of creation, of invitation, of family. When we think that God doesn't care, either because he is "too far" above us, or because we think we are not good enough, then we have rejected His covenant with us and His unconditional love for us which, necessarily, since it is a relationship, calls for our response. In not accepting Him, we don't want to belong with Him. When we refuse to wonder about the world in which we find ourselves, we fail to see any beauty in life, either physical or spiritual. And if we don't question life, then how can we ever learn or ever love? To become like little children means to renew that sense of awe for God's creation and to acknowledge that the personal God relates to us as family is meant to relate [-] with love. We do belong to Him and to each other.

Adam and Eve have been convenient scapegoats throughout the history of humankind. If only they had passed on the apple, we would be home free with regard to any difficulty that life currently presents. Adam and Eve are part of the mythical creation stories, which doesn't mean they are not real. They are. They are us. In our humanity, we have failed, and some of us have refused to accept God's gracious concern for each of us. Rather we so often try to "go it alone", to think that we could deal with life on our own, that we need only ourselves. We try to make God in our image rather than the way it should be. And so, we often build walls rather than bridges. Walls allow us to keep others out while bridges make us vulnerable because it allows others in, and we are not always comfortable with that. Of course, what that means is that we don't always agree with God.

After all, look who God invited into His life: Adam and Eve, Cain and Abel, Abraham, Moses and Aaron, David and Solomon. If you look at the Old Testament, some of these faithful people were not always so faithful. Reading the psalms closely, we can figure out when the covenant relationship is going well and when it is not. Hymns or prayers of joy and praise let us know that the people's relationship with Yahweh is healthy. When the psalms reflect confusion and sadness, the covenant is not going well. As the prophets (whom we will meet in the next chapter point out rather dramatically) these situations result from the people not being faithful to their relationship with God. In the New Testament, Jesus befriended the apostles who shared the "Last Supper" with him and then abandoned him in the Garden of Gethsemane. Some people walked away from Jesus because he proclaimed "Good News" that was simply too good to be true. In today's day and age, we have some pedophile priests, unscrupulous evangelical marketers, perverted teachers, and self-indulging politicians who claim to care for the oppressed, but only if they can be beneficial to their own goals. Over the years, God's track record with a number of us human persons is somewhat questionable, especially if we follow some of the human "standards" reflected in our vulgar and violently oriented movies and television shows. Fortunately, God's "standards" are universally non-discriminatory. The covenant is the unconditional love relationship God brings to us [-] a holy relationship. We know that relationships require both parties to contribute or it fails to be as fulfilling as it could. Through creation, God immerses Himself in the covenant relationship. Through our care-filled response, the covenant flourishes.

As someone whose artistic talent extends no further than "stick figures", I can appreciate some of the wonderful expressions of artistic talent that I have been fortunate to see in some of my travels. One that is particularly relevant to this topic is Michelangelo's "Creation of Adam" on the ceiling of the Sistine Chapel in Saint Peter's in Vatican City. The Creating God the Father is reaching out to touch the created child, Adam. This personal creation is awe inspiring. It is as wonderful a depiction of what the first human person's creation must have been as we read of it in Genesis two. It is humanity being touched by God. Instead of the contemporary "fist bump" as a sign of companionship, it is a finger touch. It allows us visually to appreciate what the Yahwist theologian writes of in this wonderful story. The love of God and the beauty of the human condition are captured in this work of art. It allows us to appreciate God's being in touch with us from the very beginning, and gives us the hope that God's touching us is as real today as it was in the beginning.

In Psalm 8, the author writes these beautiful words that capture what the human spirit is meant to be. It is a hymn which celebrates the glory of God and His creation as well as the dignity that God has bestowed upon the human person called to be caretaker of this creation.

> When I look at the heavens, the work of thy fingers,
>> The moon and the stars which thou hast established;
> What is man that thou art mindful of him,
>> And the son of man that thou dost care for him...

> Yet thou hast made him little less than God,
>> And crowned him with glory and honor.
> Thou hast given him dominion over the works of thy hands
>> And put all things under his feet...

The answer to the question, "what is man?" is simply that given our purpose in God's creation, we are the mysterious and blessed objects of God's love and intimate friendship.

When I began writing this book, someone asked what the title was. When I told him, his response was: if we don't blame Adam and Eve, then whom shall we blame for whatever goes wrong? If he were trying to be funny, it is a sad attempt at humor. If he were acknowledging the role of "passing the buck" in life, he represents far too many of us. And that is even sadder because he has missed the significance of being made "in the image and likeness of God." It has nothing to do with excuses, but it has everything to do with "loving one another as God loves us."

It is time to stop blaming Adam and Eve, or anyone else, for what we are failing to accomplish today in our lives. We are social by nature, and therefore people influence us. We influence others as well. As we journey through life, we discover that some people and experiences are positive influences and some are not. We do make choices as to who influences us more; so we have a say in selecting the people who will affect us the most. We also have a say in what we choose as important or not so important. All of this is part of our makeup as described in both the anthropological (Genesis 2-3) and cosmological (Genesis 1) accounts of creation. But we do need time to "retreat", to back up, to reflect and wonder: are we more important than the technology with which we often find ourselves mesmerized; are we more individually significant than the political and social climates that clearly affect and effect our decision making and often dampen our enthusiasm about life and those with whom we share it; and are we more important than the unfair economic situations in which so many of us find ourselves? The Genesis creation myths claim that the human person is God's most significant creation *because* He has entrusted us with being His caretakers and groundskeepers. So let's stop blaming others and take responsibility to learn from *yesterday* in order to be more consciously care-filled about *today* and then hopefully *tomorrow* will be a bit more reflective of the goodness of God's creation. Life is a process and that involves asking the better questions so that I can attempt to develop living out the best answers.

None of this is easy and the world is damaged by what we have inflicted upon it; wars, prejudice, fear; as well as by what we have failed to contribute to life; namely, taking responsibility for ourselves and others, sharing, and loving. The great thing is that it is possible to turn things around. Cures have been found for debilitating illnesses and healers have ministered to those in need. Education (e-ducere, to lead out) has led people out of the darkness of ignorance into the light of knowledge. Art has allowed us to experience the beauty of nature and the expressions and insights of individuals as they share a world we sometimes fail to see. Inventions have bridged gaps and brought more people together than we could have imagined. Heroes have emerged to rescue those in danger and in need, whether they knew those people or not. Lovers have discovered there is joy in life and hope for relationships. And so many people have come to realize that they are important to themselves and to others and that their lives changed others for the better.

Maybe it starts with our return to the real "country of origin" for us [-] Original Grace [-] Genesis one and Genesis two [-] the covenant between God and us, because we are still His greatest creation. We are His caretakers. How wonderful it could be if we acted like caretakers instead of selfish, fearful people. Selfish people refuse to see others. Fearful people can't see others. Careful people reach out to others, not always successfully, but because the others are there.

I have taught philosophy and theology for five decades and, as we philosophers know, the question is more often than not, the most important part of our quest in life. Unless we formulate the important and challenging question, we won't ever recognize the best answer. As we theologians know, the answer to our significance as human persons is our relationship to our Creating, Redeeming, and ever present God. If the question is concerned with our significance as individuals, then the answer emerges only in the living out of our lives. So let me end this chapter with a question:

If God is for us…what does it matter who is against us?

CHAPTER TWO

Don't Kill the Messenger

We are always intrigued when a person says "I have good news and bad news." Do we listen to the "good news" first in the hopes that it will soften the "bad news"? Or, do we put on a "stiff upper lip" and hear the "bad news" initially, hoping that it won't be as bad as the messenger claims? News, whether good or bad, isn't simply delivered by people. Events, possibilities, discoveries, opportunities, and even political campaigns like recent ones, can be harbingers of present or future good times, or heralds of impending doom. And, of course, there are the messengers. How do they deliver the message? Do they set us up for particular responses by carefully editing or slanting their announcements or do they make the message clear enough that our response reflects genuine understanding? Or, do they intentionally present "fake news"?

Most people don't handle difficult or bad news well, or at least what they consider to be bad news. For some people, bad news can be as superficial as changing weather patterns or the local grocery store being out of their preferred yogurt. What I am referring to as bad news concerns information or challenges which involve having to alter personal viewpoints on issues, or in more serious situations, peoples' own ways of living, which might require making dramatic adjustments to their lifestyle. It might be of a physical nature such as someone who is diagnosed with this or that bodily ailment which will hinder mobility, or lead to debilitating health. It could be psychological or emotional bad news which often are the results following upon the breaking of relationships or losing a job, or simply not being able to claim what you thought belongs to you. It might involve someone saying that "I don't want to marry you." Or "You are being downsized and all your employment benefits are gone." Or "You are terminally ill!" These messages are real and in some cases, life threatening, and in all cases, life changing."

In October 2012, the super storm "Sandy" wreaked terrible havoc in New York, New Jersey, and Connecticut. I live in this area. There are currently many homes still in need of repair or insurance monies to help in the repairing. There are many families whose residences will not be replaced. Recently, it was reported that only sixty percent of the homes have been completely restored. In this day and age, that seems terribly inadequate. It is a natural catastrophe of a lesser degree than the devastating hurricane "Katrina" which damaged homes and families in New Orleans a few years previously. That storm's message heralded over 1800 deaths and more than 100 billion dollars in damage. That is very difficult news for any of us to imagine. There are neighborhoods and parts of neighborhoods that will never be rebuilt. It is a long time, in this day and age, to be without the place you call "home." I am sure that most of the victims of "Sandy" never anticipated the length and the depth of the losses, hurt, frustration, and alienation that it brought in its aftermath. As a messenger, "Sandy" initially brought death (more than 160 people) and destruction of property, while its aftermath spawned political abandonment, economic failure, and a terrible sense of hopelessness, especially when the municipal agencies people relied upon to help turned out to be the very ones who failed to help. The storm is but a memory on the calendar for most people, but there are still many who are "under water" with little hope of making it back to shore and starting all over again. Some insurance companies who collected premiums for many years questioned whether the damage done to homes was the result of the wind or the flooding. In many cases, if you did not have flood insurance, you were without benefits. In other cases, if you failed to cover the backlash from windy conditions, there was little recompense for you. All the political life jackets residents thought would help have never been tossed to them. While a number of people have been helped and some houses restored, there are still many others for whom life as they lived it for so long will never exist in the same way. There were many political leaders and business agencies who could have and should have helped, but didn't. They appeared on the scene for the photo-ops back in October and November of 2012, but now, a few years later they are missing from the arena, and yet there are "Sandy" and "Katrina" victims still struggling to put their "American dream" back together. There were heroes, first responders, firemen and police officers, municipal workers and neighbors, just as there were after the horror of September 11, 2001. Their message was one of *hope* which eventually becomes one of new beginnings, at least for some, and even, at times, for many. Hopefully the message of everyone who was hurt by those terrible "natural" disasters will eventually be answered.

Bad news challenges hopes and realities, and calls for rearranging the way we live life. It involves changing priorities, often in ways that we had not previously envisioned and that seriously question whether our life's hopes and dreams are worth pursuing. Far too often, we blame the messenger for the bad news, whether the messenger is a person or an event. But then there are also those of us who are very quick to dismiss good news, because it sounds too good to be true; so obviously it can't be true. We sometimes blame the messenger because life can't really be that good. It seems that often we don't want to handle good news because that might lead to joy and celebrating in our lives and what could be so great about my life? We also have no desire to handle bad news, because that hurts and who wants to be hurt? To whose message, and to which messenger should we listen? Maybe this is the essence of wisdom: realizing whose message we should accept and which message we should reject. We do have to pause, not only to hear what is said, but to concentrate on listening to what we hear; so that, we can more clearly understand. Then, we are able to more consciously accept or reject the message, and/or, the messenger. What is more important: the message I heard, or the message that was said? Sometimes they are the same, which is the way it should be, but sometimes what I hear and what was said is not the same. Then the difficulties begin.

Tradition involves the handing on of stories, customs and beliefs from generation to generation. It seeks to bring people together. Its message involves "remembrance of things past" which sometimes calls for celebrations and, at other times, simply quiet reflection. I have always thought that some people are unfair in their handling of tradition. Some think tradition is meant to be unquestioned, and therefore they miss so much in life because they are afraid to attempt or even to question "something" new, or novel. There are others for whom tradition is so "old fashioned" as to be ignored as meaningless. I have always believed that tradition is meant to be questioned, either for a more contemporary appreciation of the meaning of the tradition or to acknowledge that it is time to move beyond the tradition.

Thanksgiving Day is a tradition that I think will always be significant in the United States. There is a need for us to belong to a group of people whom we can trust. For most of us, that is the message that *family gatherings* offer, even those families who have experienced hurt. The occasion calls us to gather around the table sharing a meal as well as conversation filled with familial memories, hopes, and stories. Thanksgiving is celebrated not simply for past blessings but also for future hopes. The hope that the family who is sharing a meal today will also be a family who shares meals together for years to come. Traditions are not only about the acknowledging of past blessings but also about the hopeful anticipation that the future will include similar familiar celebrations. Most of us who are "senior citizens" acknowledge the connection between this holiday and Norman Rockwell, the American painter and magazine illustrator. Most of his works relate to family scenes and to American holidays. The one I recall most vividly is one of his "Four Freedoms" paintings, entitled "Freedom from Want." It shows a large family around the dinner table with empty plates in front of them. The matriarch is serving a cooked turkey on a large platter while the patriarch smiles approvingly as he stands behind her. It is a scene of family sharing and celebrating. It has also been called "The Thanksgiving Picture" as well as "I'll be Home for Christmas" which also focuses also upon the family gathering and celebrating together. These traditions are reflected in art. They celebrate the past and anticipate future gatherings with hope. The message echoes the reality that there are good traditions worth celebrating from year to year.

Every Fourth of July in the United States, we celebrate our historical independence as a nation. The celebration is traditionally associated with fireworks and concerts originally dedicated to marching band music and Americana. A tradition such as fireworks for the Fourth of July, or Independence Day, comes into question because, unless supervised, fireworks can be harmful and even deadly. The answer in recent years has been to entrust firework displays primarily to professionals; so the annual tradition continues, with public safety features added to protect participating individuals and public spectators.

The significance of tradition is the underlying theme of "Fiddler on the Roof", a wonderful play and movie, which offers a challenge for all of us, whether of the Jewish faith or not. The 1964 musical presents Teyve and his wife Golda living on a poor farm in the late nineteenth or earlier twentieth century village of Anatevka, a rundown and rather barren place in Russia. They are raising five daughters in their Jewish faith and tradition and trying to eke out a livelihood running a small farm and delivering milk to fellow villagers. The focus is upon the three eldest daughters. When Tevye's daughters sought to marry "outside" of the traditional expectations, there were challenges to be met. His first daughter, Tzeitel, wanted to marry a poor tailor who wasn't the father's choice. Tevye had arranged (as tradition expected) an economically beneficial marriage to a wealthy widower who was the village butcher, but his daughter was "in love" with the struggling tailor, Motel. I have to conclude that this "tradition" had little consideration of romance associated with it. Motel had hopes but not much else to offer Teyve's daughter.

This was a challenge to the father's authority, but he questioned and broke with tradition to be supportive of his daughter's hopes. He had to convince his wife, and this was not an easy task; so, he tries to bring God onto his side in a theatrical and imaginative dream sequence that certainly wasn't a traditional expression of divine intervention, but a funny attempt to encourage God's intercession on behalf of his daughter. In the play and in the movie, it is a hilarious and wonderful sequence. Teyve is trying to convince Golda to accept Motel as her daughter's husband. Husband and wife are religious people and this scene aims at showing, I think, that the religious aspect of life does indeed have a humorous element. God does have a sense of humor. [After all, He created us to take care of the universe. This would be ludicrous if we were left to our own ingenuity. Thank God, we have His help in trying to care for this world.] Eventually he convinces his wife to side with him in supporting Tzeitel's choice. This scene is better viewed than explained, but finally parental agreement is achieved. Teyve questioned the traditional parental authority of arranging children's marriages, and placed his daughter's concerns above his paternal position, and God blessed them. Amen.

The second daughter, Hodel, sought to marry the "outsider" tutor, Perchik, who was involved in social and political issues far beyond the concerns of the Jewish community in which the family lived. He wasn't even a member of the community, but simply someone passing through. How could she possibly want to marry him? But, with her father's support, she eventually follows him away from the village in which she was born and raised. Perchik goes on to pursue his radical political views which ultimately lead to the events of the Russian revolution of the early 1900's.

The third daughter, Chava, said she was going to marry a "foreigner" who didn't even share the same religious background. Fyedka, a soldier, was one of the Russian oppressors of the Jewish people in this little village, but he did not agree that his overlords should be hurting these people (which meant that he went against the military tradition of the conquering oppressor.) Their romance upset the status quo of the religious community as well as raising the possibility of another daughter leaving the home and family in which she was raised. The message is changing for the traditionalists, but this will eventually lead to the beginning of new traditions.

The final scene shows a modern day exodus of the Jewish people as the Russian overlords banish them from Anatevka. The parents and the daughters go their own ways, but it was clear in that final scene that the familial love, no matter how challenged, or how far dispersed, would also remain alive, even as new traditions were born. According to the 20th chapter of the Book of Exodus (which message includes the Ten Commandments as concrete ways the people, including us contemporaries, can relate to God in their everyday lives), Yahweh is their God and the Israelites are His people. Yet, it took time and difficult experiences for the Israelites to relate to their God, and still does (even beyond the 20th century village of Anatevka.)

I do think that "Fiddler on the Roof" is important because it involves the family as both the message and the messengers. The parents lived by and embraced their religious and historical traditions and yet were willing to challenge them out of love for their children and their children's hopes. What message do husbands and wives send to each other by what they say and do? And *how* is each message sent? As parents, what messages do we send our children by our words and deeds? How do children, distracted as they are by so many contemporary sights and sounds, hear and understand our messages? Tzeitel, Hodel, and Chava all realized that their hopes were not so comforting to their parents, but that their God-loving parents' concern for them was paramount. Teyve and Golda's blessings were offered with varying degrees of enthusiasm, and apprehension, but they were offered freely and generously. Actions always speak louder than words. Love is not love until it is given away by sharing with others. That should be a universal family motto.

The events depicted in this play and movie are true not only for the Jewish people, but for other religious people, such as my fellow Christians, as well. After all, getting to know God and what He expects is not always a simple quest. Or perhaps it is a simple quest, but we, oftentimes, manage to make it more difficult that it should be. Being liberated from Egypt was wonderful, but then the wandering in the desert was a very difficult experience during which the people turned against God's liberator, Moses. It wasn't until some really problematic times were resolved that again, reconciliation took place. This wandering in the desert is the inspiration for "Fiddler on the Roof. "At the end of the play, the Jewish faithful are forced to leave their homes once again and find somewhere else to settle. It's not always easy being a believer [-] just ask God, and I know that Moses would also agree. Certainly Tevye would agree, as well.

The Exodus as an historical, political, and social event refers to the liberation of the Israelites from bondage in Egypt. At the end of the Book of Genesis, there is the story of Joseph, the last patriarch. Instead of "getting even" with his jealous brothers who sold him into slavery,

Joseph saves the Jewish people from starving because of a terrible famine. Thanks to his political status, the Jewish people are welcomed into Egypt. We know that historically, the Hyksos, a Semitic people like the Israelites, had conquered Egypt in the mid-seventeenth century BC. They were not as hostile to the refugee Israelites who were invited to settle there. However, a century and a half later, the Egyptians rose up, driving out the Hyksos and enslaving the Israelites, which is the situation we find at the beginning of the Book of Exodus. This book marks the birth of the national history of the Jewish people covering the experiences which will lead to their unification as a nation. The shared difficulties of living in bondage became the event which unified them as a distinctly historical people. The message of the Book of Exodus is also concerned with personal religious and/or spiritual liberation, which involves the freeing of any person from sin to grace, from being burdened or chained by the evils of the world to a life of companionship with God, a covenantal life.

While there have been good people throughout history, I think that there is, in varying degrees, a universal need for mankind to be purged or liberated or saved from a life of selfishness or despair which can arise from so many different temptations and persecutions. There is a time to do penance for what we did and should not have done, or for what we failed to do and should have done. The Jewish people certainly suffered during the Egyptian enslavement, and the Israelites are the religious forerunners of any of us who are so enslaved to the concerns of the material world, or a politically intolerant dictatorship, that we fail to appreciate the need for spiritual liberation. When spiritually liberated, we can not only accept that we are "made in the image and likeness of God," but also that we are our sisters' and our brothers' keepers.

Led by Moses, they were liberated from slavery. However, their wandering in the desert for many years evoked many feelings of rebellion against God and Moses. They suffered even more until they finally realized what was meant in the message of Exodus 20...*I, Yahweh, am your God and you are my people!* Like so many of us, the people would probably have preferred to win the lottery and then be generous according to their own standards. However their difficult journeying taught them that being God's chosen people was not always easy, but was always worthwhile, and always a relationship in which they were never alone. Having a sense of belonging to God, they were able to embrace Him. Any experience of religious liberation involves letting go of what can hinder one's loving or welcoming others and opens the person or persons up to embracing the goodness or holiness of life. Of course, it is not simply a willingness to say that I want to embrace goodness or holiness. Actions speak louder than words and it is in the acting, which often is slower to materialize than the saying that situations begin to change, hopefully for the better, even though sometimes, unfortunately, for the worse.

When the Israelites journeyed through the desert to the Promised Land, they experienced not only the physical struggle of finding their way through unfamiliar territory, but also the mental and emotional struggles associated with what lies ahead. The liberating journey allows us to appreciate what we have left behind, but not always how the future will unfold. The liberating process is more often than not fraught with difficult choices and consequences that are not always anticipated, but that are always possible to achieve. The word "possible" ought to be one of the most important words in our vocabulary. Far too frequently in our own day and age, we think "guaranteed" is more important. It's not; life is not as guaranteed as we would like to think, but almost anything reasonable, or relatively reasonable within life, is possible. Maybe our motto ought to be: *with God all is possible!*

It is difficult to identify the specific role of Moses in the Old Testament. He was a believer, a leader, an author, an emancipator, and a foreshadower of Jesus, especially in the New Testament Gospel of Matthew. He is also a prophet, perhaps the first prophet of the Jewish people. A prophet is a messenger and the message may emphasize good news or bad news. He, or she, has a message for the people and that message involves indictments, warnings, exhortations to change, or messages of encouragement and hope; so that we remember Yahweh cares for us in a very special way and we should take that relationship to heart. The prophets are probably the forerunners of "tough love." There are indeed consequences as to whether or not we accept God's love. They did not deal in surprise birthday greetings or funny "jib-jab" cards sent via e-mail. Essentially, they said that we have to get our acts together and if that is difficult - tough! It is not a message too many people want to hear, but it is a message all of us should heed. After all, life is tough, or at least, there are tough times in life. The real challenge is whether or not we are tough enough to deal with the confrontations we will encounter throughout life.

Friederich Nietzsche (1844 – 1900), the 19th century atheistic philosopher, would hardly seem to be a person with whom the Old Testament prophets would be in agreement. In a work entitled "Die Frohliche Wissenschaft" or "Joyful Wisdom", Nietzsche describes the madman in the marketplace announcing that "God is dead." John Paul Sartre (1905 – 1980), the 20th century Existentialist philosopher, would also be a person with whom the prophets would probably not be seen celebrating. Sartre contends that there can be no God, because the human person is "condemned to be free." He also claims that human freedom would be an illusion if there is a divine person or being, a Supreme Being. His message is that the presence of a God would thwart the human person's ability to be free to choose. And yet, I think there is a connection between them, that we ought to explore. The ancient prophets, like the modern existentialist philosophers, were messengers who were concerned with the consequences of freely chosen actions and their messages ought to be understood.

It is the importance of hearing and understanding what others have to say that I want to explore in this essay. There are common difficulties in communication, which are encountered in different areas of life. We often hear the sounds of what others are saying, but comprehending what we hear doesn't necessarily follow unless we really listen. I believe that the greater difficulty in communication [-] which essentially means coming together as one in understanding, not necessarily in agreement or disagreement, which is a judgment [-] is in listening to and appreciating what the other is saying before we answer the other person. That is why the Tower of Babel myth in the Book of Genesis deals with the inability to communicate with others, and hence the unwillingness to work with others. This story is still part of our contemporary social, political and religious landscape. We oftentimes refuse to hear what others are saying, especially if they are culturally different. In our own day and age, the political scene is a particularly dramatic expression of the Tower of Babel myth, with different factions unwilling to even acknowledge the opposition's message. We need to reflect more deeply in an effort to *understand* what the other person means. Then perhaps our judgment might make more sense, whether we agree or disagree, or agree to disagree.

The prophets of the Old Testament were religious men for whom the Mosaic Law and Jewish tradition were of primary importance in trying to appreciate and live out their covenant relationship with Yahweh, with God. They were not fortune tellers, but messengers with similar announcements to bring to the people. More often than not their message took the form of warnings that current behavior would lead to misfortune. They came at different times and in different circumstances in the history of the people, but the message was basically the same: if we don't change the way we are living our lives, if we don't rearrange our priorities in our current lifestyle, there will be very difficult times ahead. If we don't follow the message and meaning of the Ten Commandments and the traditions of the Mosaic Law, there will be dire consequences. Of course, the underlying message is that if we return God's love, and that love confirms our relationship with Him, then all will be as it should. If we only pay "lip service" to God's words, we will experience an unexpected backlash for which we are unprepared. If we don't live up to our covenant relationship with God then there are consequences that will hurt. We will bring pain into the relationship because of our refusal to love. This is because of the reminder that "actions speak louder than words" and religious people are meant primarily to be actors, not spectators.

How does anyone of us respond to messages which warn us that unless we change our lifestyles, we are going to be in trouble? Today's economic scene offers many examples of the need to change lifestyles: the unemployment figures, the underemployment figures, increasing debt, the permanent losses in the housing market and the loss of retirement benefits which so many thought were guaranteed by industry and government, both of which have callously abandoned workers over the years. Add to these individual and social setbacks, the weak economic outlook not only in the United States, but in many parts of the world, and the message is the need to rethink priorities and hopes.

Many of our children will not receive the same economic opportunities to succeed in life as their parents and grandparents have. These will include college graduates whose financial burdens will outweigh, at least for some time, their opportunity to pursue careers and goals that offer challenges to help and assist others who might be incapable of helping themselves. This is despite the current rise of the diverse stock markets, which remind us that there are fewer contributors to investing today. The decline of the middle class and the evaporating "American Dream" has seen many people slide into untenable financial positions as the worldwide gap between the wealthy and the poor increases. Some studies show, less than one percent of the population owns as much as seventy percent, or more, of the world's economic wealth. Other studies indicate a growing population of homeless people, both nationally and internationally…a universal scandal. These messages should lead people to rethink how they will embrace the future, or if they can embrace the future. This is not what the original Garden of Eden intended.

Instead of political and business leaders coming together to address the dire circumstances of their constituencies with clearly thought out plans, they have seriously developed what began in the Garden of Eden, the exercise of "passing the buck." Their primary concern is to hold onto their political offices, or business positions, and build up their own treasure chests rather than address social justice issues on either national or international stages, and to that end their energies are spent on blaming other political leaders instead of joining their efforts to work out answers that can help all the people. Washington, D.C. is as guilty as Wall Street for our country's financial collapse, but neither the government nor the financial industry take responsibility for the horrendous economic situation. They blame each other. This is a message which ignores the larger audience of financial victims by focusing only upon themselves, as they scramble to "cover up" not only their own mistakes, but also ongoing immoral and illegal practices. Oh, isn't this what Adam and Eve decided in Genesis three; namely, to focus only on themselves by "covering up" the betrayal of their covenant relationship with God?

In the seventh century B.C., the messenger-prophet Amos, who was called the prophet of social justice, preached to the Israelites of the Northern Kingdom. He admonished them for not taking care of their own poor and afflicted. Whether there is a religious, or political, or economic focus, social justice issues are timeless. Are the people in any society treated fairly with respect to expressing their rights, their opportunities, and their accessibility to shared resources? He warned them of dire consequences. The Northern Kingdom was destroyed by the Assyrians in 721 B.C. Perhaps the social justice message of Amos should be heard by world leaders today. It sounds familiar to the media's announcement of political unrest, or economic inequality, or what religious leaders might identify as spiritual lethargy, and political leaders term instability.

Political conservatives and liberals blame each other. The rich and the poor blame each other. The message is clear, "look out for number one!" These current events have led to many people being no longer willing to help others, or, in a growing number of cases [-] no longer able to help, not only others, but themselves as well. The message is that there is a widening gap between the rich and the poor. The former are being politically supported, making it more difficult for the poor to rebound economically. When I am teaching a course on Political Philosophy, I point out the naivete of so many people who live in the United States. They think that a political person is either elected or appointed to a particular position. They never see themselves as political beings, and we are. Who supports the political realm? We do. Who benefits or fails to benefit from political decision-making? We do. This is why we are political beings.

Change, which always deals with elements of the unknown because we are not sure what will happen, is more often than not fraught with varying degrees of anxiety or fear. So much of what happens seems to be beyond our control. But then the challenge is that we have to change our lifestyle, that we have to give up that with which we are comfortable, and realize that we should be sharing more of who we are and what we have. Now, that can be tough to handle! This is especially true if I don't possess as much as I used to have. Some people think they are entitled to what they have. They worked for it. Others view entitlements as undeserved benefits given by some to others. No wonder the prophets were regarded with less than affection. It is only after difficult times were experienced and understood, that the prophets were held in any esteem. The prophets faced the possibility that they could be beaten or killed for the message. Martyrs are real people, and genuine martyrs are admirable people, but not people that many of us would want to imitate. Alas, this is also something we think about, especially on those occasions when people bring us news we don't want to hear, whether they are religious teachers or modern day philosophers, or economists or political leaders, or friends and neighbors. How should we respond to the message and to the messenger?

The prophets, like the Existentialist philosophers of the twentieth century, appeared in history during times of crisis. The crisis for prophetic times involved people drifting away from the covenant relationship with Yahweh. Their relationship with God had lost its meaning (today that sounds like déjà vu "all over again.") They were starting to rely on themselves instead of their God who had brought them out of the land of Egypt and their enslavement. Following the Exodus experience, they eventually settled and soon afterwards began to prosper. They were in a period of economic and political growth that tempted them into thinking they could handle life on their own, without God, or, at least, with God kept at a distance, or treated as a decoration, like an ornament on a mantelpiece. Their attitude was similar to some investors of the past two decades who seriously thought that the stock market would only go higher; so there was no need to save for a rainy day because the sun would always shine.

As modern thinkers, Existentialist philosophers are primarily concerned with the significance, or lack of significance, of the individual human person. The crisis for the Existentialists, like the prophets, also involved a loss. The loss involved the recognition that individuals were not considered to be of much importance in an economically functioning world. The ordinary person, as a distinctively individual self was simply not someone of value. One's significance was measured by economic or political influence, or social stature, and without any of these "positions", no one was "important." The loss of any individual meaning, or significance, was rooted in the decline of religious influence and the growing secularization of society. The thrust was on how many possessions I can accumulate rather than fairness for everyone involved.

The message that I am my brothers' and sisters' keeper was replaced with "Look out for number one!" This has been true since (and before) the industrial revolution which rewarded the few at the expense of the many, and in the political scene which created an abyss between those in power and those who were powerless. Whatever "value" individuals might have depended on how they fit into the assembly line at the local manufacturing plant, or as a field worker gathering crops during the harvest. I teach a "Business Ethics" course, which is not an oxymoron, not a contradiction in terms. If ethical business practices had been followed more faithfully, then the financial collapse of 2008 would not have been so terrible. I deal with the messages of Adam Smith, the "founder" of the capitalistic system and with Karl Marx, whose message is found in the "Manifesto" of 1848. Smith's message spoke of efficiency and diversity in the manufacturing process and noted that owners of the capitalistic enterprises would be among the few who were enriched, and perhaps reasonably so, because they risked the most. The capitalistic system is, I think, still the most theoretically workable and probably the fairest possible economic process for supplying the ever increasing demands of our contemporary world. Karl Marx's message was concerned with the distribution of wealth. Did the owner get more than he or she deserved and did the worker get less than he or she deserved? Is the accumulating of wealth a guarantee of fulfillment or happiness in life? Because Karl Marx is a spokesperson for socialism and communism, should his message be ignored?

In a globally interactive economy practices affect everyone. Adam Smith theorized at the dawn of the capitalist movement. Included in his ideas was the return of profits, by the owner-entrepreneur, into the business to keep it growing. He never imagined the huge contemporary corporate enterprises of today and one can only wonder what he might say about the accounting, legal, and manufacturing processes of today. Unfortunately, the many layers of business enterprises allow for the greater possibility of illegal and immoral practices, which often aren't punished [-] or at least, the corporations are not held accountable to the public without whom they would not be in business. Today corporations may be fined for criminal activity and yet no corporate individuals are held accountable for crimes committed against the public. How can there be criminal activity without criminals? Perhaps this type of "passing the buck" only occurs in the corporate business world? The ones who are really punished are those who lost their jobs, their property, and their savings. The corporate world sends many mixed messages. There are the technological advancements which lead to the multiplication and availability of products. Due primarily to outsourcing in order to boost corporate earnings by saving on taxes, many workers lose jobs and necessary income while many new foreign employees are often exploited. Many consumers lose the ability to pay for products, not simply what they want, but what they need. Technology advancements allow us to be in constant communication with so many more people than ever before, and yet we are afraid that our privacy as individuals is too easily forfeited. Robots are replacing human persons in the work force, often more efficiently. Does this free us to pursue other interests or does this take away our livelihood and ability to raise a family? These are messages, and messengers, who concern us. We hear them all. To whom should we listen more closely? How should a socially just society respond to today's entrepreneur and to the consumer?

The Greek philosopher Socrates' concern that *"the unexamined life is not worth living"* was a reality for so many people overwhelmed by political and economic abuse and social and religious apathy in ancient Athens. Socrates' challenge was that the significance of the individual had to be fully appreciated no matter what one's status in life was. It must be appreciated by humankind; so that individuals could be seen as having value simply because of their existence. That could only happen with reflection which would lead to an implicit understanding that the individual is the point-of-departure for responding to life, whether supported and encouraged by his social environment or not. Social, political, and economic circumstances often led people to realize that he or she is not accepted by others who share the same landscape. This sense of alienation from society, or nothingness in terms of value, was fed by the frustration that many people experienced, especially in the workplace. Centuries later Nietzsche would declare that Nihilism, or Nothingness, stands at Europe's door and knocks. This was around the last decade of the nineteenth century, shortly before he went mad.

We know about the terrible world wars of the twentieth century which devastated Europe and the Far East. Was Nietzsche prophetic? Or mad? Or both? Only in hindsight was he deemed insightful, and then it was too late for so many people who did not pay attention to the message the messenger was announcing. It was not terribly unlike the audience of Socrates in the marketplace. He was eventually put to death because he upset the "status quo" by questioning what is and what should be important in life. Perhaps the idea of "not rocking the boat" stretches way beyond the contemporary scene. It is much like the prophets in the Old Testament who became important social and religious figures during the time between the writing of Genesis two (circa 950 BC) and Genesis one (circa 550 BC). The prophets and their messages addressed religious, economic and social concerns in both the northern kingdom of Israel and in the southern kingdom of Judah. They warned the people of the Northern Kingdom that unless they renewed their fidelity to Yahweh, there would be terrible consequences. The people did not listen and were destroyed by the Assyrians. Then the people in the Southern Kingdom shouted down the prophets only to be enslaved by the Babylonians around 587 BC. The prophets saw the primary contributing factor as religious infidelity, which resulted in the historical devastation of the Israelite nation. While we can understand events specifically from a religious or political or economic perspective, perhaps we should pay more attention to how they interact rather than how they reflect distinctive perspectives. In the end, it is not simply a political or economic conclusion but a *human* situation that builds up or tears down human people. Human situations refer to the covenant. And the covenantal people suffer religiously, economically, politically and socially, and, these people are us!

The "Joyful Wisdom" scene which Nietzsche describes is a very powerful indictment of the people of the times [-] both 19th century and today. The madman carries a lantern in the marketplace at noontime, looking for God. He is mocked and ridiculed by the townspeople because he is carrying a source of artificial light when the natural light is at its brightest. They laugh and ask if God is lost, or on a trip, or is not sure of where He is. Against this mocking attitude he makes his indictment: "We have murdered God!" His message cries out for contemporary humanity to answer the question: why would we do away with the best person who ever came among us. We have unchained demons and we don't even seem to realize what we are doing by distancing ourselves from God. Not only is there the tragedy of turning away from God, but people do not even realize the catastrophe they are bringing upon themselves and upon their children. What are churches now but empty tombs? Who is to replace God in our lives? Ourselves? This is more than simply a dramatic outburst. It does express reality, not only then, but today as well. Church attendance has declined, which seems to indicate that more and more people reject the community of God's people, and while they might not be rejecting God, at least in their own minds, they are choosing, it would seem, to go it alone, much like the Israelites from the time of Solomon to the Babylonian captivity. They are, perhaps, trying to create God in their own image [-] and try as they might, this simply won't work. Why? Because God is God and we are not. Thank God for that! (This observation is courtesy of a friend of mine, Father John Cush.)

Perhaps, some might argue that this scene is a preparation for some of Nietzsche's later works. In "Thus Spake Zarathustra" he will refer to the "overman" or "ubermensch" who is "Beyond Good and Evil", which is another of his works. The "overman" or "superman" becomes the substitute for God and he is not subject to any moral obligation. He is "beyond" good and evil. Today, that might refer to some governmental policies in many countries throughout the world. Some of these policies ignore the needs of many people while catering to the interests of a few. Nietzsche also speaks of a "herd mentality" referring to the overwhelming majority of people who subject themselves to moral obligations and responsibilities as if adhering to some sort of publicly published moral codification is all that is needed. These are the people who view morality primarily as a series of codes or laws to be strictly followed. They tend to see morality more as a legal requirement than as personal actions of obligation and responsibility to themselves and others. Even today, many business have "compliance" officers who were supposed to be concerned with the moral or ethical dealings of the firm, but who are, more often than not, simply addressing the corporation's legal concerns. How can the firm avoid civil or legal difficulties of the state in which they operate? Not every legal decision is ethical.

Nietzsche's herds of ordinary people are distinguished from the few who are not subject to moral regulations. These few determine what is right or wrong by how they decide to act. Nietzsche was adopted by the Nazis as their "philosopher" primarily on the concept of the "overman" or "superman" or "super race." The irony is that history suggests Nietzsche moved to Switzerland because he did not tolerate the anti-Semitism in Germany. It is safe to say that he is anti-Church and many of his conclusions stem from his disagreement with and objections to religion as practiced in his day. For many Catholics, this certainly resonates today with the pedophilia scandal. Statistically, there is a small percentage of priests in the world that have been charged with this horrible practice and yet its consequences have certainly turned far more than a small percent of followers against everything the Church represents. One wonders if those who have "left" the church are using the pedophilia scandal, which is real and heinous, as an excuse for substituting their own image of God. Or is this real scandal so offensive, they cannot relate to their fellow churchgoers, even if the latter might need forgiveness themselves? To be accused and to be guilty are not always identical.

Certainly there are those in positions of authority who allowed terrible things to happen and for this they deserve being legally punished, including imprisonment. One would hope they are certainly morally being punished! A few years ago I was questioned by a defense attorney while being considered as a potential juror in a trial. It is a process called "voir dire" in which the prospective juror is asked by the prosecutor and the defense attorney certain questions to determine the person's competence to contribute to the trial of a particular defendant. Knowing that I taught at Xavier High School and Saint Peter's University, he asked what I thought about the Catholic Church's pedophilia scandal. I thought this was a strange question in a public trial procedure, but my response was that I could think of some bishops who should be imprisoned for allowing some priests to continue ministering pain and suffering to people.

In the 2012 presidential campaign, a former student of mine was talking about the difficulty of making a decision because of the conflicting political messages being offered by the candidates. He spoke as a Catholic wrestling with issues tied to the political campaign: same sex marriage, the universal health care issue, the immigration issue, and concerns regarding religious freedom. He thought some Catholics weren't very convinced of the church teachings on which they were raised. I could certainly, intellectually and religiously, sympathize with his dilemma. So I asked: do you understand the teaching and can you explain your concern? Should the church change positions on certain issues that many younger people at least, have some difficulty in accepting? If I am a believer, Catholic, or any other religiously affiliated person, to whom should I listen and what should I accept? How does *truth* change, or does it?

There is a distinction between a faithful believer and a blind follower. The former tends to be more spiritual (and probably more in conflict with his or her conscience) while the latter tends to be more legalistic (and probably more "comfortable" with whatever is popular, or whatever the majority seem to accept.) It is not always clear, nor easy, to determine whether certain laws are means to an end, or have become the ends in themselves. Does the spirit of a religious or civil law lead to a willingness to act socially or politically? Does the letter of the law bind a person mindlessly to the interests of a certain idea, or individual, or group? There is a wonderful book, based on an historical situation, by Robert Bolt entitled "A Man for All Seasons." It is about Thomas More, the chancellor of England under Henry VIII. He was also a confidant and friend of Henry. He refused to go along with Henry's divorce from his wife because the Roman Catholic Church would not agree with the King's selfish decision. There is a very moving passage in the book in which Thomas' daughter Meg implores him simply to "make peace" in order not to incite the king to put him to death. What about the family, she pleaded, and what the family wants? Thomas chose death over dishonor and became a martyr. He was a man who followed his conscience. He was honored, I am sure, by many, but there were those who probably thought he should have compromised his convictions. He didn't. He wouldn't give in to his friend's request because it was wrong. Henry's selfishness cost Thomas More his life. Was it worth it? It clearly was to Thomas More. I believe he is far greater a personal model today than Henry VIII will ever be. What is the message any law presents?

What is the church's message today? Is it any different than it has been since the time of Christ, or have new and different legal and political and social issues and challenges arisen making it more difficult to appreciate the message, or, at least, to cloud the message? As a believer, my conviction must be based upon what I understand and how I act on that understanding. There is no "blind' faith. Faith is not the opposite of reason. We think. We understand. We commit ourselves. Faith is an ongoing committing to a person, or an idea, or a movement, or a conviction. Faith is a way of living out one's understood convictions and values. It is not simply based on feelings, which are fleeting, temporary, and subjective, but on humanity's universal values, which deal with the significance of each person born into this world.

On many occasions it is the kind of life the messenger lives that convinces us that the message is worth listening to and acting upon. This is true whether we are talking about ancient or modern prophets, or philosophers. There are some whose message we refuse to hear because of who they are or because of our own narrow views of life. Society, politics, economics are contemporary realities and they are voices we hear. How does one evaluate what is heard and seen? Where is God in all of this? If God isn't meaningful in our lives, where is meaning to be sought? It stands to reason that the creator of life will always be concerned with the life He has lovingly fashioned. If we refuse God's concern, God's care, God's love, God's covenant, then who, or what, is left to provide meaning for life as it *ought to be lived*? This really is Nietzsche's question and it should be ours as well. And this is why I think that Nietzsche is "on target."

Many of us have our favorite singers or musical groups. We have our favorite actors and actresses as well as sports figures. When you speak to some people about their favorites, they are very close-minded. Every song their favorite has sung is great. There are no movies their favorite actor or actress has been in which could possibly be a flop. If a sports figure is in a batting slump, or not playing up to his or her potential, then there must be some outside factor, or injury situation, which is the reason for whatever setback he or she experiences. This is not the human condition. No one of us, as we journey through life, is always at the top of his or her game. I have watched and listened to a number of political analysts. Some see no merit to any position other than their own. Others balance their analyses with investigative reporting which acknowledges the reality that there are varying positives or negatives to both sides of a story or a position. This is the message I try to discern when listening to the spoken word and reading attentively the written word. Is the message fairly presented, whether my judgment will agree or disagree? I think that the purpose of reading and studying philosophy, or theology, or things political, or social, is to try to understand what insightful people have to say about life, and in reflecting, decide how it can be related or incorporated into my own life. I admire Nietzsche, even if I do not agree with everything he wrote. I think that "The madman in the marketplace" is a great and insightful piece of writing that opens the human mind to wonder about what is going on in his or her life. If I am concerned with whether or not my government is on my side, then even more seriously I ask the question: Where is God in my life? Sometimes I find him in the writings of atheists, or in worshipping in Church, in my marriage and in the classroom, as well as in conversations with others, or simply walking through life. His covenant message is not limited to only certain messengers.

Nietzsche's madman scene is as philosophically important as the ancient philosopher, Plato's (427-347 BC) scene in the *Republic*. "The allegory of the cave" depicts the human condition as a struggle, or a journey to reach some attainable spiritual fulfillment. We have to take the steps to move forward in life, but there is always the temptation to stay where we are, hidden in our own man made caves. Or we can respond to the "sunlight" which draws us from outside our little caves and calls us to new challenges, future adventures, and the possible fulfilling of ourselves as human people. Initially it may temporarily blind us, but like everything worthwhile in life, it takes adjusting one's vision in order to more clearly focus on what matters. An allegory, as distinct from a myth, involves each level as representing something. In Plato's Allegory of the Cave (Book VII of *The Republic*) people are chained together facing a wall, the back of the cave. They represent the majority of mankind, who more often than not, live in the darkness of ignorance. They see shadows on the wall, because behind them is a fire which is casting the shadows from the flames. Reality as "shadows on the wall" refers to simply accepting what others say and refusing to think for ourselves. It says that everything the television newscaster says must be true [-] after all, it is on television.

Then one of the individuals breaks loose of his chains. Turning around he "sees" that the light is artificial, manmade, a bonfire made by another. He looks at what is happening in front of him and realizes that it is not what he initially thought it was. The "shadows" are not reality. The *first* move is made by the individual, not knowing where that will lead. He moves beyond his "comfort" zone and is willing to take a risk. He is not sure what lies ahead, but is willing to begin a new journey. Plato's man looks beyond the fire and sees some light coming in through a hole at the end of the cave. He turns towards the light, which instinctively makes him blink, and he tries to adjust. This requires effort and is not always rewarded with immediate success. How do we take in unfamiliar sights and sounds of life; so that we can begin to appreciate them? How do we hear the voices of new realities and try to judge which ones are more important than others? How do we prioritize the varying values that life offers? Attracted to the light coming through the mouth of the cave, Plato's man slowly moves out of the cave entering a new dimension, the sunlit landscape. The adjustment is even more difficult here, because it involves trying to understand how differing experiences can lead to an accepting and developing of one's own meaning in life. It involves more than uncritically accepting what others say. It involves exploring what lies in front of you. This choice to move challenges all the messengers and the messages with which you have already confronted, both those that are clearly stated and those that are questionable. It seeks to discover and embrace new meaning. In the cave you can look to the side and there is darkness which helps your eyes adjust. But in the sunlight you either close your eyes completely or you squint. By squinting you can see a little at a time and eventually your eyes can adjust to the natural world, illumined by the sun, which is all around. The sun is the source of real light, and looking at the world outside of the cave yields far more to reflect upon and to appreciate than the darkness of the cave could ever offer. There is so much to learn.

Of course, Plato's concern is the "inner eye" of the soul, or psyche, or mind, without which there is no human access to what is "really real" and to what is "really good." He goes on to discover and to describe varying realities in life, from material to spiritual in what becomes his epistemology, his "theory of knowledge." This knowledge will eventually lead to his discerning, to his figuring out, what is more important in life [-] spiritual reality or material reality. It will lead to his foundational outlook on life which favors the spiritual over the material. This outlook involves recognizing and identifying priorities in life which, in turn, will shape his or her ethical view: how *should I act in this life?* Initially, I come to understand, then I choose to prioritize what is valuable, and then I act upon it. This is the reasonable way to approach life. Plato, Aristotle and Aquinas did this, and even if you and I are not in their philosophic circle, this is the approach all of us should be taking in life. Knowledge leads to prioritizing values upon which we live our lives. Clearly, Plato's "allegory of the cave" message is all about risk and reward: our own. What are the messages that I experience in life which will help to prioritize what is most important? Who are the messengers I ought to accept and who are the messengers I ought to reject?

There are two aspects of my buddy Plato's philosophic message that strike me as being of paramount importance. The first is that there exists a hierarchy of reality and of value. Some aspects of life are more important than others, and I believe that is true for all people. We may not agree on the specific ranking of different priorities, but whatever the priority, it will influence greatly how we act and how others are affected by our actions. Some seek power, others money. Some seek understanding. Others reach out to care for those who come in and out of their life's journey. For some, things are most important, and for others, people are more important. In the time I have been a Eucharistic minister in my parish, I bring Communion to people who are homebound and want to receive Our Lord, even though they cannot join in communal worship. As a messenger I come to keep them in touch with God, because they cannot shuffle the few streets to their church where they had worshipped for years. They value His presence in their lives. Their message is that it affirms His love and this is their priority.

A value is not simply an arbitrary name I give to some aspect of life. Values are discovered by us, or not, on our shared life's journey. What is important is present to all of us. We all breathe the same air and walk the same earth. How we should be treated belongs equally to all of us who share human nature. This is the objective dimension to life. This is the dimension we share, the arena in which we interact. When we make it our own, it becomes our priority, our value. This refers to our subjective dimension [-] the aspect of choice which calls me to identify what I believe to be important as I journey. Given that there is an objective dimension [-] that which is there for all of us because we are social by nature [-] we may not agree on what is most significant, and yet, it seems to me and hopefully to many, our life's concern involves coming into contact with others every day in the hopes of sharing similar priorities or values.

Everyone's life journey is a discovery quest. The second aspect of Plato's allegory that I think is crucial is that the individual makes the initial move. The individual breaks his or her chains and begins the journeying out of the darkness into the light. Education is the process whereby one is led out of the darkness of ignorance into the light of knowledge. The educational process has never been simply the mastering of examination techniques, no matter what all the for profit "college prep" programs suggest. Like any journey, there are wonderful views or experiences in life which bring joy to the individual and to those with whom he or she can share. But some journeys have "bumps" in the road or detours that have to be taken and which involve struggling and difficulty in trying to decide how much further we can go. The primary consideration here is that it is the individual who must move, or motivate, himself or herself in order for any journey of discovery to happen. Part of the significance of being an individual is that our choices come from within, from an inner strength, which is a developing of our learning experiences, which others invite us to appreciate. This strength may emerge with the encouraging of those around us, or may emerge in our individual struggles to overcome our fears and hesitancies.

One might downplay Plato's approach because ultimately he views the human person as a "soul imprisoned in a body." This suggests the material or bodily aspect of the human person is a negative aspect of the human condition. One may envision the self as an embodied spirit (as St. Thomas Aquinas essentially did) giving the body a more significant role in our earthly journey than Plato does. I think most of us would agree that the spiritual aspect of the human person is more important than the material. The adjective "more" clearly indicates that the material, like the spiritual, is not only important, but is necessary for human existence. Not every aspect of our lives is of equal value. I believe, with most other thinkers throughout history, that our spiritual or "inner" self is more important to nourish and develop than our physical or "outer" or "bodily" self. I would always prefer to be able to think and remember rather than being able to run and to jump. I hope I never have to make a decision about any of these activities.

At times I think that my bride, Dona, is an Aristotelian. The message of Plato's pupil, Aristotle (384 – 322 BC), in his *Nicomachean Ethics*, focuses upon virtue. He speaks of the "mean of virtue" as a balancing action in ethical or moral conduct. Virtue is a balance between conduct which is *either* excessive *or* defective with respect to how one *ought* to interact with others in life. He speaks of the necessity for striking a balance in life if one seeks to develop character or virtue. For example, one should be neither withdrawn nor excessively outgoing in terms of treating the self and others with respect. If deserved, I shouldn't avoid showing respect because the other person differs racially or religiously from me. Nor should I fawn over someone in the hopes of gaining something for myself. The person of courage is the one who seeks a balance in life between the defective vice of cowardice in which one does not speak out against injustice in life and the excessive vice of rashness in which one bellows loudly but ignores the need to take into consideration the climate of the particular situation. He speaks of life as a balancing act, a mean between extremes. For him, as for my bride, virtue is not the result of an action, but the motivation for an action. A virtuous person is not one who doesn't get caught doing something stupid, but rather is one whose actions are guided by his or her concern for the other person, whether everything turns out as intended or not.

Dona agrees with those who speak of "everything in moderation", a wonderfully philosophic approach which aims at a concept of justice or fairness in dealing with people. In business ethics terms it means treating "equals equally and unequals unequally" because unequals need more help. If you and I are financially equal, then we need not help each other as much as someone who is not financially fit. I think again of that terrible storm, "Sandy" that struck in the "tri state" area of the east coast where many people lost homes and possessions. Clearly, these people are financially "unequal" to those whose homes were left standing. Those who suffered from lack of electric power and the necessities of life are clearly not as equal to those who didn't. In justice, they need to be given more assistance and support than others. In charity, they are God's people and we are obliged to reach out to them as best we can. In one's individual life, it involves steering a course which avoids giving into peer pressure (surrendering your own self worth) while offering to others the benefits of your own understanding and appreciation of life. For Aristotle, generosity is the "mean of virtue" because it is a balance between being (excessively) wasteful and being (deficiently) stingy. To care for someone would be a virtuous balance between the excessive vice of hurting others and the deficient vice of ignoring others. The message is that an ethical person balances how he or she treats others. Those who are more in need should be more carefully treated than those who are less in need. I don't think that Aristotle was terribly influenced by insurance companies, but they should be influenced by Aristotelian ethics, because as customers, there were some Sandy victims who needed more help than they received.

Immanuel Kant (1711 – 1804) is a difficult philosopher to study, and yet he has so much to offer for reflection. His ethical message is a deontological one. The word "Deon" means duty. His emphasis is on how everyone *ought* to act by reason of our human nature. We are bound by duty to act in certain ways. Most Americans are guided by "rights." How "far" can we go without being legally accountable? Kant's message emphasizes that we should be far more concerned with our obligations, or responsibilities, than with our rights. He certainly would focus on the idea that we are our brothers' and sisters' keepers rather than "what is in it for me?" He is probably not someone you would tweet about because he is not someone who can be understood casually. There is little spontaneity about his life, and his biographical information tells us he was a very organized and routine-oriented person. He certainly would not be characterized as someone who would likely "go with the flow." There is one aspect of his message upon which I would like to focus. In developing his ethical outlook, he arrives at what is labeled the "categorical imperative." Categorical means without qualification, or unconditional, and an imperative is a command. A description of his ethical approach is: *Act only that you treat others as ends in themselves, never as means to an end.* Each person is significant because of the individual he or she is, not because of how people can be used by others. It resonates with the idea that we should love people and use things rather than the other way around.

However, this doesn't always happen in everyday life. Often in life we act primarily on our feelings, or our emotions. Yet we must realize that feelings are fleeting because they come and they go. Kant's approach to how we ought to act stems from with his idea of the *categorical imperative* rather than from the impulse of feelings. It might seem to interfere with a casualness or spontaneity in responding to others, but it is a message worth hearing. There are ways we ought to act towards others, simply because they share our human nature. The difficult part of this for many people is the idea of obligation. When we treat other people well, it makes us "feel good." However, there are people we meet in life who certainly don't seem to "deserve" our treating them well. They don't treat us well. Kant's message is that we have an obligation to treat them (ethically) well even if they don't reciprocate. That is the hard part of this approach.

What are the consequences of not accepting responsibility towards others? Some students of mine have asked whether I believe in the existence of hell. After all, Jesus is the loving Son of God and hell is identified with the place of eternal damnation. My answer was of course I believe in hell because I believe in the significance of the individual person to make his or her own free choices. I am not sure who, if anyone, is in hell [-] although there are some people I have met in life who might be candidates, but then, my judgment, is human judgment. Since being human involves being in process, then perhaps my judgment might be lacking at times, even if, at other times it is completely "on target." Since we are free to choose from different courses of action, there are consequences to our choices. I envision heaven and hell as consequences of the way we live our lives with consistency. And the way we live our lives is tied into the relationships we have with others, including God as another person.

How different is Kant's approach from Jesus' answer to the Pharisee's question in the New Testament: What is the greatest commandment? Jesus says to love God as fully and completely as one possibly can and to love your neighbor as you love yourself. The words are different, but the meaning is similar and more importantly what both are saying is *possible* to do. It is always *possible* to love. Kant claims that we are obligated to love. This sounds more legalistic than spontaneous and generous, but then, so does Jesus' greatest commandment. We are obligated, by our very nature, by the covenantal calling to love others; we are responsible for loving others At times it can be difficult and at times not so difficult, but always possible. The "ought" of Jesus comes, I believe, with much more compassion and both empathy and sympathy for individuals than the Kantian approach, but there is a similarity in the purpose of the message. Jesus' focus is on the universality of God's love for us. Our goal is to love as God loves and Jesus claims that, with Him, all is possible. Kant's focus is on the idea of "obligation to others." I suspect Kant is far less confident in the goodness of people than Jesus is, but there is a kinship. It might seem strange that Jesus would speak of a commandment to love; that it is our obligation, our responsibility, to love those who come in and out of our lives. Since love is primarily a relationship, it requires both parties to contribute if the love relationship is to grow and prosper. They both offer a serious message for an important audience – us.

Jesus is certainly not a legalist. He opposed the Pharisees, the legalists of the Old Testament inheritance. There are a number of instances in the gospels where He is confronted by them regarding the minutiae of the Mosaic Law. Jesus is always respectful towards the Law, but He is always conscious of the reality that law is a means to an end, not an end in itself. So what could He mean when He speaks of a commandment to love? He is reminding us that it is our created nature to love. We have been created out of God's love to express His love for His creation in the ways we love others, including God. He is repeating the message of Genesis one and two. Yet, we realize how impossible it would be for us to love others if we didn't love ourselves. How can I give lovingly to you if I am unable to love who I am? The idea of "commandment", I believe, reminds us of our purpose in life, which is to love as God loves. God doesn't need a reminder, a commandment, encouragement, because His nature is to love. Creation is the proof. But there are levels of loving. There are priorities. Isn't this the meaning, and the message, of what Jean Valjean sings in "Les Miserables", the Victor Hugo classic which is a triumph as a Broadway musical? "To love another person is to see the face of God." Our obligation to love is our purpose in life. The Genesis creation accounts are the biblical foundation of this idea and practice. And all the theologians and philosophers whom we encounter continually challenge us to discover life's meaning. There is no unanimity regarding the specific or particular meaning, but all of them are worth being heard simply because their search for meaning is the same as ours. We are ultimately responsible for what we say and what we do, but none of us lives in a vacuum. We live today appreciative of yesterday and anticipating tomorrow, or burdened by yesterday and wary of tomorrow. And the people we have encountered in life will be supportive of what we come in contact with tomorrow, or they will not.

Whether philosophers or theologians, poets or artists, fellow workers or neighbors, friends or enemies, or the most unlikely people we could imagine, there are so many people we encounter in life who are pointing us toward or away from a meaningful experience with the God. He made us to be caretakers and wants only our love shown to Him through the people we have experienced and will encounter throughout our earthly journey. The content of the message stays essentially the same but it takes on wonderfully different forms as time and history evolve. Sometimes it is harder to understand and appreciate what we are called to do and maybe that is why many of us don't pay as much attention to all the messengers as we ought. Maybe we are inclined to listen more attentively only to the messengers with whom we more readily agree, or with which we are comfortable. But the question always remains: why do we agree with these messengers and not the other messengers?

Nietzsche's madman is a spokesman for so many of us who turn our back on God, primarily, I think, because God doesn't always want to do what we want to do and when we want to do it. So we pay lip service to God, but not heart felt service. Many of us adhere to the letter of the law, rather than to the spirit of the law. Many of us go through the motions; we are concerned about appearances, not about what really matters.

Actions do speak louder than words, but unless we have understood, then what we act upon may have little or no lasting effect on ourselves or on others. In the first grade of grammar school, many years ago, I had a "Think and Do" book. I did not realize at the time how philosophic that was. The human person is designed to think and to make choices on the basis of what he thinks. If I think that the message I am receiving is going to make me uncomfortable, or is going to challenge me to change my outlook, I should neither accept nor reject it until I have closely examined it. What does this mean? What is going on in this scene or situation? Nietzsche's madman is "in our face" challenging us to make a decision about our relationship with God, and that is not necessarily a relationship with which I am always comfortable. I think that the audience of Nietzsche's madman is very similar to the audiences of the prophets, and to today's audiences. The message of both Nietzsche and the prophets demand answers from the audience, answers which have consequences for what happens next: what am I going to do, and how am I going to act?

The Existentialist philosophers, by and large, are not simply academic people, but are insightful people who bring their thought and feelings about their experiences into their writings. They differ from their predecessors in philosophy in their willingness to highlight emotions and contemporary situations, and not simply intellectual concerns. Their writings are focused on the world and surroundings in which they live. Jean Paul Sartre lived in France during the Second World War and was a member of the French resistance, organized to interrupt anything their Nazi invaders attempted to accomplish. The circumstances of his life were not conducive to a life of leisure or to the quiet intensity of academic study. Some of his works, I think, reflect the "nihilism" and "alienation" he encountered: "No Exit", "Being and Nothingness", "Nausea", "The Flies", "Troubled Sleep". He was concerned about the lack of significance the individual experienced in life and his approach to capturing some value to the human person was to focus upon human freedom. For him, atheism was a reasonable conclusion to the issue of human freedom. If there is a God, then the human person is determined in his and her actions. I do not think the God-man scene is an either/or situation: either there is a God and the human person cannot be free or there is no God which allows for the "free" expression of the human person. I think the relationship that exists or can exist between God and man is because both of us are Persons! A divine person and a human person [-] this is why there are personal relationships. I spoke of this in chapter one. We will explore this more deeply as we journey throughout this book.

I think one of Sartre's greatest insights, from "Being and Nothingness" as well as a famous talk he delivered entitled "Existentialism as Humanism" is the following wonderful one-liner: *Man is condemned to be free!* Certainly, the connotation of being condemned claims that the individual cannot escape making decisions. Indeed, for Sartre, this is what makes the individual so distinct, so significant, from every other being. To put it another way, "not to decide is itself a decision." This certainly contends that each of us is ultimately unable "to cop a plea", to say that we cannot in a particular situation make a decision [-] we do [-] in every situation, even if the decision is to surrender, to give up, to excuse one's self. These are decisions which stem from what Sartre concludes is the burden of freedom to the human person. This is human freedom from which the individual can neither escape nor excuse himself. The power to choose is the power to help or to hurt the self and/or others by what one says or does. While the significance of human freedom is a characteristic of all the Existentialist philosophers, I think that Sartre deals with this concept most deeply, and most insightfully. I really think that the concept of human freedom is what challenges the interest of the atheist and the theist philosopher, as well as the agnostic. And what the individual chooses to do or to say is what distinguishes the atheist's, the theist's and the agnostic's outlook on life and how he or she acts with consistency.

Let me digress for a moment. I went to Catholic grammar school, high school and college. I graduated college at 32 years of age; so it wasn't planned according to the social calendar of educational expectations. Actually, it took me thirteen years from beginning college to graduation and probably would not have happened if I didn't have the wisdom to marry an Italian Language major from Brooklyn College. I went to Fordham University as an undergraduate and transferred from a Business major (I was in business at the time) to a Philosophy major. I had

had taken three philosophy courses and enjoyed them. After graduating as a Philosophy major and with the urging of my professors at Fordham, a Jesuit University, I pursued post graduate studies at the New School for Social Research while working at General Motors Overseas Operations. Among my professors was Hannah Arendt, who was not a very good lecturer. She admitted that. According to her contract, she had to lecture for at least fifteen minutes, and then she would light up a cigarette, sit down and answer questions and engage us in conversation in which she held the students spellbound with her knowledge and wisdom. She was the most amazing intellectual person I had ever met. Of course, what contributed to her being so insightful was that she had experienced the beginnings of the Nazi occupation, and had fled into exile. I also was honored enough to have Aron Gurwitsch and Hans Jonas as teachers. All of them had fled the Nazi onslaught that was taking over Germany in the 1930's. I was taught by and in the company of people who had existentially experienced the brutality of oppression against people simply because they were different. I did learn about Existentialism from people who were "in the field." Also among my professors was Quentin Lauer S.J., a Jesuit priest and philosopher who majored in the works of "subjectivity" and Edmund Husserl, a contemporary of Martin Heidegger. Now, the reason I mentioned these people is that I have been honored to be in the presence of philosophical greats both at Fordham University and the New School for Social Research. I have heard many of them. I hope I have understood most of what they presented, and I pray that I have passed along much of it to the thousands of students I have been privileged to teach and for whose learning I have been responsible. I became the messenger of my messengers.

The uniqueness of the individual, stemming from his or her freedom, distinguishes each of us from any other person. Sartre also wrote that "hell is other people." I doubt there is any theological implication in that phrase, but it is a phrase that I suspect many of us have experienced in life. The temptation to go with the phrase is related to those times and incidents when we feel, when we think, that other people don't understand us. It is a phenomenon well known to children because of their parent's uncompromising actions on occasion; to students because of their teachers' random grading evaluations; to employees because of their employers' lack of appreciation; and the list goes on. The adversities people create for us religiously, morally, politically, or economically contribute to the difficult atmospheres we sometimes encounter on our journey [-] hence, "hell is other people."

Philosophically, I subscribe to the Sartrian idea that the human person is *condemned* to be free. We make decisions with which we are comfortable, and relatively convinced of the goodness of the possible outcome. We make decisions with which we are uncomfortable and not as sure of the outcome as we would like to be. We make decisions that we shouldn't make, or are afraid not to make. I take "condemned" not to be simply, or primarily, a negative condition, but rather to describe the significance of the human person to be powerful enough to choose from alternative courses of action. In choosing a particular course of action to follow, the individual influences an outcome which can call others to respond positively or negatively. In other words: bring about change. I do not agree with Sartre's implication that human freedom eliminates God. As we saw in the last chapter, the Genesis' description of the covenant relationship between God and us is not a deterministic relationship but rather a relationship based on God's unconditional love for us which calls for a response because love essentially is a relationship. If the response, freely chosen, is refusal, than the relationship fails to become what it could be. If the response, freely chosen is acceptance, then the relationship has the possibility of varying degrees of fulfillment.

Also, I do not agree with Sartre's claim that "Hell is other people", although I will admit to the few temptations in life that I might have thought of this in relation to a few people I have met. I do believe that the human person is social by nature. This means, psychologically, I need others in order to become who I could be. Morally and religiously, this means that I am my brother's and sister's keeper. I have obligations to those with whom I come into contact throughout my life's journey. My obligation, or responsibility, towards others varies with the nature of the relationship. My greatest human responsibility is to my wife because of the intimacy of our relationship. Part of the mystery of relationships, is that because of the knowledge we have shared, she is the one person who could most deeply hurt me; at the same time, she is the one person who most completely fulfills me. The mystery of personal relationships is indeed amazing. Human nature is a mystery to be lived rather than a problem to be solved. I acknowledge the French Existentialist teacher, Gabriel Marcel, for this distinction: we live with life's mysteries, and, we attempt to solve life's problems. Dona and my relationship is the lived expression of our love, which includes at times temporal problems which we either solve with little difficulty or perhaps minor *agita*, because, after all, life's problems are always fleeting.

I would like to take another digression to examine the notion of human freedom and the idea that the human person is social by nature. These run throughout all of the thoughts that are being shared in these essays. I would like to make a distinction between free will and freedom. *Free will is the power to choose from alternatives, from differing courses of action.* This statement presupposes the ability to think. In the natural course of human activity, thinking allows me to understand what my possible choices entail and to some extent what some possible consequences of my choice could be. For instance, in trying to make a career choice I think through certain considerations. Will this choice involve relocating and what does that mean with respect to my relationships with family and friends? Will this choice bring some degree of economic stability, or does this choice offer personal satisfaction with only minimum financial reward? Do I see this as a long term activity or as a relatively temporal situation? Do I have other family considerations to address [-] my spouse, my children, my parents, my siblings? How might this change affect them? The understanding I develop in the face of an unknown future helps to make a decision, but, of course, does not guarantee that the future will play out completely the way I hope it will. And yet, without the thoughtful consideration, without consciously "listening" to my thoughts, my choice becomes simply "a shot in the dark", which is really no help at all. My ability to think contributes to how free a choice I can make. This free choice is made from alternative courses of action which I could seek; financial reward, prestige, or personal satisfaction? family ties or relocation? a long term commitment or a temporary arrangement? a life of service to others or a life focused upon one's own self interest? support another person or be self-serving? return God's love or reject God's love? The choice is mine, the consequences differ. When I chose to leave the business world to become a teacher, there was only one family member who supported me: my bride. The rest of the family basically told me that my obligation to our five children outweighed any desire or inclination I had to enter the world of education. The benefits, especially the financial, weren't the same. These people were correct, of course, but the benefits of becoming a teacher with my bride's support wonderfully outweighed whatever "big business" could offer. My serving as a teacher for these past fifty years has made our Christian married life even more rewarding. It was never guaranteed, but it has, blessedly, become a reality.

My choice is still free whether it is an attractive choice or not. I may have to decide whether or not to remove a hospitalized parent from a life supporting machine. I must choose whether to turn my friend over to the lawful authorities for embezzling funds from our company or overlook his criminal activities. Having discovered that my spouse has cheated on me, I am faced with choosing between forgiveness, revenge, or divorce. I learn that the fetus in my womb is physically or psychologically damaged and I must choose whether to abort this child or give birth to this child. He or she is still a child whether able to fully function or not. And my choice does not take into consideration any choice the fetus, the potential child, might have. This is indeed a very difficult choice, with incredible consequences. To steal from another person when I am in need is a free choice. It may be an understandable choice, but it is a wrong choice. The choice may be a very difficult one, but that doesn't make it "less" free. It does highlight the idea that the power of free will is both a *blessing* and a *burden*. It is a blessing in the sense that it attests to the significance of the individual person who makes a choice, a decision that has consequences not only for oneself but also for others. I can affect outcomes that also change what others might say and do. That is certainly powerful. I am certainly powerful. Yet there are decisions that we wish we did not have to make, or decisions that we wish others would make for us because we are so overwhelmed at times by what we have to choose. The burden of having to make choices at times can and does negatively influence our lives at times. I can hurt others by the choices I make, whether they are particular choices, or whether they express a pattern of choices. But the bottom line is that "free will" is what most characterizes the human person as "imago dei" [-] an image of God.

As distinct from free will, but obviously intimately linked to it is the following statement: *Freedom refers to those actions, freely chosen, which are purposeful; that is, they aim at those actions which fulfill our purpose as human agents.* Remember the Adam and Eve story. We are called to complement one another and to live in familiarity with God. To the extent that our freely chosen actions embrace this Genesis two purpose in life, they are acts of freedom. I support you because your circumstances are such that you cannot help yourself. I counsel you in the hopes of advising you in some kind of life's decision-making. I act kindly towards you. These are acts of freedom rooted in the idea of Genesis two that we are called to complement one another. When I steal from you, or slander you, my purpose is to tear you down. When I rape or murder someone, I am consciously making a free choice to hurt, to damage you. These are acts of *unfreedom*. They are purposely designed to tear down self and others. They are freely chosen distortions of personal freedom. When Cain killed Abel out of jealousy, he freely chose to tear down his relationship with his brother. God freely forgave Cain through the mark on his forehead so that no one would do to him what he did to Abel. His sin is far worse in nature than Adam and Eve's, and as Genesis continues, things get worse. By the way, God's forgiving the person does not mean acceptance of the action.

The Noah story is about "general" or "public" immorality with people tearing each other down through their freely chosen actions. It is described in chapter six of Genesis which reads "how great was man's wickedness on earth, and how no desire that his heart conceived was ever anything but evil..." God's forgiveness is mythically expressed through the salvation of Noah and his family. Unfortunately, humankind doesn't always understand the message and so the finale to the Genesis creation myths is the Tower of Babel story which casts society in a situation in which they are unable to communicate with one another. For the human person, who, of course is you and me, and we are social by nature, not to be able to communicate will not allow us to be able to learn, to grow, to act. In short, it will not allow human persons to fulfill themselves. God's response to this human failure, to this human condition, is the next section of the Bible: the beginning of the Patriarchal history with the call of Abraham and through Abraham, the Israelite people, who are further called to renew the covenant with God and His people.

The situation improves as we move through the legends of the patriarchs following Abraham; namely, Isaac, Jacob and Joseph. What follows is the Book of Exodus and slavery under the Egyptians. Then Moses comes and liberation follows. Joshua leads the people into the Promised Land, and then the developing of the Kingdom, especially under David and Solomon. It is only when the political bickering and infighting begins and the Kingdom is divided into two parts, northern and southern, that we begin to experience the lure of capital gains and the loss of moral and religious concerns. Then enter some of the most important people in salvation history, the prophets. Their preaching and their praying, their suffering and their leadership shape the mission of the Israelites through the Babylonian captivity and eventually to the reestablishing of the religious kingdom of the covenant people.

Let me return for a moment to the existentialist philosophers. Not all of them are atheists or leaning towards atheism. There were the theists. A theist is essentially someone for whom God is important. God gives meaning to human life and without a sense of God's presence there is a vacuum or emptiness in life that needs to be filled. Soren Kierkegaard (1813 – 1854), the Danish philosopher, also acknowledged as the "Father of Existentialism," wrote of the need for people to make a "leap of faith" to the Judaic-Christian God. The Christian God of 19th century Denmark had gotten lost in the "appearance and reality" question. In philosophic terms, the "appearance and reality" issue is rooted in the idea that "things" are not always the way they appear to be. This issue is a favorite of the "con" artists in life. If it sounds too good to be true, it often is. Sometimes people are really as nice as they appear to be. At other times, they are not what they appear to be. In Kierkegaard's time, Christians were often more concerned with "appearances" and sought to go through the motions as church goers rather than "really" acting as Christians and expressing in word and deed how they loved their fellow men and women. They followed the "letter of the law" more often than they lived out the "spirit of the law." Church attendance had in far too many instances become social gatherings rather than motivations for serving and ministering to those in need. This was really not too different from the scene which faced the prophets. Instead of taking care of the "widows and orphans" as the prophet Amos reminded the people, too many people had become so comfortable in their own lifestyles that they could not see those who were in need. When we look around today, how different is the church scene, or economic scene, or moral scene, or political scene, or social scene? The most important difference is that today, you and I are the ones responding to and delivering the messages!

Too often, it seems, there is a lack of compassion or even consideration for those who don't share our social and political and religious situations. As an aside here, maybe we should ask why people should try to care for others, if, in the past, it didn't always work? The answer is that we should care because in the past, it did sometimes work and real people were helped. It worked often enough that we are still here trying to understand and be understood by others. Furthermore, to care for others is what God calls us to do, whether or not those others are appreciative. God is. Today and tomorrow are always more important than yesterday. What we do today for ourselves and to others is what really counts. Maybe we can attribute some of the reluctant attitudes to fear or to ignorance (one of Kierkegaard's works is "Fear and Trembling") but whatever the motive, actions that should be practiced among people don't always happen, but sometimes, oftentimes, they do. It would be unfair to say that all the Israelites and all the Christians of Kierkegaard's Denmark and all of today's worshipping peoples do not live out their true religious challenge "to love one another as God loves us…" But the scenes that the prophets and the Existentialist philosophers described are similar in that many people experienced a kind of futility, or abandonment, brought about by a sense of disconnect with those around them. They need messages that will help them to realize the God loves them. Will we be those messengers?

The response of some contemporaries to Kierkegaard was to ridicule him. He wasn't a particularly good looking man, disfigured and bent over. He was certainly not one of "the beautiful people." He would not measure up to today's tabloid image of a celebrity, but then I think that is in his favor. Mocking and ridicule are chosen ways to silence the message of people when we don't want to hear what they are saying, because we know that the message is a challenge to us to respond. So much of our contemporary "comedy" has become exercises in mocking and ridiculing others, and through vulgarity in words and expressions are messages of hurt and hate. They have become ways in which we judge that people who are different from us are worthless, or, at least, not worthy of our consideration, never mind our compassion. Just consider our contemporary political scene. Instead of debating and compromising, the opposition is dismissed as being irrelevant or blind to the real issues. In political circles, "liberals" are dismissed as being fiscally immature and hence not worthy of being heard. "Conservatives" are treated as "spoiled brats" who only want to hold on to their financial gains and care nothing about the rest of the nation. When the vision on each side is so narrow, there is no room for coming together in conversation. I put in quotation marks, "liberal" and "conservative," because at one time they had valid meanings. A liberal education was a process in which one freed himself or herself from the bonds of ignorance by being open to hearing and evaluating different sides of issues and viewpoints. A conservative was one who would take the time to weigh varying approaches to issues and develop clearly what he or she valued, without ignoring the other stands. She was open to moving forward on political and social justice issues, but with patience and caution. Liberal and conservative ought to be more meaningful terms in today's society. They are not.

Consider some of our contemporary television personalities who mock religion, church, and people. The person we ridicule can't possibly have anything significant to say. To ridicule another person or group of people is to attempt to remove them from any significant consideration in life. It makes no difference whether it is an ethnic or religious or political group, the idea of ridiculing is to reject them. It is then a relatively short distance between mocking and ridiculing and bullying or intimidating these people. While bullying sends, at least to all appearances, a terrible message both to victims and onlookers, it arises from humorless mocking and undeserved ridicule. And make no mistake, while bullying flows from mocking and ridiculing, they are all rooted in prejudice.

This philosopher's interest was similar to the concern of the prophets, including John the Baptist in the New Testament, who was considered, at least by the author of Luke's gospel to be the last prophet of the Old Testament tradition, even though he appears in the New Testament. Too many church or synagogue leaders weren't challenging God's followers to lead lives of service and concern. They were more concerned, as are some contemporary leaders, with their standing in the community. Personal status, at times, replaces service as the leading concern of many communities.

Kierkegaard's writings described three types of people, the *aesthetic* person, the *ethical* person, and the *religious* person. The first person was one who is essentially selfish. Don Juan was his model for this type of person. He avoided any kind of personal relationship because he used the people with whom he came into contact. There was nothing genuine or authentic about this type of person. He or she is the contemporary person who is convinced that their office in life, whether in a business or a social position, whether as a political or a "religious" figure; is enough to guarantee the respect of his or her peers, no matter what the accomplishments or failures. They are focused entirely upon themselves. Our newspaper stories are filled with narcissistic people who are concerned only with themselves. Many of them are referred to as celebrities, but it stretches the imagination to try to understand what is "celebratory" about their lives. Selfishness and arrogance would be the leading criteria in many lives. Most of these people today are defined by their wealth or physical appearances. We know that wealth is useful, but not descriptive of goodness. And we know that appearances change, for better or for worse. Neither criterion is particularly valid. A different kind of person, the ethical person, was the one who did care for people and he named Socrates as this type of person. Socrates was so influential on Kierkegaard that he would rather be identified as a "Neo-Socratic" philosopher than as an Existentialist. I do believe, however, that this Danish philosopher's interests qualify him as belonging to the Existentialist tradition. Socrates challenged others to seriously reflect on their own lives and their own values. Few of us are comfortable when we are confronted with our own shortcomings. Eventually, Socrates was put to death because he bothered people and many of them did not appreciate his message, because it meant that they (like us) were responsible, in varying degrees, for all those who come into and out of our lives.

In a real sense Socrates is a political and ethical martyr because his primary concerns were for the people he encountered in the marketplace, the people of Athens. I think that among the points Kierkegaard was trying to make is that while the Socrates type is clearly a more caring and moral person, and his actions towards others were admirable, the human person motivated exclusively by political and social concerns, human concerns, is unable to fully appreciate goodness in life. There is something missing in this type of person. He or she means well in life and has good intentions, but there is a lack of fulfillment in appreciating only what the limited human condition can offer. Perhaps his point is that "reason" or "rationality" can only take us so far in life. There are people and issues which can be understood and appreciated, and yet there is a sense that there is more to one's significance or value in life that can be captured or understood simply through interpersonal activities. Is life's meaning simply temporal, or is there more to life than what we experience within time and space? It is difficult to capture what draws one to another simply on the basis of reasonable attraction. Kierkegaard's notion of the fully human person, the religious person, is one who is consciously related to God in his life, and responds to others as God's creation, as one who relates to God.

Sometimes reason is simply not enough to give us the strength to reach out and care for others. Unlike Sartre, who denied God's existence in order for the human person to be free [-] and unlike Nietzsche who claimed that God has lost meaning in contemporary society [-] Kierkegaard claimed that only when God is primary in one's life can life be meaningful. He used Abraham as his model for the religious or spiritual person. Abraham was willing to sacrifice his only son, born after a very long childless marriage. Isaac was most important in the lives of Abraham and Sarah and to sacrifice him was an attempt to show what Abraham thought was his love for God. A sacrifice should involve the best one could offer. Isaac was the best. At this time in history, human sacrifice was socially and religiously accepted in different cultures, though I doubt, very much, whether it was a popular option. Human sacrifice was offered to appease the gods primarily out of fear or misguided respect. I do think that the primary purpose of the Abraham-Isaac story, in the Book of Genesis, is that contrary to the accepted practices of that time, God does *not* want human sacrifice. In the story, the angel stops Abraham from executing this ritual of human sacrifice. It does reflect the depth of Abraham's love for the God Who called him to be the "father of a great nation." But far more than this, it theologically explains that God seeks our love, not our sacrifices, especially not human sacrifices of those whom He created in "His image and likeness."

We return again and again to the Genesis creation stories, to the covenantal foundation of the world. God wants our love and since actions speak louder than words, this love must be practiced in and with the people whom God has brought into our lives. His message is constant. As time passes, and we develop deeper insights and understandings in life, how do we continue to appreciate and adapt this message to our contemporary times? Among the many things for which we have Abraham to thank, is the need to rethink how we offer sacrifice to the God Who made us. The word "sacrifice" means to "make holy" and killing a person has nothing to do with "making holy." This is why a "holy war", or any war, makes no sense. Sacrifice means making the ordinary holy by responding to the needs of God's creatures. For me, one of the great images of sacrifice is the mother (far more frequently than anyone else) of the new born child rising at two or three o'clock, morning after morning, to feed and change the baby, because of love. The child needs and Mom responds lovingly by sacrificing her own need for necessary rest in order to take care of the one whose needs, at the time, are greater. This is sacrifice, making holy, what God has given us to nourish and to nurture. Abraham did what he thought God wanted, and for his fidelity, not his culturally accepted action, he was rewarded. The patriarchal history of the Old Testament does indulge in legendary expressions. I believe the "sacrifice" of Isaac is a story which shows (like Kierkegaard's "leap to faith") the significance of Abraham's trust in God, but it also demonstrates a sacrifice, making something holy, has to do with affirming life, not destroying life.

When Existentialism as a philosophic message was initially being heard in the United States, it was viewed as a "negative" approach to life drawing primarily upon the works of Sartre. In time it became obvious that this critical and concrete approach to life is a much deeper questioning of life's concerns. Whether the Existentialist philosopher was atheistic or theist, and hence the approach to the resolving of the individual's crisis in life would differ, they did share some common characteristics. Their focus was on the significance of human existence, the human person. I offer the following four Existential characteristics. These, not only apply to the thinkers being considered, but are also expressive of those who are involved in the quest for life's meaning.

The individual person is (1) a *being-in-the-world;* that is, each of us confronts an everyday existence fraught with possibilities resulting sometimes in success and sometimes in failure. The human person doesn't live in a bubble, or in an ivory tower, apart from all the flaws and the gems of this world. The human person acts within the temporal and spatial context of the everyday world and society and culture into which she and he is born. In other words, whatever significance an individual contributes to life will occur between womb and tomb. Marriages aren't made in heaven, they are created on earth. Whatever significance, or failure, the human person creates or contributes, it will be during our earthly life's journey. For each of us, this is where the action happens or doesn't happen as it should. For the theist heaven or hell is the goal or consequence of one's life choices. For the nihilist, this life is all there is.

The Existentialists agree that (2) *personal freedom* is crucial for there to be any response to or any message about the human condition, and that there are consequences for the actions which follow from our choices. They believe that freedom is both a blessing and a burden. Ultimately the reasonable human person is *primarily* responsible for whoever he or she becomes. Whether one's responsibility is played out in the loneliness of avoiding interaction with others, or in community with family and friends or in a covenantal relationship with God, or in the interweaving of those relationships, the individual bears the *primary* responsibility for contributing to his or her own life's meaning, whether eventually that will be positive or negative. We are social by nature and certainly others will influence us, either to be creative or to be destructive, but ultimately how the human person responds to life will characterize his or her individual significance, or his or her lack of significance or distortion of significance or value. The importance will include not only the results of our actions, but also the sincerity and understanding of our reasonably chosen attempts. The Existential message is focused on the individual and her or his response to life; otherwise, we lose any significant meaning as persons. I do think that the question of God is an integral part of the Existentialist quest, especially with respect to the necessity of our ability to choose from alternative courses of action. Does God's existence hinder man's freedom? Such would be the case in the approaches of Sartre and Nietzsche. Or does God's presence and companionship answer the human person's yearning for fulfillment. Certainly Kierkegaard would agree along with others. Martin Buber, the Jewish philosopher, would distinguish between the "I-Thou" relationship and the I-it" relationship, championing the former as more significant. It is in personal interrelationship, the personal "encounter", especially the one between the self and God that would lead to human fulfillment. Gabriel Marcel, an ambulance driver in the First World War, witnessed the terrible destruction and its effects on the human condition. This experience plus his philosophic, music and drama backgrounds steered him towards the concerns of Existentialism. Like Kierkegaard, he would probably want to be considered a "Neo-Socratic" philosopher because he did not want to be identified in the same school of thought as Sartre. After his conversion to Catholicism, his philosophic message focused upon life as a mystery to be lived rather than as a problem to be solved. He saw the significance of the individual being fulfilled in and through his relationships, his communion, with others. His notion of "intersubjectivity" which is the relation between persons as subjects rather than objects, raises the significance the individual. His expression of the human person as "homo viator" or wayfarer, or wandering man, or pilgrim man and his need for communion with others, including God, is another approach to God being the answer to human fulfillment.

The Existentialist message recognizes that the individual is (3) *self creating*, not in the sense of bringing himself into existence but in the sense of responding to the existence in which she finds herself. What kind of a person do I become through how I respond to my life's experience? There are the four great "no's" in life associated with this idea. I have shared these *"positive" negatives* with my students.

> *No one makes you learn!*
> *No one makes you forgive!*
> *No one makes you believe!*
> *No one makes you love!*

All these life responses come from within; however, since we are social by nature, there will always be those who continually invite you to learn; family, teachers and friends. There will be those who ask you to forgive them for their mistakes or to forgive yourself for your failures. There will be those who encourage you to believe in a good and loving God even when you have difficulty in finding Him in the smokescreens that life tosses in our way. And there will be those who need and want you to love them: so that they can hope and grow and enjoy life. Your response will make all the difference in the world to some people, or to many people, along your life's journey.

Finally, included in the significance of each individual is the realization that our meaning in life, both good and bad, both beneficial and destructive (4) *transcends our temporal and spatial situation.* What I say and what I do goes beyond, in terms of influence, the time and the place where I acted. We remember those people who influence us in life whether they are now living or dead. We recall their goodness or their evil. We might remember them fondly or with anger or hurt, or dismiss them as meaningless. And so our meaning in life will go beyond, or transcend, the number of days we walk upon this earth. How will people remember us as messengers? They will remember the message we expressed through our lives. They will remember whether we were care-full persons, or care-less persons.

Now the prophets of the Old Testament were religious people steeped in a religious tradition. Their concern was fidelity to the covenant between Yahweh and His people; so there clearly wasn't any priority other than a relationship with God. Their appearance on the scene stemmed from the religious crises of the Israelites drifting away from God. The Israelite people were caught up in their own accomplishments and livelihood which were viewed as rewards for their own initiatives. They became comfortable with themselves and casual in their relationship with Yahweh. The prophets, however, agree with the Existentialist philosophers in that one's response is of primary importance. There can be no "passing the buck" in dealing with God and "appearance" in the synagogue is no substitute for "really" caring for God's people. So how people acted was of primary importance, and this, I think, is where the existentialists and prophets are both extremely important messengers.

I would tend to characterize the philosophers as teachers and the prophets as preachers. A teacher's purpose is *primarily* to inform. A preacher's *primary* purpose is: to form or reform or conform. The teacher imparts knowledge to the students in the *hope* that he or she will prize this knowledge and use it to form their own life's priorities or values. The teacher invites the student to learn. No teacher can make a student learn because learning ultimately comes from within (remember Plato's cave.) The preacher challenges the audience to change to a particular viewpoint and act on it or there could be dire consequences. The preacher tends more to indict rather than invite. Teachers cross over into the arena of preaching depending upon the conviction of what they are offering to others. This goes along with the idea of education not being "value free." As a teacher, I firmly believe that education is NOT value free. How convinced a teacher is of what he or she is imparting will come across in the enthusiasm (meaning being "filled with God") with which they present to students what they know. The preacher enters into the teaching arena to the extent he or she explains why the audience should respond to the message by changing their ways. To repeat, in general, the teacher invites others to learn through knowledge while the preacher challenges and encourages others to change in order to embrace certain consequences rather than others. Actions have consequences. The Existentialists taught the significance of the individual person in a world which is not always supportive. The Prophets preached that embracing the covenant relationship with God makes one's life significant, whether or not the world is supportive.

As mentioned above, after the reign of Solomon, the Israelites divided into the northern kingdom (Israel) and the southern kingdom (Judah). Prophets associated with the northern kingdom include Elijah and Elisha, Amos and Hosea. Prophets associated with the southern kingdom include Proto-Isaiah (or first Isaiah) and Micah, as well as Jeremiah along with Zephaniah and Habakkuk. Israel was destroyed by the Assyrians in 722 BC while Judah was conquered in 587 BC by the Babylonians. The prophets associated with the Babylonian Captivity included Deutero (or Second)-Isaiah and Ezekiel. After returning from exile, the prophets include Trito (or Third)-Isaiah, along with Zachariah, Malachi, and Joel. I mentioned different prophets who appeared at different times because obviously their messages, while containing most of same themes, would be presented slightly differently because of the changing circumstances of their audiences. Warnings were mostly the theme before the fall. During the exile, the theme would focus on hope and the theme of encouragement would be more evident during the restoration of Jerusalem.

I would like to focus upon two [reworded] general prophetic themes important to the Jewish people as well as to those of us who are Christian. One theme deals with the nature of the relationship between God and us and the message is very clear: *God loves us!* Since love is, by nature, a relationship, we are the important party called upon to respond to the relationship with God. The second theme is closely related. *If we return God's love, there are consequences. If we don't return God's love, there are different consequences!* In a nutshell, the consequences are everlasting life or eternal loss because death is a transition, not a termination. Both themes are very important messages not only to the people of the time of the prophets, but also to us, today.

The nature of the relationship between God and us is repeated in different prophetic messages such as: *the new paradise* (Amos 9:13-15) rooted in God's concern to bring His people home. This theme aims at making permanent the love which established the "Garden of Eden." Among the consequences of fidelity to Yahweh is everlasting life, everlasting fulfillment. There is eternal life after temporal death. *The marriage theme* (Hosea 1 through 3) in which the covenant is presented as the intimate love relationship intended between the bride and groom, unlike the relation between Hosea and his faithless bride, Gomer. Yahweh is the groom and the Israelites the bride. The love between God and His people is meant to be intimate and life giving. The promise of God's presence in their lives is as sacred as the promise made by the bride and groom at the time of the wedding. This is not simply a legal obligation, but an existential obligation, one that is supposed to be lived out in and through our daily expressions.

Israel is God's beloved son (especially throughout Isaiah and Jeremiah). Just as Isaac was so precious to Abraham and Sarah; so Israel is as precious to the God Who called them out of slavery to belong to His family, to be His own special children. This theme foreshadows the

Lord's Prayer in the New Testament. The Our Father is the prayer in which we, the children, recognize that the love between us and God, the Father, is the same as the way parents and children are meant to love. These are among the most encouraging and hope-filled prophetic themes which echo God's concern for His people. The prophets recognize that we need reminders of our significance in life, because the settings and situations in life are not always peaceful.

Reflecting on the message of the "Our Father", we are called to recognize that there is a personal relationship between humanity and divinity. We address "Our Father Who art in heaven" which means we are personally related to Him, the divine person. We petition that His love which permeates the creative heavenly kingdom be the same for us in the earthly kingdom which includes our earthly journey. We ask for what we need today to live life as fully as possible. We implore that He forgive us for having failed to love and we claim that we will forgive those who have failed to love us (to me this is the most important part of the prayer Jesus gave to us, because He is inviting, encouraging, urging us, to redeem the world, just as He is doing.) And He promises that He will be with us in those times when we are tempted to deny or renounce Him and He will not abandon us. He is on our side. He is with us. Either I believe this and act upon it, or I don't, and the consequences are incredibly different.

God's love is not dependent upon our love, but is freely given in creation with the hope that we will return His love and contribute to bringing about the fulfilling which love promises. Family situations and marital situations do not always bring the joy we hope to experience in this life. When failed earthly relationships happen, we live in the confidence that being created in His "image and likeness" we will never be abandoned by Him. Earthly relationships fail for any number of reasons, sometimes understandable, and other times, incomprehensible. But each of us, His individual creation, will always be special to Him. When earthly relationships reflect the wonder and goodness of God's creation, we live in the comfort that our earthly journey will lead eventually to the table of the Father whose friendship we experience here and which we will enjoy more fully hereafter. The covenant relationship confirms the significance of humanity's creation.

Balancing these themes are other prophetic announcements which remind people of the consequences of certain human actions. God doesn't want us simply to go through the motions in life. We have never been called to be spectators in life; rather we have been called to be caretakers, to be actors in life's drama. *The Day of the Lord* referred to God's intervention against Israel's and other nation's refusal to love as God has called us to love. Actions speak louder than words and the covenant is intended to be practiced. The failure, or refusal, to act as we ought will result in consequences which will hinder rather than foster good will in the world. *Formalism in worship is hateful to God* (found in Amos, Hosea, Jeremiah and Isaiah.) This reminded the Israelites that it is their love God wants, not their sacrifice. Their presence in the temple should not simply be for the sake of appearance. If God hates anything, it is hypocrisy. This is as true today as it was during the time of the Old Testament prophets. Don't say that we love God, if we act in such a way that proves we don't. One's presence in God's holy places should be to speak to and to listen to what God calls us to do. God speaks to us in the silence of our hearts, which are holy places, and in the liturgical settings in which we acknowledge, individually and as a community, our dependence on Him and our willingness to serve Him. Then we should go out and do it. To worship God is to acknowledge Him through thanksgiving, through petitioning, or asking, for what we, and others, might need, for forgiveness because we have failed to love, and finally to praise God for having given us His creation and having made us His caretakers. The forms of liturgical worship are meant to help us to focus on our relationship, and to carry on the love relationship which will fulfill the nature of our worship.

The futility of dependence on human aid as opposed to dependence on God (Hosea, Micah, Isaiah and Jeremiah) remind the people of the need to keep their priorities in focus. Before the Babylonian Captivity, during the exile, and after the return of the remnant of Israelites to Jerusalem, the themes were proclaimed with varying qualifications but they all followed the same basic Book of Exodus formula established on Mount Sinai: I, Yahweh, am your God, and you are my people!

Messages and messengers don't exist in a vacuum. They are presented in social, religious, political and economic contexts. They are heard by people who are doing well financially and people living in poverty. They are heard by the oppressed and by those who are happy. They are heard by optimists and pessimists, by loving people and by frightened people, and what these people hear and what the messengers say are not always the same. The messengers can be caring people or despicable people. They are parents and teachers and preachers who care for others as well as bullies, thieves or hackers, and despots who do not care for anyone but themselves, and, of course, by media outlets who try to push their own agendas by the way they report "the news." The messengers can be events created by nature or by mankind, or by God. There are consequences to the messages which help others or hurt others. For these reasons, it is always important not only to hear the message, but to reflect upon it in order to understand. Then it is time to act on it. Perhaps the worst situation is to routinely dismiss life's message, and not take the time or the effort to know who the messenger is. Care-filled messengers respect their audience and their aim is to share the message in the hope that it will move people to care for others, just as Yahweh did with Adam and Eve in the Garden of Eden. Care-less messengers try to manipulate the audience into "caring" for the messenger whose only concern is to "look out for number one" just as the serpent did with Adam and Eve in the Garden of Eden.

The digital age has certainly quantified the number of messages and supplied the ease through which they are relayed to others. We must be careful not to confuse the amount of messages with the importance of the message. Quantity and quality are not the same, and never have been identical measuring tools. There are so many messages that are "wifi-ed" today; so that it seems we can never get away from our business situations, or from social situations, some of which may be important, but not necessary, and many of which are frivolous. When we cannot find time to be alone, it becomes difficult to reflect and difficult to recreate ourselves. Recreation means the necessity to re-create ourselves in order to be more fully involved with what is important in life. It helps us to re-focus on priorities, on the hierarchy of values which belong to our earthly journeying. Our "smart" phones and other devices often prevent so many of us from retreating a bit to decide what is really important in life and what is simply connecting to others, whether that is important or not. We can't get away from messages and messengers because they are part of how we communicate with others. We rely on different forms of communication for news. We are social by nature; we need communication. The word itself means to "come together as one in understanding." Without understanding, there is no meaning in life and thanks to Socrates and Plato we know that "the unexamined life is not worth living." Thanks to the message of the Existentialist philosophers, we can understand the significance and worth of the individual person in this created world. Thanks to the message of the prophets we can appreciate the significance of our covenantal relationship with God and the consequences of this relationship being exercised through life's journeys.

All of life, each one of our lives, is a continuing self-revelation. We reveal to ourselves and to others what kind of person each of us is [-] what we value [-] what we don't value. Essentially, these are our messages. We reveal ourselves through what we say and how we act. What we think about, what we reflect upon, in order to reach a sense of who each of us is, is found in the messages to which we listen and the messengers with whom we identify. We are social by nature; so, the self is a point–of–departure for action, but not a definitive dictionary of all meaning. The messages to which we listen and the messengers whom we accept become motivators and models for what we decide to do in life and how we decide to do it. The Existentialist philosophers and the Jewish prophets are not the only ones with messages for us, but I believe they are certainly among the messengers we should acknowledge very closely because they identify *who* is important in life and *why*. The "who" in the message is the individual who needs others in order to be himself or herself and the creating God who lives in familiarity with us. The "why" in the message is the covenantal responsibility of being caretakers for the world created by God. The Priestly author and the Yahwist author introduced us to the covenant, the message of love [-] God's love for us and our need to return His love. They identify our purpose as God's caretakers. The Prophets and the Existentialists built on this foundation in the hopes of prodding us, bothering us, teaching us to more fully understand the consequences of our accepting or rejecting the message.

I think that our traditional spiritual advisors and even our psychological messengers, or "professionals" have lost some, if not much, of their significance in influencing us in these modern times. Perhaps they have been replaced by gym instructors and personal trainers who lead people through physical exercises designed to improve the body. This is good. After all, we are responsible for our bodily health. But the question still remains, what is more important: our bodies or our souls [-] our physical health or our mental health [-] how we look or for whom we care? I really believe that Socrates' message proclaimed hundreds of years before Christ should still resonant with us: *The unexamined life is not worth living!*

I think the message of the atheist Nietzsche is really important: *Have we killed God (at least in our own thoughts and deeds)?* And what are we going to do about this now?

As I have mentioned, the philosopher's concern includes framing the challenging question. Nietzsche's question is one that we must answer if we are to discover that "life is worth living."

Finally, the message of the prophet Amos cuts right to the heart of the matter, and it is as valid today as it was in the last years before the fall of the Northern Kingdom, because some of those who heard his words did not listen:

Seek good and not evil/ That you may live...

Let's not kill any of these messengers who come in and out of our daily lives. But let's not ignore any of them. Instead, let us listen to them; so that we can decide who is "for us" and who is "against us." We shouldn't ignore the messages or the messengers, because we are "condemned to be free" to decide to whom we shall listen and whom we shall follow. Since our journey lasts a lifetime, there is time to change, but only if we listen to the message and the messenger. We simply don't know how long our own journey will last, or how many messengers we have yet to meet.

When I was very young, a long time ago, the radio served both as the messenger and the message for all of us. We listened eagerly to hear the world's news as well as to be entertained. *Captain Midnight* was one of my favorite champions of justice. He always offered a signet ring which would allow us to decode messages announced at the end of each program. Without the decoder, there was no way to know what the message said.

As a sign that I have grown a little wiser in life, I know that there is no one decoder instrument that opens life's mysteries to us in simple terms, because God can be found in *all things.* With the Creator's gifts of understanding and choice, I can hear life's messages and appreciate life's messengers so that I know I am loved and I can love those who come in and out of my own life's journey.

To each of us, the message always has two elements: who said it and what is said.

Wisdom asks: which is more important? Love always answers correctly!

CHAPTER THREE

Why Me, God?

Two of our sons played rugby in high school and college, and well into their allegedly maturing post graduate years. They coached and refereed. When I grew up I never heard of rugby. We played baseball in the public park, in which the boulder in right field elevated that area by twenty feet. Whoever played the position had to climb to catch a fly ball or repel down the rock to field a grounder. We played football in the "Greenies" by the East River in what is now known as High Bridge Park. We played basketball in the school yard, and on weekends it was only accessible by climbing over the wall. We did not realize at the time that we were developing our rock climbing skills, since, at that time, rock climbing was an obstacle rather than the current pastime it has become. It wasn't considered a sport, or recreation; it was a necessity. One had to climb to get there from here. There was no rugby. When I inquired about the game, I was told it was a "Hooligan's game played by Gentlemen." The key playing situation is the "scrum" in which the larger behemoths on each side gather in a pack, hooking their arms around each other while they try to dislodge the other team's giants, grab possession of the ball, and "run for glory" unless a number of opponents tackle them and the adventure begins to move in the other direction. There are fifteen players per side, each of whom is intent on hurling himself, or herself [-] our son, Pat, coached an All-Star Women's Rugby Team, the

"Wiverns" [-] at the other team's ball carrier. I suppose this is the "hooligan" part of the game's description. Since I have always been an avid American football fan over the years, and maybe because I played both as an offensive and defensive lineman, I think that rugby is a great game. Yes, I am aware of the current and sad "concussion" problem in football. I think it is ironic that the advancements in protective gear have often been the reason for a number of injuries in the sport. I still enjoy watching contact sports. In rugby which touts unprotected bodily gear, the battle cry that accompanies the players is "No pain! No gain!" It was the first time I heard this phrase and I would like to explore its meaning for us contemporaries, focusing upon one of my favorite Old Testament books as the point-of-departure, the Book of Job, where there is lots of pain, and, I believe, eventually, lots of gain.

The Book of Job belongs to the "philosophic" works of scripture, which suggests, that while it is rooted in Old Testament theology, it might stand on its own as a secular or reason-oriented work of literature. It is part of what is called Wisdom Literature. Wisdom involves living life with all its bruises and bumps, with its laughter and celebrating, its hurts and sorrows, and with its empty moments and its fulfilling occasions. Further, it means putting these events into a somewhat reasonable understanding while learning from them and growing as a person because of or despite all these adventures. Wisdom is associated with Philosophy and more closely, with my hero Socrates, whose mantra, as you know by now, is "the unexamined life is not worth living!" My referring to this message often emphasizes how important I think that it is. Whether these are his words or the words of his student, Plato, they capture the meaning of what is involved in the pursuit of living life as fully and as worthwhile as possible. Until and unless one looks inwardly, growth, which is not automatic, will never happen. Wisdom is the gift that allows one to know when to laugh and when to cry, when to lean on another person and when to let the other lean on you. One of the more moving books of Wisdom Literature in the Old Testament is entitled "Ecclesiastes" or "Qoheleth" or the Book of Wisdom. A passage from this book which my bride and I think is very significant and which we read during our silver anniversary thanksgiving liturgy is:

There is an appointed time for everything, and a time
for every affair under the heavens.
A time to be born, and a time to die;
a time to plant, and a time to uproot the plant.
A time to kill, and a time to heal;
a time to tear down, and a time to build.
A time to weep, and a time to laugh;
a time to mourn and a time to dance.
A time to scatter stones, and a time to gather them;
a time to embrace, and a time to be far from embraces.
A time to seek, and a time to lose;
a time to keep, and a time to cast away.
A time to rend, and a time to sew;
a time to be silent, and a time to speak.
A time to love, and a time to hate;
a time of war, and a time of peace.

We chose this reading because we have shared the experiences identified in this passage. We have experienced the different occasions and the different responses we have had to make at different times. The times are filled with the possibilities of wise, and unwise, decisions. Life is neither a clear path nor a continuous line in which everything falls into place, and everyone knows his and her stationary place on life's stage. It is more a series of events, many of which don't follow clearly upon what went previously. It is a winding path calling for us to wander and gaze at the surroundings. That makes it more interesting if only we could appreciate the differing views. It is encountering Van Gogh's "Starry Night" rather than looking at a carefully calibrated road map found at a local gas station. The road map shows you precisely where you are, and where you want to go. The art invites your attention, your vision, and offers you something to savor, rather than simply moving from point A to point B, without taking notice of life's varied scenery along the journey. Too many of us look for continuity and routine and perhaps are bothered when that doesn't happen, even if we don't admit this. What is more important, getting the job done, or stopping to "smell the roses?" It does seem much "cooler" to be an adventurer who discovers and explores, rather than as someone who expects life's adventures to unfold in an agreed-upon script. People seeking wisdom realize that life is neither smooth nor scripted, and what makes that exciting is that life is never easily planned nor easily executed. *There is an appointed time for everything.* We simply don't know beforehand, when that time will come. Only God knows. It is His creation. It is His time. He is the author of life.

Life is more like a labyrinth with unexpected twists and turns than it is like a stairway leading directly from one level to the next. Or, if life is viewed as a roadway, there are plenty of detours and potholes. The gift of wisdom allows one to appreciate how to respond as appropriately as possible to the different people and situations and times, who and which are encountered throughout our life journey.

Wisdom signals when we should take initiative and begin a conversation with others, because there are those who need our presence in their lives at times that are not necessarily convenient for us. Wisdom prompts us to listen for the "voices crying in the wilderness." They may be whispering and we fail to hear, or they may be shouting but because of our own self concerns and distractions, we ignore them. They are hoping we can give them some direction. At other times, wisdom beckons us to follow the "please be quiet" signs. They want us simply to hear their story. There are different times in life which call for different responses. There are also the times we need the intercession of others so that we can regain a lost sense of direction, or understand more clearly the type of situation we are confronting. We need others in order to be ourselves. But even more than our own individual needs for seeking or dispensing wisdom, Ecclesiastes warns against the "vanity" of human wisdom that fails to realize and acknowledge the Creator God of all life is also involved in the journey. In failing to acknowledge the Creator of all life, we fall into the trap of trying to rearrange what life should be like according to our own unsolicited plan. Perhaps this might initially not seem to be so terrible a thing, but it is impossible simply because none of us creatures is life's creator. The sooner we realize this, the better our life choices can be. It certainly doesn't mean we are powerless, but we are not the ultimate designers, and we should spend more time and effort in trying to appreciate and work and play with life's designs rather that trying simply to redesign them to fit our outlook. None of us has created the unusual and beautiful original works of art that nature reveals but all of us can appreciate the power and the beauty of the landscapes and seascapes we encounter. It is true that at times we are called to be the gracious host to others, but that is temporary. Essentially we are the guests in this life who have been invited to share our journey by the eternal host, the God Who created us.

We are not the necessary being in the scheme of life. We are contingent, or dependent beings. The necessary being is the one who must exist in order for any other beings to exist. We do not have to exist. We come into existence, a gift. And we will go out of existence, hopefully, as a worthy gift to be remembered and appreciated forever, especially by those we will leave behind. This is why "wisdom" belongs in scripture, ultimately tied to the covenant theology of the Old Testament. True wisdom consists in freely surrendering to the love of the Creator God, Who can only be most truly encountered in the love we express for one another. All love involves surrendering, but that is not always easy; hence, the pain. The reward is, of course, the gain, which is friendship with God, and through Him friendship with those whom we love, and care for and are cared by, throughout life's journey. To surrender in this approach does not mean to give up, but rather to refocus, or to re-prioritize what is most important in our life's journey. This is why there are different times in life when different responses, like Qoheleth suggests, are called for by us journeying pilgrims. We simply hope they are the more appropriate, or wiser, responses at the time. We are not always sure, but that is okay, because the ones with whom we share life's journey are not always sure either.

Now, let's reflect on the adventures of Job. Wisdom literature deals more with the individual as a human person than most of the other books in the Old Testament which focus more directly on God's "up front" relationship with us and our response or lack of response to Him as covenant partners. Philosophy seeks truth through reason. My own "spin" on this is that Philosophy is the seeking after the truth of what it means to be as fully human as possible during our earthly journey. Our ability to think should spur us to wonder about the world around us and beckon us to explore what is behind and beyond whatever path in life we choose to travel. We are called in life to be philosophic, to be thinkers, to use our primary contact with reality, reason, so that our actions will at least be thoughtful ones. It is the reasonable search for what our own humanity means, and how we can best reflect upon and express the significance of what it means to become the people we do. I have arrived at this description of wisdom, because I am a philosopher who has taught this wonderful and exciting topic for five decades (maybe some day I will even get it "right".) When you really think about it, the only "thing" that I have is my own humanity, and I am *primarily* responsible for what becomes of me as I journey through my life. I say "primarily" because I choose to make decisions, but since I am social by nature, I am certainly influenced, but not determined, by those who come in and out of my life. In rugby terms, it refers to those who share life's "scrum" with me. This is true whether they come into my life for a short period of time, like students and colleagues or neighbors or coworkers, or for a long period of time, like parents and siblings or a spouse and children, or friends. This is certainly going to be the situation for Job, which is why most all of us can relate to him in some way.

Dona and I like to read, because it is wonderful to be drawn into the world of imagination and interest and inquiry. Confession: we read books, the printed word. We like to turn pages because that helps us to anticipate, to look forward to a new adventure. Whether the object of reading is information or enjoyment, it transports us into a realm for an afternoon or evening which allows us to encounter aspects of life we don't always embrace or reflect upon, but which are part and parcel of our own life's sojourn. It pulls the reader into the action, unlike say, television, to which one is essentially a spectator, even if a willing one for a time. While much of television "entertainment" is aimed at mocking and ridiculing and "tearing" people down, there are some shows that acknowledge the human condition, no matter how challenged, and involve people who care. I do like "NCIS" and "Blue Bloods" because the cast of characters in each drama contribute to what has to be done to confront the issue at hand. There is teamwork and interaction, agreement and disagreement, but respect for the other person is always a primary ingredient. They recognize that we are social by nature and that we are our brother's and sister's keepers [-] just as philosophy insists. If it weren't for sports events, a few news shows and Dona's cooking and home improvements shows, I am afraid our television life would be fairly dormant. But to get back to our favorite form of recreation, of re-creating ourselves, which is reading, it allows our imagination to expand and our knowledge to grow more deeply than any other form of intellectual pursuit. I used to tell students that one of the best ways to appreciate and interpret scripture is to read good mystery books. Granted that the popular mystery books are concerned with solving the individual crime or mystery, the mystery in scripture is to try to solve the meaning of one's own life in order for us to live in communion with God in such a way that we are partners, friends, children of a Father Who passionately wants us to succeed by living our own lives as fully and faithfully as possible. In teaching the introduction to Philosophy, like many other teachers I focus on Socrates and Plato. A life worth living demands reflection, no matter what pains, or setbacks, we might experience. Scripture is filled with mysteries which we are called to untangle and penetrate in order to see how they apply in our own earthly journeys. To read, to imagine, to reflect gives us an opportunity to take a deep breath and a step back so we can more completely plunge into life's experiences, both those which are anticipated and those which are unexpected.

Literature, whether poetry or drama, history or humor, challenges the imagination by involving characters and weaving plots which engage our thought processes and prod us to wonder what will happen. By the end of the story, the reader always hopes that the plots make sense and the characters are more transparent and appreciated. This is also true of the characters we meet in the Old and the New Testaments. When inviting oneself into a novel, or a textbook, or a biography, or a fairy tale, it is always important how the beginning of a book, of a story, grabs your interest. The more inviting the beginning of a book is, (e.g. Genesis one and two) the more likely you are to immerse yourself into it, and doggedly pursue it until the closing chapter. C.S. Lewis is a favorite author of mine, both his apologetic works (his defense of the

Christian faith) and his fantasies or fairy tales. Fairy tales are very important because they deal with good and evil and are usually the first stories that little children and other people like me, who never outgrow childhood, want to hear and explore. Lewis is the author of the "Chronicles of Narnia." These are seven fantasy stories which are filled with the interacting of characters, with good and evil, with temptation and redemption, and with fulfilling and failing relationships. The first of the series is entitled *The Lion, the Witch, and the Wardrobe* (which, I think, happens to be the best of the series.)

It deals with four young English children who are sent out into the countryside during World War II, in the hopes that they would be safe from the impending attacks by the German air force on London. They are being removed from the horrors of everyday existence, but wind up being immersed in the horrors and the joys of the fantasy world of Narnia which are experiences they undergo in a parallel universe. One day while playing hide and seek, a traditional children's game, Lucy Pevensie, the youngest child, hides in a wardrobe in an old bedroom that has become a spare room. As she moves further back into the wardrobe so as to be better concealed, she steps out into a new world [-] a winter wonderland in which she doesn't need the clothing that we usually identify with dropping temperatures and gusty winds. It is decorated with snow that looks beautiful just as we first see it cover the landscape. It is not like the homeowner's vision of snow which we know will turn ugly, and icy, and resist attempts to tame it with our shovels, while chiseling out a path to walk. In this introduction the winter wonderland (or, at least what appears to be a winter wonderland) persists as the adventures begin. This wonderfully imaginative beginning leads Lucy and Peter and Susan and Edmund into a series of experiences dealing with the conflict between "good and evil" and which includes both a crucifixion and a resurrection scene. The siblings eventually experience adventures in this different, fantasy world: love and fear, courage and betrayal, hope and despair, abandonment and rescue, and ultimately, redemption. In short, this book addresses our contemporary experiences starting with an "eye-opener" of a beginning.

We are also faithful "Harry Potter" fans. The books and movies are invitations for enjoyment and for reflection. One of the messages is apocalyptic. An apocalyptic message or description deals with the ultimate struggle between good and evil with good (God) emerging as the ultimate victor. When Harry is a baby, Voldemort who is the personification of evil kills Harry's parents. He attempts to kill Harry but is unable. He does leave a visible scar on his head, but as Harry will emerge as the personification of good, he survives to live another day and will ultimately be instrumental in conquering evil in the end. The apocalyptic battle between good and evil continues to be waged, but not without the pain and suffering of those who journey with us. The love of Harry's parents saved him from dying while he was an infant. Their love is but a reflection of God's covenantal love. It reflects the New Testament adventures of God's only Begotten Son Who also died that we might have life and life to the fullest.

There is another message in this series which is also biblical; our God is a caring God, and through friendship, the care we show for one another will lead us to triumph over any attempt to destroy our human, and created, goodness. The message, no matter how it is articulated, is always the same; God loves us! Since love is a relationship, requiring all involved to participate, the individual concern is: how will I respond? After all, by what we say and by what we do, each of us is a messenger. What the main characters, Harry Potter and his companions, Ron Weasley and Hermione Granger communicate is a message which emphasizes the challenges and the rewards of friendship. What their teachers and advisors, Dumbledore and Professor McGonigle and Hagrid, the groundskeeper, and their fellow classmate and peer, Neville Longbottom, communicate is the support necessary for friendship to be recognized, to be nurtured and to blossom. We are social by nature, which reminds us that we need others in order to become whoever we can. What the antagonist, Voldemort and his serpent Nagini (reminiscent of the serpent in Genesis three), the Draco family and their minions communicate is a force in the world which doesn't want good people to enjoy what God has created. Isn't this the truth? Just read the "temptation" stories in the synoptic gospels.

I do not mean to suggest that Harry Potter is the Messiah promised in the Old Testament, nor do I profess that magical incantations are prayers. I do think, however, that friendships are rooted in covenant relationships, and that good and evil are realities, whether confronted in everyday experiences or wonderfully told in imaginative books. Finding God in all things includes fantasy literature. The bottom line for me is that we can gain insights into our relationships with God even in the Harry Potter books. So thanks J.K. Rowling.

You have to marvel at the beginning of each year at Hogwarts School of Magic when Harry and the Weasley family board the train to school through track 9 ¾ at London's King Cross Station. They overcome an obvious rock solid obstacle; so that they can enter into life's wonderful and frequently frightening episodes. It is such an imaginative opening. This beginning cleverly invites you to the adventures that will follow throughout the seven books. These are adventures which continually deal with good and evil, with friendships gained and challenged and lost, with suffering and celebrating. In short they deal universally with all the life and death experiences we encounter, and with the wisdom necessary to persist through life's experiences. They remind us that in our earthly journeys, joy is not simply the absence of sorrow but the presence of God Who is usually revealed through those people who touch us in various ways as we go throughout life. Like the amazing creation stories of Genesis one and two, which lead us to an appreciation of God's covenantal love for all of us, the beginning of any life adventure is always significant because of how and why it invites each of us to embrace life.

Another one of our other favorite fantasy series as descriptive of reality is Tolkien's "Lord of the Rings." It is a trilogy of books (and movies), dealing with "good and evil." My concern with "good and evil" is motivated because for years I have been teaching theoretical and practical ethics, business ethics, and medical ethics. The latter afforded me the privilege of teaching nurses, whom I came to admire as among the most caring and compassionate of people in our world. I am certainly not downplaying the compassion of doctors, but my opinion is that they are often more concerned with *how* to help patients while nurses are more concerned with *who* the patients are. "The Lord of the Rings" trilogy begins with the *Fellowship of the Ring*. The story is about an "evil" ring which must be destroyed in order for the world to continue and it takes all sorts of people to eventually accomplish this: humans and wizards and dwarfs and elves and, of course, hobbits. It is a great story about the necessity and willingness of different kinds of peoples to carry out God's purpose for a good and wonder-filled world; in other words, it deals with the universality of God's love. These different characters, with different talents and abilities, as well as weaknesses and temptations, come together for the good of humankind. The gathering of these diverse characters highlights the need for all good people to struggle against evil. We need each other and our differences ought to be a call to unite instead of what is so often the case, a call to defend ourselves against each other simply because we are different. Our differences should call for unity rather than opposition. We hear so much about violent acts against people simply because they are not the same color or religious or political conviction or some other physical or economic difference in life. Sadly, instead of appreciating these differences, we use them to enter into combat with one another. The adventures of the "fellowship" are varied and manifold, bizarre and ordinary, but isn't that life? Their gathering together for a common purpose is a challenge to any kind of social (or religious, or racial, or political) prejudice which aims at crippling the wonder-filled diverse universality of human existence.

The second book is entitled *The Two Towers* and it identifies the enemy. Saruman and Sauron are the opposition leaders of their kingdoms (towers) of Isengard and Mordor. We encounter these same towers in our own journeying through life. Their names may be fear and bullying, or poverty and insecurity, or sickness and war, or pride and prejudice. The names change, but the towers which we must encounter in battle are there for all of us. After all, the world as created is a world in process [-] not yet fully created. Remember Genesis. God created us and gave us the purpose of "taking care of His creation." Some of us have responded to that purpose through caring for others and there are those (the Sarumans and Saurons) in life who don't care for anyone but themselves and consequently are not concerned with whether the world is a better place for all of us to live. Sometimes they are political or religious leaders, from whom we expect more, and sometimes they even masquerade as "friends" and that is the saddest of all.

The final book is *The Return of the King*. It rekindles the hope which empowered the original "fellowship" and which was severely challenged by Saruman's and Sauron's forces. It is hope resurrected and brought to fulfillment in the true king's return to his throne. We look for the hope that will restore us to being able to comfort and console, to encourage and entertain, to laugh with and love others [-] to be fulfilled. When I read and reflect upon the Book of Job, I follow him through his fellowship with three friends which didn't turn out the same way as the fellowship developed in Tolkien's trilogy. Job encounters the two towers of individual pain and suffering and the lack of compassion from those whom he thought were friends. Finally there is the return of the King, of God, Whom Job thought had gone missing in his own life. Tolkien's trilogy and the Book of Job reflect human events gone "sour" and pain and suffering shared before there is an eventual reconciliation and happiness. I suspect that these series of events are relived in the lives of many us who are God's guests in life, individuals and communities.

The Book of Job is a psychological drama, written by an imaginative literary artist and theologian, whose message is that God loves us unconditionally, no matter what happens in life, and despite how we respond. A drama is a literary (as well as a real life) composition which deals with some kind of human conflict [-] some kind of inner torment the subject or actor has to confront and struggle to resolve. Whether there is or isn't resolution, there are consequences. We recall such dramatic literary figures as Shakespeare's Hamlet or MacBeth, or the struggle between family, faith, and king which consumed Sir Thomas More in Robert Bolt's "A Man for All Seasons." When we speak of "psychological" drama, we refer to inner conflicts or conflicts of conscience, triggered by external events. For Job, external events will definitely trigger the internal religious conflict he will undergo in this magnificent theological and literary masterpiece. It consists of a prologue, the body of the work which begins with dialogues and continues with monologues, and finally concludes in an epilogue. It is a deeply religious poem with a prose beginning and a prose ending.

As previously mentioned, religious language is more like poetry than scientific language, because like poetry it points to meaning beyond the words [-] meaning which is sometimes more hidden than we would like, but meaning which can always be unearthed. The poem of Job really invades our feelings as well as our thoughts about God

Who is not always as willing to conform to our image of Him as we would like, but the interacting is fascinating. It is really important to understand the prologue or we might simply think that God is "setting up" Job to be whacked by the difficulties of life. The opening scene of the Book of Job, like the "Chronicles of Narnia" or the Harry Potter books is also very unusual. In this work of Wisdom Literature, the prologue takes place in heaven. God is holding court because many people, at that time, envisioned heaven as a court, not unlike the king's courts on earth. The king has a council (called the "Sod") made up of those who advise him as well as those who try His patience. In this scene God and Satan (who isn't quite yet the fallen figure he becomes in religious tradition, although we can get some hints in this book as to why he does become the personification of evil in history) make a wager, a bet. Satan, I guess, qualifies as the devil's advocate, the one who challenges certain judgments so that associates can decide what might triumph in the face of possible adversarial situations.

God and Satan bet on Job and why Job is a prosperous person at least in human terms. God bets that Job is really a good guy because he has been developing his relation with God throughout his life. God bets that Job is a believer who trusts in the God Who created him. Satan's bet is that Job is a good guy, because of the way things are in life for him, because of the "accidents" in his life. He has a family who cares for him. He has property and wealth. He is healthy. Why wouldn't he be a good guy? After all, he has "got it all." But if circumstances were to change, then Job would change his outlook on life and God wouldn't be so important for him. Take away his circumstances, his worldly goods, Satan says, and Job will no longer be God's good and faithful servant. God says that Job will be faithful, that Job will remain His friend, no matter what happens to him. It is the person who is most important, not the conditions or situations in his life. It is the personal relationship between people rather than the circumstance in life that lead people to encounter and engage in life fulfilling experiences. You have to admit that this is a very different opening for an Old Testament book, and it is a great way to speak of God's relation with us. He bets on us; what are the odds? When you stop to think about it, God has been wagering bets on us since Genesis two. When God wins, so do we.

Many of us have heard of the "patience of Job." It refers to Job still accepting God after enduring more pain and suffering in his life than most of us could even imagine. I am not sure I would label Job as "patient" as much as "persistent" or "persevering." He is a great character and one to dwell upon when we encounter serious bumps in life and say, "Why me, God?" The Wisdom literature of the Old Testament shows signs of the influence of philosophers and theologians throughout the ages. People wonder about the significance of the human person and they wonder about the mystery of life, and they think about a Supreme Being and question how all of this comes together and what it means for me, the individual human person!

Well, by the end of the prologue, Job has lost family, property, wealth, health, and just about anything else one might imagine. He is suffering physically and psychologically, emotionally and socially, economically and religiously. He is the contemporary person whose wife has abandoned him for his best friend. He is the person who has entrusted his 401K retirement account to a "Bernie Madoff" type and has lost everything. He is the person who has unwittingly contributed to a political figure who supports terrorist organizations. He is the epitome of one who suffers dramatically and has contributed nothing consciously to the suffering he is experiencing. He really is a pitiable and pitiful figure. He is the poster child for the "innocent who suffer." Even though most of us will not suffer as Job is described as suffering, any kind of suffering weighs heavily on a person. Granted some people bear suffering "better" than others, I think it is reasonable to say that all things considered, any of us would rather be healthy and comfortable than be diseased and in constant pain. I suppose that masochists or sadists might qualify as exceptions, but I am trying to think in terms of reasonable people, and for them, healthy is preferable to suffering. Yet there are probably very few people who don't experience some kind of suffering or pain in life, whether that suffering is real or imagined.

Because of our own experiences, Job's painful experiences allow people to identify and to sympathize with him recognizing that what he goes through is often reflective of our own confrontations with pain and suffering. His own wife urges him to be done with God because God is somehow responsible for his pain. She cried out, "Why us, God? What did we do to deserve this affliction?" She blamed God and wanted Job to follow suit. Some years ago, a book entitled "When Bad Things Happen to Good People" became a best seller. That is because people find it offensive that those who try to live life as upright and responsible persons sometimes have to endure terrible experiences of loss and hurt. It is not fair [-] at least as we view life from our perspective of human reason alone [-] and we are right; it isn't fair. Now this might suggest that justice and injustice, fairness and unfairness, are not the primary reasons for why there is suffering in life. Job was clearly presented as a God-fearing man, a righteous man. The biblical meaning of righteousness involves loving God as fully and unconditionally as one can, and loving one's fellow men and women as openly and obviously as one can. I think it is more clearly expressed in the New Testament. In Matthew's gospel (chapter 22) a Pharisee asks Jesus what is the greatest commandment? The answer is to love God as fully as one humanly can and to love one's neighbor as openly and completely as one is capable of doing. While this is easier said than done, the point really is that it is *possible* for each one of us. Job is presented in the prologue as a righteous person. Is it because "things" and circumstances are going well in his life, or is it because of the person, Job, himself, no matter what the circumstances? In a small way, or in a large way, all of us can identify with some of what Job is experiencing.

My "love" of philosophy, the pursuit of wisdom, originated in the Platonic dialogues starring Socrates. Plato's focus is on that grand old timer who wrote "nothing" but whose life and mission, or ministry, or activity, or vocation, led to writings which have influenced people for over twenty-five hundred years. That is more than impressive. He is a truly "awesome" figure in human history. In what he has taught the world, he is not unlike Jesus, who did not write anything either, but who also has been incredibly influential in life. Anticipated by the Old Testament and the subject of the New Testament, the historical Jesus, Who becomes the Risen Christ, is, I believe, the most significant person who walked this earth. The historical situations, or scenes in which they found themselves, certainly influenced how both of them responded to life, just like us. Socrates taught in the marketplace in post war Athens. They had been defeated by the Spartans in a war in which Socrates had fought for Athens. The overall scene was not too great for those who had been born and raised in Athens. It is like trying to imagine life in the United States if we had not "won" in World War II. The Jewish born and educated Jesus taught and healed and shared the table in the Roman ruled territory of what is modern day Israel, but the Israelites had to grudgingly dance and play to the political and social tunes of the despised Roman Legions. They had survived imprisonment in Egypt and captivity in Babylon, and they had not planned for Caesar to dictate how they were to live in those contemporary times. What philosophy has taught me is that a philosopher is a seeker after life's significant meanings. He is not necessarily an accomplished academic figure. He doesn't know "everything." The philosopher confronts reality and wants to know "why." The pursuit of the philosopher for wisdom is a journey no one of us should ever ignore no matter whether rich or poor, healthy or suffering. Come to think of it, I suspect that very few of us can avoid philosophizing [-] we can't avoid seeking meaning, or prioritizing what is more important to us in life. Maybe this is what is meant when we realize "the buck stops here, with me." The burden of freedom reminds me that I cannot escape making decisions.

It is no different for each of us journeying through life. My bride and I grew up in the 1930's and 1940's, during the Second World War, followed by the "Cold War" and the Korean War, and the Vietnam War. We worshipped in the pre-Vatican II Church and survived without television and "smart phones", or actually without any phones until we were in high school. These were very different times than when our children grew up in the 1960's and 1970's, which saw the assassinations of the Kennedy's and Martin Luther King, the exit of the disgraced Richard Nixon from the presidency of the country and the end of the Vietnam War They grew up in the church as recreated, or at least challenged by Vatican II. The Beatles, Johnny Cash, and "Rock Around the Clock" had replaced Nat King Cole, Frank Sinatra, Lena Horne (my favorite singer of all time) and the Andrews Sisters, as well as the "lindy" which is a traditional American dance. You had to hold onto your partner, unlike so many of today's dances which seem to involve jumping up and down in one's own private space. I have to admit that I think traditional dancing is closer to life because you have to hold onto your partner, whether doing a fast lindy, or a slow foxtrot. Holding onto your dancing partner symbolizes the "togetherness of people." That is more enjoyable and sensitive that jumping across from your partner until you wind up opposite someone with whom you did not start. We didn't have generational titles like the "baby boomers" or "gen x" or "millennials." We were simply people journeying through life like those who went before us. The times they were a'changing, but there was still good and bad, hope and despair, joy and sadness. Our grandchildren began in the early 1990's with the Gulf War, the Iraq War and the War in Afghanistan, the horrific events of September 11, 2001, hip-hop, the X-men and the brutal and immoral financial collapse of 2008 with the damning injustice of good people being hurt and selfish people escaping responsibilities. Life is still evolving, sometimes better and sometimes, to be optimistic, very questionable. They are journeying through a technological environment which we could not ever have imagined sixty years ago. Had I belonged to my parents' generation, I probably never would have been able, as a lay person, to teach Religious Education in a Catholic high school; so I am happy to have appeared in life when I did. There are aspects to our children's and grandchildren's lives that we never dreamed we would experience. Some of them, I think, are great and others, I fear, are not as fulfilling as my bride and I would hope; but then their hopes aren't quite the same as our hopes were. Life certainly goes forward, at least in time, as it did for Job and his family. I sincerely hope that our grandchildren can enjoy some aspects of contemporary society that my bride and I have difficulty in accepting, and yet, the bottom line is that "life is good" because created by God and "there is hope" because God loves us whom He created. That makes us His special creatures, whether we are conscious of that or not. We continue to love, to hope, to have children, to plan, to endure pain, to blossom in life, and to try our best to get up when we fall down. In the years that I have served as a Eucharistic Minister visiting the sick and homebound is always a privilege and at the same time, a very humbling experience. I bring them the Body of Christ in the Eucharist. When we pray together, we always ask for the wisdom of knowing that God is with us. The Creator, who gave us life, will never abandon us; we are never alone, no matter how deeply we are suffering. And the people to whom

I bring the body of Christ continue to help me to grow and to appreciate the fragileness of life. A great gift! Perhaps their greatest gift to me has been to appreciate today and to hope for tomorrow.

Job envisioned no hope as he began to assess his situation. Even though his wife urged him to turn away from the God to Whom he had been so faithful, Job doesn't. He is baffled, bewildered, and somewhat beaten, which is not strange. He knows that he has been clobbered, but has no idea why. Brooding, he sinks so low as to "curse the day he was born." Job doesn't curse God, at least not directly. He does curse the day of his birth, crying out that it would have been better had he not been born. In the next essay we are going to see this cry repeated again in one of the best movies ever filmed, "It's a Wonderful Life." To curse the day of one's birth is tantamount to saying that one's life is meaningless, is not *worthwhile*. And since Job sees Yahweh, God, as the creator of all, this certainly questions his fidelity, if nothing else. It is understandable that his faith in God is challenged and somewhat shaken. He is a good man living a good life [-] and isn't there a connection between being good and living well? I am doing what God expects, or at least what I think God expects, and therefore living well should be a consequence, but that is not happening now. He wished he had never set foot on this earth.

I think that this describes what later thinkers like the 16th century Spanish mystic, Saint John of the Cross, called "the dark night of the soul." Instead of resorting to pain killers and other medication, he like others, before and after, painfully experienced a sense of "nothingness" and questioned and prayed to climb out of the depths onto the heights. In Plato's "allegory of the cave" in one of the greatest philosophic books ever written, "The Republic," the struggle for true knowledge is one that begins with the self motivation of the individual to search for the truth that will allow him to appreciate the significance of life no matter how difficult. We move slowly out of the cave into the sunlight where we can begin to appreciate life as it is truly meant to be lived. The brightness of the sun may blind us temporarily, but then as we begin to adjust our vision, we are led into appreciating the world in which we live, not sheltered as in a cave, but open to the experiences we encounter on the road of life. That is, unless, of course, fear drives us back into the darkness, which we mistake for safety. The "dark night of the soul" for mystics involves experiencing the hurt and pain and suffering in life so that there can be the possibility of an ascent to the realization that joy is not the absence of suffering, but the presence of God, whose primary concern, from Creation to the Cross, has always been to bring us to Him for all eternity. In the midst of one's own pain and suffering, it is sometimes difficult to imagine that there is a God Who cares, a God Who loves, a God with Whom I can relate. When one is hurting, there is little to appreciate in life, except to deal with the hurting, and there's no appreciation in that. There are a number of people who have shared similar experiences involving real and perceived setbacks and spiritual wrestling in one's hoping to journey with God. In the Old Testament we read about Jacob wrestling with the angel, describing a spiritual combat in which the human person tries to understand and eventually accept what the divine is calling him to do. The wrestling is with the established customs of those times. Specifically, the law in question is that of primogeniture, which establishes the traditional and legal significance of the first born son. However, God's ways are not simply man's ways. The elder son inherits the property and the land, but Jacob wrestles this away from his elder brother, Esau, and answers God's call to lead His people. It wasn't easy then, nor is leadership easy today. Maybe God takes to wrestling with us because we are too complacent or willing to let an unjust situation continue to hurt people, maybe even ourselves. Sometimes a well placed kick to a certain part of the anatomy (rhetorically speaking, of course) is more convincing than a "please do this." Victory in a divine wrestling situation ends with fidelity to God and to His covenant. Our relationship with God is not always comfortable, nor easy. Maybe that is because He knows us so well and that He is wise enough to know that there are "different strokes for different folks." We don't all respond to wisdom's advice in the same manner.

Recently a biographer mentioned Mother Theresa of Calcutta's "dark night of the soul." Any kind of spiritual or difficult mental experience is going to be accompanied by physical struggling and suffering as well. And so it is with Job, the struggling is the pain; the reconciliation, as we shall see, is the gain. Not too long ago, Nelson Mandela, the South African leader died and continues to be acknowledged by people around the globe. The movie, "Invictus" depicted his love of and affection for rugby. He certainly represents the significance of the rugby motto "no pain, no gain." The pain involved twenty-seven years of imprisonment; the gain was reconciliation through forgiveness and the rebuilding of his country rather than the retaliation and destruction which could have been the choices made after Mandela's liberation from prison. His actual path of peaceful coexistence highlights the perennial struggle between legality and morality and whether or not the legal judiciary is itself moral. This is difficult for some to assess and easy for others to judge, but perhaps this is why wisdom, while elusive, is always possible. Wisdom requires patience because it takes time [-] its own time, not ours.

When any of us have been hurt, we turn to other people, consciously or unconsciously, for some kind of support. Initially we probably don't have specific questions or issues for which we seek answers, but we simply seek help to survive, help to ask the right questions, help to recognize useful answers, help to set us on the path to some kind of positive direction. We seek help to make some kind of sense of what is happening to us because we don't fully understand why we are in this dilemma. The experiences of so many people in the recent disaster of the super storm "Sandy" are reminders. While the storm brought physical damage initially, its aftermath of psychological, emotional, and economic damage were, and continue to be, lingering examples of human pain and suffering. A few years after this terrible storm, there are still so many people attempting to rebuild their homes and their lives [-] people who have not received the financial aid from insurance companies, and government agencies, and charitable organizations who promised them that help is available for the asking. Many people asked, but did not receive. We need to be consoled, to be comforted, and to be nourished by the milk of human kindness which comes not only from the lips of others, but also and more importantly from their consistent and ongoing actions. However there are still promises from people, from government agencies, from charitable organizations, which haven't been met. Perhaps one of the reasons I mention this disaster so often is because it is a contemporary situation which could have, and should have, been resolved. The resources are available, but innocent people are still hurting. Why?

Help comes to Job in the form of three friends. They come to console Job in his grief and suffering, but, as we all know, intentions and actions don't always complement each other. So begins a series of dialogues, or conversations, between the friends and Job. I do believe they initially really intended to console him, but whenever we set out to help others, we do so with a history. That history includes our own value system, our own sense of what should be done, and our own approach to how reconciliation and hope will take place. It usually includes an understanding of the other person's hurt, but we rarely experience the depth of the hurt which the other person is undergoing. If someone in my family is injured or dies tragically and you come to console me, to offer your sympathy for me and my family, you understand that I am hurting, but you don't fully experience my hurt. You cannot feel my feelings. I appreciate your sympathy, your comfort, but you could never experience the depth of my hurt, because my relation to the person who is sick or has died is not the same as yours; yet, I appreciate your reaching out because you share a concern for and with me. You appreciate the reality that the human condition offers many occasions for joyous celebration but at the same time is interrupted by setbacks and suffering. After all, the world is still in process. It is not yet fully perfected. It is not yet fully created, which is why Genesis one calls us to be caretakers. This is the case with Job's friends. They understand he is hurting. They understand his need for support, but it turns out that instead of helping to support him in his pain and suffering, they wind up condemning him because they were *more* concerned with their own convictions regarding life than they were with his individual experience. They end up judging Job by what they consider important rather than reaching out to help him carry his own cross. They heard Job's cry but didn't listen carefully to him, because their interpretation of life took precedence over Job's pain and suffering. They got bogged down with their own thoughts and priorities rather than addressing Job's pain and responding to it. They got in their own way while trying to help their friend and their own concerns prevented them from comforting him. Has that happened to us? People mean well, but they just don't deliver. Or are we guilty of advising others because of what we think should be done rather than what they need, now, at this moment in time.

In the first cycle of dialogues, Job is cursing the day of his birth exhibiting his despair at having been born. This is serious because if I think, or believe, that my existence has little or no value in life, then how do I proceed, how do I journey through life? How do I not "throw in the towel" and give up attempting to discover whatever meaning I might have in this earthly existence? This is the beginning of his feeling sorry for himself and while this is understandable, it is a sure path to self-destruction. I don't think there are many of us who have not experienced some degree of self-pity at different times in life. Some of us thrive on it, and some of us are ashamed of it, and some of us are destroyed by it. I think that most of us can understand Job's self pity. His cursing also suggests that, unlike Genesis one and two, perhaps God's creation is not good. It is clear in the Genesis myths that God's creation is good. Here, the particularly unfair suffering of the individual raises the question of whether God's purpose in creating the covenant experience is good, or arbitrary and whimsical, as in subject to change without notice, or unpredictable.

The three friends who stop by to "console" Job are named Eliphaz, Bildad, and Zophar. Eliphaz, the most patient of the friends, reminds him of the good he has done in life. Job has helped others. This confirms the fact that Job is "a righteous person." He has befriended people and they have been helped by him. He has to balance his torment with the good deeds that he has done. Bildad, who tends to be more demonstrative and self assured, attempts to remind Job of the need to trust God because of the suffering their ancestors experienced during history and the fact that God cared for them. After all, Job is simply suffering like those who went before him; so there is no big deal. (At least it is no big deal for Bildad, because he is not one who is suffering.)

At this point it is important to acknowledge that Job is not a flesh and blood historical person of the Israelite faith, as are Moses and Joshua, David and Solomon. He is essentially a model [-] he is a type of the innocent person who suffers unjustly. This is why the book is philosophical as well as theological. It could be viewed without the historical roots of the covenant people. The reality is there are innocent people who suffer unjustly in life, both in the historical past and in the contemporary present. It seems upon investigation that only the circumstances of the suffering changes. However, since this story appears in the Old Testament and the characters involved are clearly related to the covenant experience [-] even though all the characters do not understand nor appreciate their covenantal relationship with God [-] we can accept the theological foundation of this wonderful piece of literature. While it is both sad and a reality that people suffer, there is a depth of empathy, sympathy, and sadness for people who are innocent and hurting, whether young or old. Acts of terrorism and the presence of incurable diseases highlight the suffering of the innocent, but are reminders of what the Book of Job is trying to teach [-] innocent people suffer in life's journeying. This is a reality which is neither easily learned nor easily accepted. Let's try to follow the story through.

The third friend, who is called Zophar reminds Job of the "hidden depths of Divine Wisdom." Only God knows" is his answer. In a sense, he is absolutely correct. We are not divine; we come into existence and we go out of existence, while "God is!" Yet the covenant tells us of our significant relationship with God, and the messenger-prophets remind us that in good times and in terrible times that God cares for us, and our response to this is acceptance or rejection, faith or disbelief. The consequences of our choices are life enhancing or life threatening. Zophar, in his self-righteousness, "passes the buck" to God and seems to suggest we don't have a chance (don't have a prayer) in trying to understand what is happening. What a terrible way for a human person to go through life, thinking or believing that he or she has no role in what constitutes their ultimate reward, or punishment. How terrible it is to think that there is nothing significant or valuable to what I contribute in life. Everything is arbitrarily decided. This is certainly not a description of the covenantal relationship between God and us as described throughout the Old Testament. These conversations go on for three cycles of speeches with an increasing distancing between the "consolers" and the one seeking "consolation."

Initially, Eliphaz, Bildad, and Zophar come as friends to comfort Job in his grieving. The philosophic question of "appearance and reality" emerges as the conversations continue. They appear to be solicitous, appear to be comforters, but are they really who they appear to be? With each cycle of speeches, there are attitude changes as the sensitive

Eliphaz, the argumentative Bildad, and the blunt Zophar engage Job. They really get "in his face." Like Job, they also are types of people. They typify the different kinds of people we meet in life. There are those who try to influence us by suggestion, by offering ways through which we might deal with our pain. Some use reasonable arguments suggesting that we are blinded by our own suffering and cannot see things as they really are. Finally, there are those who simply try to "bully" us into accepting our situation, our fate, as beyond anything we can understand. Just accept what is happening and move on. These types are exemplified by the friends in this poem. Since no one functions in a vacuum in life, it is important to note that their theological frame of reference is narrow and legalistically grounded. Throughout the Old and New Testaments, blessings and curses are used to emphasize the importance of the consequences of keeping or not keeping the covenant. Blessed is one who does, and woe (or cursed) is the one who does not remain faithful to the covenant demands. After all, the covenant, or the unconditional friendship between God and us, requires each party to contribute or the relationship will fail to become what it is meant to be. This refers back not only to the Adam and Eve myth in Genesis, but also to the historical developing of the Israelite people who "blessedly" kept the covenant alive at times, and "woefully" broke the covenant relationship more often than not. We may also substitute, or least I may substitute "Christian" for "Israelite" as history continues [-] sometimes "blessedly" keeping God's covenant with us, and at other times, "woefully" breaking, or at least, trying to rearrange the covenant relationship to become more user friendly [-] to ourselves.

As an aside, the theoretical purpose of the Crusades could probably be considered as somewhat "noble", to regain the Promised Land upon which Jesus walked and taught. The means are certainly suspect [-] war. I am aware in discussing the concept of war, that there is such an ethical notion as "just defense." One should question whether the Crusades fit this category. I doubt it, no matter how well intentioned it might historically have seemed at the time. There was no clearly identifiable question of defense, and the issue of justice seems more suspect than righteous. Did the Crusades reflect the purpose of the Genesis covenant or did they "misuse" the covenant relationship to seek support for questionable activities? After all, poor God has been called upon and used to justify certain actions of some people against other people. "In God's name" has not always been used as God intends. I won't get into the "Inquisition" which clearly misrepresented God's covenant with His people, because some leaders unjustly and sinfully interpreted what God wanted to satisfy their own agendas. Their decisions, in no way, attempted to appreciate God's universal care for all of us. Sometimes, when we think we know what God wants us to do, we simply don't. We substitute what we want. As a Christian, on behalf of all the "Inquisitors", I apologize. Please God, accept this apology. And in apologizing to God, I pray for all the unjustly treated victims of the Inquisition. This is a painful and unjust event in our Church History. Jesus recognizes this in the New Testament when He says, "Not everyone who says "Lord, Lord, shall enter the Kingdom of Heaven." (Matthew 7:21) He said it because not everyone means to do God's will, or because there are those of us who "use the Lord's name in vain." To be sorry involves a very conscious effort to "right a wrong" as well as to engage in an effort to avoid the same and similar wrongs in the future. For example, in today's day and age, the issue of a "just defense war" is certainly questionable given the nuclear and long distance missile abilities to attack and inflict lasting damage on other nations. Nuclear weaponry, which inflicts tremendous earthly suffering and death challenges the philosophic issue of whether or not a just war theory is valid in this day and age.

When we attempt to understand contemporary situations like the United States invasion of Iraq, or the "Arab Spring uprisings", or the "Occupy Wall Street" movement, we will find interpretations of support and opposition to each of them. It seems there were no "weapons of mass destruction." Why invade Iraq? The uprisings against dictatorial Arab leaders fell short of any peaceful resolution. Were the protests reasonable? Why were protestors jailed? The protests against the immoral agents of Wall Street yielded few, if any, ethical resolutions. Why weren't they held accountable for their unethical and/or criminal activity? Are these revolutionary decisions justified by the circumstances which preceded them or are they unjustifiable actions on the part of some people who are "out of control"? In terms of social justice, we read of "pros" and "cons" and yet we know that particular invasions, or uprisings, or movements are not equally just or righteous. Some are real attempts to right wrongs, but some are just "cover ups" to wrongful actions.

The pedophilia issue facing the Catholic church I love is scandalous both with respect to the actions perpetrated on innocent victims and the cowardice of some religious officials in failing to serve God's people with either justice or mercy. "Defending" the integrity of the Catholic church as an institution in no way justifies the human perversion executed by some of our usually, highly regarded clerical leaders and the question remains: are we, the laity, guilty of enabling the sinful actions by the way we treat the clergy, or, like the victims, are we also victims? There are consequences to hurting people and there are consequences to those who allow the hurting to continue. There is no obvious blanket answer to all experiences of social and political and religious confrontations. Do the above mentioned situations reflect an understanding of our covenant relationship or a false interpretation? This is not an easy question to ignore because of so many people have suffered and are still suffering because of the decisions that were made. Consequences followed these social and political decisions, and like Job's particular situation, many people suffered and never understood why they were suffering; but they, and we, and Job still have to respond to the suffering.

Let us return once again to the Book of Job. The doctrine of reward and punishment is a major concern in the lives of most people. The punishment aspect is identified with suffering, especially temporal or earthly suffering. As of this time in history, the Israelite people had not fully developed the afterlife consequences of heaven and hell. The friends, therefore, are in agreement with a prevailing theological notion of the time; namely, *to sin is to suffer*. This is also the case in Saint John's Gospel in the New Testament. In the story of the man born blind (chapter 9), the disciples ask Jesus whose fault is it that the man suffers from blindness, his or his parents? So the prevailing understanding in the Book of Job continues six hundred years into the future to the time of Christ and beyond. I suspect it is found in some contemporary situations as well, just like the "just war" theory. Any kind of suffering, at the time of Job, suggested, and was believed by many, that the one suffering was obviously a sinner; hence, their escalating attempt to get Job to confess his sins. It was obvious to his friends that the bottom line was: Job is a sinner, no matter how many good deeds he had done. These deeds masked a sinner and Job refused to acknowledge the "wisdom" of their collective judgment. Consolation and compassion are replaced by condemnation. The cycles of speeches are expressions of the tensions or clashes between the traditional emphasizing of the covenant rooted in the observances of laws, rules and rituals versus the modern (and original theological intention) emphasizing of the covenant as the living expressions of love for God and for fellow man. (Perhaps this is the primary message of our current Pope Francis: it is God's love which should be the primary motivator of our lives, forgiveness is an expression of love. Laws are a means to an end, and have as their purpose to clarify and direct, but ultimately one embraces the covenant by how he or she acts with consistency in our everyday lives.) The clash involves the friends who adhere to the letter of the (Mosaic) Law and Job who has embraced the spirit of the Law. Basically, I think, the conflict between Job and his friends stems from their different images of God. The friends' image of God as a legalistically demanding judge begins to influence Job until he is "brought up short" and recognizes their image of God is false; then his eyes are opened and he repents.

The conversations break down in disagreement. Job is mired in his sufferings, which he still cannot understand. The "friends" see Job as a "loser" primarily because he won't listen to them and do as they say: admit you are a sinner, confess your sins, and then all will be fine. They are living examples of those who follow the "letter of the law" but not the "spirit of the law." If Job would just say the words of repentance, everything will be fine. But Job knows that there is more involved in this experience than can simply be resolved through a liturgical expression. For Job any liturgical expression ought to reflect the relationship with God. For the friends, their concern is only with the appearance of penance, not with the reality of Job's situation.

On the other hand, Job is emboldened. He challenges God to a duel of words. The dialog has become a monolog and Job engages in a "war of words" with God, initially within his own sub-consciousness, and eventually in a face to face confrontation. I have often thought that it is this point in the story where Job begins to emerge from his self pity. He was certainly involved in pitying himself, and understandably so. But now Job is angry. By the way, anger, in and of itself, is not necessary a "bad thing." It depends upon the object of one's anger. I certainly ought to be angered by injustice, by some people manipulating others, by people who refuse to exercise their talents and abilities, by prejudice. I ought to be angered by my own refusal to reach out to others in support when I could and should. I ought to be angry with the time I waste in life playing computer games or not returning phone calls to friends or not seeking to understand why so many people are hurting when I am not. I am my sister's and brother's keeper. Am I expressing that with consistency in my life? Anger is an emotion, a response, which has justification given the object of anger and the particular situation. Job's anger is directed at God because he is suffering and according to his friends, he is suffering because he is a sinner. He has broken the relationship with God. Job is protesting this because he claims that he is not what his friends suggest he is. He is a good person. He has tried to be a faithful and caring person. He is a believer. At the beginning of the story, it is pointed out that Job is a faithful follower and a religious believer in good standing. He resents that his friends are accusing him of being a sinner, and, of course, the difficulty is that he has begun to believe his friends are right. And if they are right, then it is God Who is unfair. To this point, the external drama has been magnificently played out, the self pitying is coming to an end, and the real internal conflict is about to be embraced as Job wrestles with God.

There are movies dealing with suffering and death. "Life is Beautiful" is a movie which takes place during World War II. Roberto Benigni (who won an Oscar for this role) plays a Jewish book keeper married to an Italian woman. They have a son, Joshua. The Nazis arrest them and the child is hidden in the prison by Benigni in a series of hilarious situations. The situation is a tragedy, and if you can believe it, the movie is a comedy, or perhaps a tragic-comedy. Humor is used to cover up the human suffering, all because he is a Jew, his only crime. By playing games he eventually saves his son who is freed by the conquering US armed forces. Benigni is killed by a firing squad. He handled his imprisonment with humor and saved his child by making believe they were playing a game. He cared and used what he was comfortable with to insure the safety of his son.

Another movie that deals with suffering is "The Way." It is a movie in which Martin Sheen plays a successful American eye doctor. His son, Emilio Estavez, drops out of the university to go traveling, and Sheen is greatly upset by his son's unwillingness to follow in his father's footsteps. His father sees him as ungrateful. The son wants to walk the 500 mile "Camino de Santiago" in Spain in honor of Saint James. It is a journey during which the religious, or spiritual, pilgrim is afforded the opportunity to reflect on his or her own earthly journey against the landscape of the Pyrenees Mountains and the alongside the seascape of the Atlantic Ocean. Sadly, the son dies as he is about to begin the journey and Martin Sheen travels overseas to claim his body. While there, he decides to deal with the pain of losing a son by completing the pilgrimage for him and in honor of him. He completes the difficult journey with the companionship of other pilgrims, along the way [-] a companionship he would not ever have imagined sharing.

A third movie is "Sleepless in Seattle" with Tom Hanks and Meg Ryan (one of my favorite films because I am a romantic.) The occasion for the movie is sad because his young wife has died and as part of the grieving process he decides to move to Seattle with his eight or nine year old son, in the hopes of "beginning over." In these tragic events, the suffering people responded differently; but in each case, the concern was someone other than themselves, namely, their sons. Benigni's concern was to save his son. Sheen's concern was to honor his son. Hanks' concern was to give his son an opportunity to embrace life differently. All were suffering, but all "triumphed" because their primary concern was focused on someone else.

In Job's case, initially his primary concern was himself and why he was suffering. As he began to question, to reach out to someone else, to challenge God as to why he was suffering, he began the process of liberation. His real prison, thanks to the ineffective, or rather selfish, "consolation" of his friends, was not only the physical sufferings he was undergoing, but the self pity. He reached out to friends for support, but they failed him. His concern became focused inwards. In the movies, Roberto Begnini, Martin Sheen and Tom Hanks saw a purpose in their suffering, and they acted upon it. In each case, it was their children. So far, Job's primary concern has been himself, and it is this aspect of his life that has begun to cripple

135

him and make him angry. The object of his anger is God, Whom at one time He revered and glorified, because they were friends!

Job has lost all his land and property and that would suggest that people who relied upon Job for employment and for what his land yielded in terms of produce and trade have certainly been affected. Realistically, therefore, a number of social dependents have suffered losses in the aftermath of Job's situation. My parents always provided a roof over my head while growing up. I never missed a meal, even though perhaps I should have missed some, and I have benefited from their social and religious education and upbringing. As a husband, my wife and I have provided, as best as we could (I hope) a home in which five sons began their journeys to manhood. There weren't others economically dependent on our actions, at least not primarily dependent on what we did. I sympathize with Job and his "failure" to provide for many people, but I cannot fully appreciate his situation because my responsibilities have been identified almost exclusively as immediate family responsibilities. I was never wealthy enough, in worldly terms, to be economically responsible for large numbers of people, as Job obviously was. While I have assisted in some community activities, and I have been responsible for thousands of students' educational progress, I was never responsible for the very immediate livelihood of many people. I participate in the community, but haven't been a community leader, and provider, in the sense that Job seems to have been. I can appreciate some of the difficulty he encountered because I can empathize with some contemporaries who have lost jobs, savings, and homes. Many are victims of the recent immoral or unethical financial upheavals, both in our city, nationwide and worldwide, but not in the sense that my decisions and my situation led directly to their difficulties. By the way, I mention unethical, because in the same way as Job suffered, it is not primarily the fault of some, if not many, people who suffer, especially economically. Their economic, and consequently social downfall, stems from decisions made by others, who should not have made those decisions. These "other" people should have been held more responsible for the suffering they brought into many people's lives. Job is not guilty of any unethical decision making. And yet, many obviously innocent people suffered from what happened to him.

Job also lost his family. His children were murdered or died in natural disasters. The suffering that follows from the loss of children is devastating. We recall that a few short years ago some twenty first and second graders, along with six teachers, were murdered at Newton in Connecticut. Instead of a national mourning period and outrage over the numbers of lethal weapons available to people who weren't responsible, there were "arguments" about the amount and nature of governmental gun control legislation. Some will say this stems from cowardice on the part of those in "leadership" positions, while others will argue for the "right to bear arms." Both positions are understandable, but the very disconcerting question arises: is *understanding* enough? Are the understandings of both positions equally valid? Does one position (social and political leadership) have a more valid reason for being followed than the other position (right to bear arms) in a country where there are national armed forces as well as numerous local police authorities. I guess that is why some "arguments" are more "smokescreens" than reasoned concerns.

We have been blessed with five sons and eight grandchildren. After Pat was born and before John appeared on the scene, we lost a baby, which is medically described as a miscarriage. The doctor explained this as nature's attempt to address the reality that the baby would not have been born. The growth process had not proceeded as nature intended. Reason allows us, in time, to understand that some events in life do not come about as intended. We have to remember that nature, including the human condition, is a process which is not yet completed, or perfected. There are flaws in life [-] unexpected happenings. What was particularly painful at the time was that I saw our baby, a few months old, being carried by the doctor in a bed pan. The baby was beginning to form with noticeable little arms and legs and a head, but he was all bloody and in two parts. I can't recall the particulars of why I saw the baby, but I did, and it is as vivid today as it was many years ago. It led to what we would call a spiritual experience. Pat was almost a year old, and developing wonderfully like any baby naturally should, and indeed the boys who followed him did as well. Both Dona and I prayed and reflected and accepted what happened. Not well, initially, but in time. I mentioned a spiritual experience, which is not always an event that happens at a certain moment in time, but can be "something" that occurs over a prolonged period of time. We regularly encounter events in life, and through reflection, they become experiences. They become experiences when we realize that "something" has changed in our lives because of what we encountered, whether that change is positive or negative in terms of how we view reality.

The bottom line is that we look at life differently than we had. Maybe the experiential change is "something" we see, or realize, for the first time. As I reflected upon our first born and our "not born," I gradually came to realize that I hadn't thought much about the significance of beginnings, or endings, in life. Pat's developing as a normal, active little baby allowed me, as a proud parent, to realize how each human life is *powerful*. Each of us has the possibility of learning, of growing, of changing, of affecting those around us. Each of us is powerful because we can influence the way others respond to us, even little babies. Think of how we respond to babies. We try to interact with them and that means that we try to "get down" to their level, not in any condescending way, but so we can relate to them. They draw us to them, not only to feed and clothe and care for them, but to share life at their level with them. Babies are powerful. The death of our second-to-be child led me to appreciate another aspect of human life [-] we are *fragile*. There are aspects of life we cannot control nor influence nor overcome without the help of others. There are aspects of life that highlight our vulnerability, our utter dependence on others [-] simply to exist [-] hopefully, to exist well. I came to embrace in this experience "something" as a father, and as a husband, and later as a teacher, that to me is the most significant appreciation of created humanity. The mystery of human existence is that each of us is powerful and fragile *simultaneously*. Not only do we have the power to make decisions and originate actions which have consequences not only for ourselves but for others as well (we are individuals), but we are subject to being influenced well or poorly by the consequences which follow upon decisions by and to others (we are social by nature.) In other words, we are powerful thanks to what we decide and simultaneously, we are fragile because of what happens beyond our ability to decide, to choose. Thanks to the baby who was never born, I began to appreciate that everyone in my life with whom I come into contact is this mystery of power and fragility. Thank God, Pat and his four brothers John, Marty, Chris and Mike all grew to become good men. They and their wonderful wives brought forth children, grandsons and granddaughters who are also becoming terrific young women and men. Later, as I began to teach I came to embrace the notion of "cura personalis" in Jesuit education, which is a principle I have tried to live not only as an educator but as a human person. It means to care for the individual person. It doesn't matter whether she or he is a student or colleague, or a family member, or a neighbor or a stranger. Anyone we meet is both powerful and fragile simultaneously. This, of course, is not confined to the classroom but extends to all life contexts. At the time, I suspect that Eliphaz, Bildad, and Zophar saw themselves as powerful and Job as fragile. They had no concept of "cura personalis", the care-filled response which Job needed to respond to his suffering.

I do believe this experience helped me as a father, a grandfather, and a teacher. I still cry in remembering our baby. Unlike Job, I never knew him. The doctor confirmed he was a boy. The pain of losing a child, with whom you hadn't shared life, is not as great a burden as losing a child whom you know and with whom you have shared life, whether that lifetime is brief or extended. I can identify with Job in this aspect of his loss, but not, thankfully, to the same depth. There is, in Job's loss of his children, another aspect of the depth of Job's loss and the intensity of his pain.

In September of 2001, I had retired from Xavier High School but was still teaching Philosophy at St. Peter's College, a Jesuit university in Jersey City. I was teaching on Tuesdays at Newark Airport as part of a college program with Port Authority personnel. On the 11th of that month I would be going through the World Trade Center around four in the afternoon [-] except, on that afternoon, there was no World Trade Center, no PATH trains, no transportation to school. A former student of mine, who was working on the "clean up" took me onto the site a few weeks later. I wrote in a short article:

"The skeletal steel burnt remains of Tower One might remind one of a giant harp with no tune ever to come from it again. It is only a few stories high and just one part of a side of what had been a magnificent one hundred story building. To its side are the charred remains of a few floors of Building Five against which some of Tower One crashed. Behind Building Five is a copy...the charred remains of Building Six... into which some of Tower Two hurled steel and brick. There is no Tower Two...no Marriott Hotel...only a hole in the ground with lots and lots of debris to mark where it once proudly stood against the New York skyline. Where we were standing marked the overpass that connected the World Trade Center to the wonderful atrium alongside the Hudson River path. There is no more connection.

"It is difficult to sort out the thoughts with which one is bombarded as you walk around. Perhaps the thought that screamed at me initially was that no one should suffer like this, should die like this. No one should be ripped from his or her life journey like this...but that is what happened. As a Christian, I thought of Christ hanging on the Cross. That was unjust. There was pain and suffering and a horrible death, just as there was on the tip of Manhattan Island, New York City, on September 11, 2001. The rubble, the debris, the bare remains of some parts of building is a reminder of suffering and death and vengeance and terror in our world. And yet I believe Our God is a God of life and hope and peace. I prayed that those who on that day were prepared to meet their God were embraced by Him and led to the banquet table of the Father. And I suspect, like many of us, there were some who weren't prepared to meet their God. For them I pray that the God of life, in His mercy, forgives them whatever might have delayed their meeting Him. I think that the reason we cry and are in pain when someone dies is that we miss him or her because we love him or her. Our human love, which is real and which can be deep and generously given to others, is a pale reflection of the love God has for every one of us. His is the love that begins our earthly journey in the womb of a mother and continues throughout a lifetime of relationships and concludes with the God Who made us looking for us at death. I believe this. And while it doesn't make sense of the disastrous scene in front of me, it allows me to accept it, even while I don't understand it.

"One is reminded of the incredible fragileness of life. In literally the blink of an eye, people who shared our world, our life, are no longer with us as they have been...some for many years and through many experiences. Yet, as I watched the water trucks pour their streams on smoldering ruins, I could image the burning towers in their last moments filled with heroic people, fire and police personnel, accountants and store clerks, security guards and maintenance people, directing, leading, helping others to escape [-] while many of them did not. We are not only fragile, but we also possess a strength that encourages us to act, to more forward. Among the mysteries of the human person is that we are fragile and powerful simultaneously."

On that day, ten of my former Xavier students and two St. Peter's students died. Ten other former students lost spouses and siblings. I finished the article by writing...

"A final thought as I gaze at the twisted steel, the smoke, the dirt and the incredible number of good people who risked their lives in rescuing and restoring is that everyone who died and everyone who mourns for them is more important to God than all the buildings and monuments that were ever built or will ever be built."

Job's story is not up to the scale of the September 11, 2001 horror, or Hiroshima, or the Holocaust. But as an individual's story, it has the same elements, the same proportionate amount of suffering and pain, but to a lesser degree. Job's pain includes the loss, at least of affection and support of his wife. In short, the love necessary for a husband and wife to share, and on which little else can be built in married life, was no longer present. And if it is no longer present, then neither can the joys be shared as they should, nor could the sufferings be endured as they ought. I cannot imagine what this entails. When I left the business world to go into high school teaching with five children, and far fewer benefits, in my family only Dona supported my decision. Other family members pointed out that the business world offered far many more incentives to me as a father than did Catholic education, at least financially, and, of course, they were right. But the point here is that, unlike Job, I had and have the support of my wife. I have had her support and been her support for over fifty-nine years. Without it, life would lose vision, interest, and encouragement. It would include neither the support necessary when life's burdens become too heavy to bear, nor would it allow for the reason to celebrate when life's joys called for sharing. To lose the support of one's closest friend, the one with whom I share both the seriousness and frivolousness of life, would be devastating [-] and so it must have been with Job. He had lost "everything."

Now, the reason I bring this up, is that, intellectually, I can understand pain and suffering. Intellectually, I can understand that family tragedies and the lack of family support can exacerbate difficulties. I can understand physical hurt as well as psychological and emotional hurt. I can try to enter into Job's suffering using my own experiences in life and I can get a part of the way into his scene. I cannot get there completely, but I can begin to realize the depth of his suffering. I have one more way of getting close to embracing Job's pain.

In 1971, Mike was a student of mine at Xavier High School. He was intelligent, athletic, musically gifted and ambitious enough to want to develop his various God given talents. He went to college and on to graduate studies where he became a doctrinal candidate. While studying for his degree, he returned to Xavier and became an administrator while also teaching mathematics. My student had become my colleague. He ran a New York City marathon, played the piano and had composed some forty songs. He was a black belt instructor in Tae Kwon Do. He was a mainstay on the Faculty basketball team against the senior football students in the annual Christmas game. He married and they brought their first son into the world. He had become my friend. While his wife was pregnant with son number two, Mike went for a routine eye examination. What he discovered was that he had a massive brain tumor which, at first, was diagnosed as inoperable. A second medical opinion, thanks to a Xavier classmate who had become a doctor, led to the possibility of addressing this "irreversible situation" which resulted in a series of operations. Scientifically speaking, the operations were successful. Mike lived. The warnings were clear. He wouldn't walk again, nor would he probably ever be gainfully employed. In August 1984, his life had changed as dramatically as Job's life changed. He had lost the capability and resources to live life as he had for the first thirty years of his existence in this world, just like Job.

In the time that followed, Mike's life as a loving husband, father and teacher was replaced by treatment and rehabilitation at the Brain Injury Association of New York State, and the Coma Recovery Association. His right side was paralyzed. He couldn't walk. He experienced memory loss. He wouldn't ever play ball with his two sons. Running marathons would no longer be a possibility. Playing the piano was a thing of the past. Returning to work was out of the question. If anyone was a modern day Job, Mike had all the credentials to take over the biblical situation. Eventually, Mike, courageously, did get out of the wheelchair for which he substituted a cane, and that was, in time, discarded for the brace he still must strap on today to limp his way through life. He plays the piano, but with only one hand. He addresses his memory loss by writing everything down and following the large calendar on the kitchen wall. He returned to Xavier High School. Administration was replaced by teaching freshmen as well as a senior calculus course. None of this "success" was easy and none of it was expected by the neurosurgeons.

In 2004, Mike threw a "Thank You" party for family and friends to celebrate twenty years of life that medical people never thought he would have had. He gave all his guests a binder in which he included welcoming all of us to a party to celebrate his life after August 1984. After all, he wasn't expected to be around the last twenty years. It was clearly more enjoyable and entertaining than any party ever celebrated on television. Our personal program for the evening also included a list of "50 Things I'm Tired Of" and a list of "50 Things I'm Thankful For." He wrote a poem of thanksgiving to a rehabilitation counselor for helping him to articulate why he was appreciative for being alive. There were tributes from both his sons and other people whom he had influenced. As part of his rehabilitation he decided to answer questions like "Why Me?' and "What if?" and "Twenty Questions I'd like God to answer for me." I can only guess that these are the same questions that occurred to Job as he wondered and became increasingly more angry about his own situation. The one that really resonates with me is entitled "Who will ever know?" Mike ended answering this question with:

> "...Life after a traumatic brain injury is never easy and never simple, but it does go on. I've often wondered "What would life be like if I had accepted either neurosurgeon's prognosis? I've also asked myself the question 'Who will ever know?' I can't answer the former, but as for the latter question 'who will ever know?'...well, ultimately, you and God will know and that's really all that matters."

My student, my colleague, my friend, is a man of faith, but that doesn't mean that anger and frustration aren't still present at times. In Robert Bolt's "A Man for All Seasons," Thomas More is in his prison cell trying to convince his law clerk, Richard Rich, to pursue teaching rather than a political career. Rich thinks that a political career would be much more exciting because he would possibly be in the "public eye." He asks More, "who would know whether I am a teacher or not?" Thomas More's reply is "Why God would know and you would know...great company that!" Saint Thomas More is a martyr. Mike, and the students who were murdered on 9/11, are not martyrs, commemorated on a religious calendar, or martyrs in our ecclesial sense, but like Thomas More, in his suffering, he placed himself in God's hands, as I am sure many people in the twin towers did on 9/11. He surrendered himself to God like every genuine martyr does.

We can "explain" Thomas More's suffering because of a political confrontation with Henry VIII in the sixteenth century. We can "explain" Mike's suffering because of a medical condition in the twentieth century. We can "explain" Job's suffering as a sixth century BC biblical experience typifying his own as well as More's and Mike's situations as "innocents who suffer." We can "explain" the victims of 9/11 as victims of an unwarranted terrorist attack. Different centuries, different times, different people attest to the reality of suffering as part of life's ongoing process.

God keeps turning up in the experience of people's suffering. Is God a cause, or what? The short answer to this question is that if God is the cause of suffering, then the covenant is a charade, and the Cross might not be the sign of hope that we believe it is. If there are "innocents who suffer" *arbitrarily* because of God' whimsical nature [-] if there are people whom God picks out to suffer terribly, through no fault of their own, or even if they do deserve to suffer in our own worldly human understanding [-] then there is no joyful meaning to life [-] and my buddies, Socrates and Plato are wrong when they speak of life being worth living. Both Saint Thomas More and Mike, my student, my colleague, my friend believe that God's presence in all of this is significant, is important, and after all, they are the ones who suffered terribly. God created each one of us, so our sufferings are His sufferings and our joys are His joys. He created us and we respond to life and He always responds to us. We can only appreciate Job's sufferings because of our own experiences of suffering in life, whether it affects our own person directly or whether it is part of our growing experiences in life. After all, life is a process and the process is not finished until each of us dies. We are not finished with suffering, but let us return to Job and see what happens, when in his frustration, he challenges God, Yahweh, to answer him as to why he is suffering so terribly. God is in the sufferings of all the people I have mentioned, not as cause, but as companion. I will speak more of God's involvement in our suffering in the last chapter.

The conversations between Job and his "friends" break down with Job being sarcastic in dismissing their admonitions, because they really haven't presented anything comforting. Their message is repetitive: "you're a sinner, Job, and if you go through the motions of a penitential ritual, then everything will be okay [-] and, if you don't, then it is obvious to everyone that what happened to you is your fault." Job doesn't even let Zophar finish his last remarks but rather finishes them for him. He knows what to expect and realizes his friends haven't really focused on his suffering, but rather on why they feel he's suffering: he is a sinner. They were, like so many of the people we meet in life, legalists. The rules, or conventions, to follow were always more important than the people we encounter. Well, Job hasn't succumbed to their "judging" but has maintained his innocence. He begins to reminisce about how things went well when God loved him, and when he believed God was on his side.

Job basically cries out to Yahweh, "Why me?" What he did not expect is that God would answer him. More than this, he never expected the answer God gave.

Let's give Job credit here. He realized that he simply hadn't given up on what he was convinced was true. He loved God, and God loved him. So he did what was left to him: he challenged God to "man up" or better, to "God up" and answer him. He wasn't being flippant. He was sincere. He was convinced that he didn't sin as his friends suggested he did, but he also knew that he didn't have all the answers. There is a genuine humility about Job and humility essentially means that I know my place in life and my place in life is a good place, whatever it is. It simply isn't the final place. I really think that it is great that Job believes he is close enough to God to expect Him to answer, but as I said above, what surprises him is the answer.

God's response to Job in this book is certainly one neither Job expected, nor, I think, that anyone reading this book expects. The author's popular title for this section is "the Voice from the Whirlwind." God's words as they are heard echoing out of a cloud, or a storm, or a whirlwind, are often part of the covenantal dialogue in the Old Testament. What God does say however makes me, even today, sit up and pay attention. I can only imagine what it did to Job:

> Who is this that obscures divine plans with words of
> ignorance?
> Gird up your loins now, like a man...
> Where were you when I founded the earth...
> Who determined its size...Who laid the cornerstone...
>
> Have you ever in your lifetime commanded the morning
> and shown the dawn its place...
>
> Do you know the ordinances of the heavens; can you put
> into effect their plan on earth?
> Do you know about the birth of the mountain goats...

Will we have arguing with the Almighty by the critic? This is one of my favorite lines because sometimes I have been God's "critic" without having any significant understanding of the big picture. I probably have argued the "little picture" ad nauseum and, like Job, have frequently and incredibly missed the "big picture."

Job tries to "cop a plea" but Yahweh isn't finished with him yet. And God continues... Gird up your loins now, like a man...Now we are not going to say "gird up your loins" but we certainly don't need a translation of what that mean. It means "man up!"

And far too many of us, women and men, have refused to do this... to take responsibility for our actions and our inactions. Far too many of us have fallen into the "Adam and Eve" approach to life..."passing the buck" on our responsibility for our own actions.

Yahweh continues...*Would you refuse to acknowledge my right? Would you condemn me that you may be justified?*

Job finally answers "I know that you can do all things, and that no purpose of yours can be hindered. I have dealt with great things that I do not understand; things too wonderful for me, which I cannot know. I had heard of you by word of mouth, but now my eye (of faith) has seen you. Therefore I disown what I have said, and repent in dust and ashes." Job has let go of the image of God that his "friends" pressed him to accept [-] a legalistic image [-] an image of God projected by laws and rituals, rather than by love.

Maybe the Book of Job is a continuing of the prophet's expression of "tough love."

I remember an incident when I was a teenager. My father suffered what we thought was a heart attack. The doctor came and after awhile diagnosed something milder than what we had supposed. I had gone out to the living room and on my knees prayed that he would be okay and promised God all sorts of things *if* my Dad would be all right. Things worked out and later on I realized something important in my life. I didn't have to suppose that God cared for my father *because* of something I would do. He always cared for my father, my mother, and my brother and me. My trying to bargain with God and make promises didn't change God's love one iota. I believe that is what my student, colleague, and friend, Mike came to appreciate also. I think that is what Job finally came to realize. What he suffered was not God, Yahweh, turning against him because of something he did or failed to do, but rather that God was with him no matter what happened in this journey through life, which is neither guaranteed to be only painful, nor guaranteed to be only joyful. The guarantee is simply that our Creating God is always with us. After all, each of us is special because God fashioned us out of "nothing" to be "something" [-] His covenant friend.

The epilogue to the Book of Job is also fascinating. Job prays for the friends who *appeared* to be supportive, but *in reality* condemned him because he did not follow their advice. But Job prays for them and Yahweh, Who lets the "friends" know in no uncertain terms that they were "out of line," forgives them. He restores Job to health and to wealth and to family blessings. Three lessons immediately come to mind. One is that we never suffer alone because even though one might individually feel the pain, there are others who will be affected by our suffering and pain. There will be people who hurt because we are hurting. The second lesson is that there will always be the heavenly reconciliation to which each of us is invited, and this has been so from the beginning of earthly time. Earthly suffering is never an end-in-itself. The third lesson is distinctively an insight taken from the Book of Job; namely, earthly suffering is not punishment for one's human lifestyle.

In chapter one, I wrote that the world is in process. That process includes pain and suffering, as well as joy and friendship. The world though incomplete begins with the loving creation of the God Who enters into a covenant with us. The prophets remind us of our need to return God's love through how we act. The Book of Job reminds us that suffering in life is not punishment, but it will take the Crucifixion to help us to realize that suffering, while not joyful as an experience can become an act of love [-] and then, maybe, we will realize the significance of our creation, of our covenant. And, if nothing else, we have learned a tremendous lesson thanks to Job: suffering is neither only punishment nor only evil. There is, or could be, a redeeming element in it. Maybe, in time, we will more fully understand this.

Viktor Frankel, who wrote the deeply insightful book, "Man's Search for Meaning" which focused on suffering in the concentration camps, quoted Nietzsche when he wrote that "to live is to suffer, and to survive is to find meaning in the suffering." I am not quite sure what my friend, Nietzsche, means by "surviving", but I do think there is, or at least, can be meaning in suffering, because it is so much an aspect of the human condition. I would paraphrase it by saying that "often, to live might involve suffering, but to persist in loving overcomes all suffering." On a personal note, I hope that as I approach the end of my earthly life, I don't suffer terribly. But if I do, I will pray for the wisdom of knowing that the God Who made me is with me; so that I am never alone. After all, if anyone knows suffering [-] He does!

Towards the beginning of this chapter, I quoted from the Book of Ecclesiastes about the wisdom necessary for recognizing there are different times in life which call for different responses in our life's journey. I would like to finish with a reference to the Book of Psalms, specifically Psalm

139, which I believe is related to Wisdom Literature and teaches us about God's persistence in responding to the covenant relationship.

> *O Lord, you have probed me and you know me;*
> *You know when I sit and when I stand...*
>
> *With all my ways you are familiar.*
> *Even before a word is on my tongue,*
> *Behold, O Lord, you know the whole of it...*
>
> *Where can I go from your spirit?*
> *From your presence where can I flee?*
> *If I go to the heavens, you are there,*
> *If I sink to the nether world, you are present there...*
>
> *Truly you have formed my inmost being;*
> *You knit me in my mother's womb...*
>
> *Your eyes have seen my actions;*
> *In your book they are all written...*

This psalm, this song, this prayer teaches us that the God Who made us will never abandon us, whether we accept Him or reject Him. He will persist in loving us and pursuing us; so that we may join Him at the eternal banquet table. It is not unlike the 19th century poem by Francis Thompson entitled "The Hound of Heaven." In this poem which takes place in the hunt on the English countryside, God is the divine hound and we are the human hare. The divine hound pursues the human hare in the hunt for an eternal mutual embrace. It is not a hunt to the death, but a hunt to reconciliation and salvation, to fulfillment in life.

Wisdom involves accepting that the Creator God gives life to us as earthly guests so that at death, whether through much suffering, or little suffering, He once again, and for all eternity, is our eternal Host. Could the answer to the question "Why Me, God?" be:

And God saw everything that he had made, and behold, it was very good.

CHAPTER FOUR

Thanks for the Gift

"This is for me? Oh, thanks, you shouldn't have! But I really appreciate this gift." A genuine gift is something or someone offered freely by one person to another. It is the action through which someone wants another person to benefit, or to enjoy, from what is given freely and without reservation. The giver hopes the receiver will appreciate what he/or she has received. Gifts may be accepted or rejected by the one who is the recipient. Whatever you give me, I may respond with a "yes" or "no", whether that gift is "something" or whether the gift is "yourself." Either acceptance or rejection become the possible responses to any gift one is offered in life, and that includes the gift of life.

I believe that any created life is a gift. Human existence is a gift. None of us had to be born. We are not the causes of our own birth, of our own earthly existence. My philosopher friend, Aristotle, spoke of the distinction between the necessary being and contingent, or dependent, beings. We are not responsible for bringing ourselves into human existence. Philosophically speaking, we are contingent beings, dependent upon a necessary being, not only as the source of our existence, but also to keep us in existence from moment to moment. But this doesn't mean we are powerless. Aristotle also speaks of the act/potency principle in each created being in life. Each of us has the potential or power to grow in accordance with our (human) or its (animal or plant) nature. He began as a biologist and carried that understanding of "potential" into his philosophy. That means we have the power to *actualize*, or *realize* ourselves as mature and caring persons by what we do and say as we journey through life. An infant cannot become a tree, nor can a plant become a dog. Each created being has the power, or potential, to grow in accordance with his, her, or its own nature. There is tremendous power even in little infants as they lie in the crib waiting to be feed, changed and hugged. They smile, they coo, they cry and immediately and carefully, we respond. As they grow, they develop the power to respond to others, both those who are in need and those who are not. In other words, they will actualize or realize [make real] their own potential to become mature and caring people for the next generation they will eventually bring into God's created world.

I cannot guarantee I will finish typing the next sentence. My birth, my life, is a gift to my family, initially to my mother and father, and eventually to me as I grow. The gift of my life is originally offered to my parents, or whoever nourishes and nurtures me during that stage in which I am not fully conscious of who I am, nor capable of taking care of myself. I don't know during that time that I am a gift, but I do come to learn, with the help of those who care for me, that the gift of my life has a process to it: being a child, becoming an adolescent, and hopefully embracing what it means to be an adult. At least those are the sociological stages of the human growth process. Any gift includes someone who gives and someone who receives, and motives for giving and the appreciation for receiving can differ dramatically. Motives can vary from freely offered generosity to deceitfully trying to manipulate another person through one's falsely offered "gift." The response from the recipient can vary from "thanks" to "no thanks." Hopefully, most of us come to realize we are gifts, but unfortunately, experience reveals that some of us never come to that appreciation. The way we disrespect ourselves and others is testimony that not all of us accept life as a gift.

The original Christmas gift to humanity is the Christ Child, God's very *Person-al* gift to all of us. We can either accept or reject the gift of this Person. During the process of life, we come to embrace that "unto us is born a Savior, Jesus" or we reject His love through what we say and how we act. This event scripturally marks the beginning of what we Christians call the New Testament. We distinguish it from the Old

Testament. It is not a substitution for the Old Testament, but rather it is or should be a complementary expression bringing to fruition the promises made to the patriarchs and prophets. In a real sense, the Old Testament is a preparation for the New Testament. The Old Testament carries the promise, or potential, of the Anointed One, the Messiah promised by God. This Messiah is to be the Savior of His people. The New Testament, for us Christians, is the real or actual presence of the Messiah in time and history. However, there is a "surprise party" aspect which wasn't expected by those who patiently and eagerly awaited the coming of the Messiah. Most believers expected a man, perhaps a new and greater David who would lead his people to earthly victory. Instead of a new man [-] surprise [-] our Christmas gift is God become man - Emmanuel – God is with us in a way that not even the original Genesis II Garden of Eden covenant projected. We already have the most significant purpose in life as the primary created caretakers. But when God embraced our humanity as His own, we received an even more significant value which we still have difficulty in fully appreciating. We are quite a gift with quite a challenge. If only we could more fully appreciate the gift of being a human person. God certainly does. After all, He embraced our humanity.

The terms new and old (testaments, or otherwise) can be very relative terms. When I was a child, or a teenager, someone who was 40 or 50 years old was an old person, and that meant to me that he or she was more ancient and moldy than "cool" and in touch with what is happening in life. (Probably saying "cool" already dates me.) Old people were to be "respected" which, as an adolescent, basically meant to be tolerated rather than admired, or held in esteem. What can you learn from an old person, or an old document, or an old custom? After all, there is a saying, "You can't teach an old dog, new tricks." What a horrible insight into life! It means there are no more possibilities for one to change, to grow. That would take all wonder out of life. As I aged, I came to better understand the statement that "The child is the parent to the adult." Whether we mature or not, neither the adolescent, nor the parent, abandons being a child. We are always children, no matter how long our life's journey is. Thanks to my bride and our raising our own family, age distinctions lost any importance. It was now our family: my wife and I, and our five boys forging ahead…or not. This recognition triggered a realization that young children need the "older" parents to guide them and the "older" parents need the younger children to keep them open to what is viable in life. After all, it is the two year old who constantly keeps the philosophic enterprise and search alive through his deep and penetrating questioning, "Why Mommy?" "How come, Daddy?"

Unless the wise parent continues to answer that question, there won't be much to explore for any members of the family. There would be little to learn on the part of the younger children, and little to wonder about on the part of the older children…aka…the parents. The growth process requires the interacting of the new and the old; so that both can be alive to what is happening *now* in life. The present is the converging of the past and the future. The old and the new come together in the *now*. For me, the Old Testament is the founding and nurturing of God's covenant relationship with us, while the New Testament represents the appreciating and fulfilling of His covenant relationship with and through us. The Old Testament is our background, our spiritual roots, our initial religious impressions and the New Testament is our present, our spiritual blooming and flourishing. With each new gift of life, the founding of the old covenant relationship continues; while, with each accepting of the new covenant relationship the fulfilling of the covenant grows or deepens. Sadly, with each covenantal refusal, the relationship fails to become what it is intended to be, a love relationship between God and us that can only be experienced through what we value and in how we express these values with consistency. Maybe that is why "today" is a mixed bag. There are some of us trying to move ahead with care and concern for others, while there are those who are so fearful of change that everyone else becomes a threat. What will tomorrow bring? No one knows with certainty and yet some of us eagerly look ahead to what might happen and others are afraid of what might happen. Maybe the answer to this is how well each of us handles the adventures of being a child, now and throughout the rest of our lives. We are always children.

Like the Old Testament, the content of the New Testament is theology. Its forms are expressed through the four gospels according to Mark, Matthew, Luke and John, as well as letters or epistles written by, among others, Paul and Peter. There is also the Acts of the Apostles which is really "Part Two" of Luke's gospel. It is sometimes referred to as an historical expression of the early Church, but since it is primarily theological in content, I think it is more appropriately considered to be the response of Jesus' followers to the Good News. What Jesus does in the gospel of Luke, the disciples, the followers of Jesus, the Church, are called upon to serve others in the world after Jesus has risen from the dead. Their service should be modeled after their teacher. As Jesus journeys to Jerusalem to embrace the Cross, which becomes the symbol of salvation, so the disciples journey to Rome, which at that time was the seat of pagan or secular power, in order to spread the Good News even at the cost of martyrdom. Finally, there is the Book of Revelation which is an apocalyptic expression of the ultimate triumph of good over evil. Apocalyptic literature speaks in imaginative terms of the ongoing earthly struggle between good and evil waged by those who believe in God's goodness and those who do not. It points to the ultimate triumph of good over evil.

Our focus over the next three chapters will be on the Gospels. We will examine the audiences, the Christological focus on Jesus in each gospel, and some of the differences and similarities between the gospel authors. Jesus' name is not Jesus Christ to whom we might mail a greeting card. He is Jesus, Who is the "anointed one", the Messiah promised of old. The surprise of Bethlehem is that the Messiah promised in the Old Testament is God become man in the New Testament. The Christ!

I will, with the insights of biblical scholars, supply background information which will help us to better understand what the gospels are attempting to say to us. The gospels give us a context in which to more fully appreciate God's message to us and our response to God. It is very difficult to use tools in any area of life unless you have some understanding of what they can do and how you can use them properly. Since we are dealing with the Christmas story in this essay, I do want to shed some light on the two gospels that present an infancy narrative or the story of Jesus' birthday. This scriptural section is where the Old Testament acknowledges the fulfilling of the

Messianic promise and the New Testament heralds the beginning of the Messiah's promise of universal salvation. The birth of Jesus is the heart and soul of the Christmas story. There is a popular saying that goes, "Jesus is the reason for the season." Each of the gospels has a beginning, and then they explore the public ministry of Jesus, and finally they relive the passion narrative. The first gospel, according to Mark, begins with the public ministry of Jesus. The last gospel, according to John, begins with a theological prologue, or preface, linking Jesus to the beginnings of the world and especially to the Old Testament. The gospels according to Matthew and Luke begin with infancy narratives which are stories about Jesus' birth. I will say something of these stories in this essay and we will investigate the gospels in greater depth in the next two essays.

The word "Gospel" means "Good News." The Good News begins with:

God loves us so much that He became like us

This is the basis for our Christmas story reflection, the Nativity or birth of Jesus.

The Good News continues with:

He shares life with us

This will be the basis for our next essay, "Getting to Know You." It will deal with the public ministry of Jesus.

The Good News continues with:

He gives all He is for us, Himself on the Cross

The passion narrative is the primary focus of each gospel account. We will address this in our final chapter, "The Price of Love."

The purpose of the Good News, in both the Synoptic (Mark, Matthew, and Luke) and Johannine (John) traditions, is the same:

That we might be with Him now and forever.

155

This we will address as we try to appreciate why God loves us so much. To put it together: The Gospel or "**The Good News**" is that

> **God loves us so much, that He became like us, and shares life with us, and gives all He is for us, Himself on the Cross; so that we might be with Him now and forever.**

Both Matthew's and Luke's gospels are written some fifty years after Jesus died on the Cross. They are expressions of the early communities of Christian believers. They are attempts to address the question of beginnings or origins, but the gospels are neither biography nor history. They are theology and theology, as we know, is the study of God revealed in time and/or history and the human response which is either yes or no, acceptance or rejection, or faith or disbelief. This is as important to keep in mind while trying to appreciate the New Testament as it is for trying to appreciate the Old Testament.

When we decorate our homes at Christmas time, many of us include the stable or manger of Bethlehem as part of our Christmas remembrance, and for some of us, this is the centerpiece of our Christmas celebrating. Besides the Holy Family, Jesus, Mary and Joseph, we include the shepherds and the magi, or wise men, and the animals and the angels. What we are doing basically is trying to put the different elements of the Matthean and Lucan infancy narratives together so that we can enjoy the fullest representation of the Christmas story. We have Saint Francis of Assisi to thank for this wonderful holyday and holiday reminder as he is the original architect of the Christmas Crib, or crèche.

As I have previously mentioned, I like to read. Everyday I prefer getting information, whether national or international, from the newspapers, rather than the internet. I can recall paying two cents for the "New York Daily News", which my father insisted upon reading each day. Today, that same daily paper costs one dollar. My Dad is probably the reason I still read this and other papers to obtain news. Many of us, each day, read newspapers, magazines and books. I am not a "smart phone" person, or a person who searches the internet continuously for news blurbs. I don't own a "Kindle" because I would rather turn the pages of a book in anticipation of what comes next. I have a phone because of the convenience it offers in keeping in touch with family and friends. I treasure the printed word because I think that this medium of information allows one the best opportunity to take a breath and try to absorb intellectually what is unfolding locally, nationally and globally. It allows us to reflect on what is presented in fiction and in non fiction. Certainly the visual "news" grasps the senses more dramatically, but the printed news allows for deeper reflection and understanding. You can close the paper or book and take time to appreciate what is happening. The visual and the written expressions obviously complement each other. Each access to reality balances the other; the printed word allows one to reflect and the visual expression allows one to witness. Between them we can come to a fuller appreciation of life's meanings.

In 1223, St. Francis, who loved the feast of Christmas, wanted to encourage people to have a more vivid sense of the Bethlehem story. The birth of Jesus already was written in the gospel accounts; so people were able to hear and reflect upon them. He thought that a visual encounter would provide a balanced appreciation for celebrating this feast. He believed that when people could see life's events played out in front of them, they would be better able to sense more deeply how it touches them. It would help people to reflect more fully on what they have heard through the gospel proclamation of the Nativity scene. To have a clear picture in one's mind is invaluable in reflecting upon its ultimate meaning. He was trying to emphasize that Jesus, Emmanuel, is the center of the Christmas festivities, rather than the secular materialism which had sprung up around this feast. If St. Francis were to return to our day and age, he would be disappointed with the commercialism of the Christmas season, but I do think he would still encourage us to prioritize the meaning of the feast by focusing on Jesus, the center and meaning of this season, both visually and intellectually.

He arranged with people of the area of Grecchio, a short distance from Assisi, to come together to have the Christmas story experienced in a way that the people would more openly embrace the scriptural depiction of the humble surroundings of Jesus' birth. He made sure that animals were present, that there was an ass and an ox to be part of the scenario. These animals were to be the created guardians who would make sure that the newly born infant is protected from the elements of the barren countryside. Hay was strewn on the ground and a manger was set up within the wooded surroundings. The people from the area gathered with candles and torches and sang in joyous exultation, probably not unlike the angels who proclaimed the "Glory to God" at Jesus' birth. The Franciscan communities from the surrounding areas came to celebrate, not unlike the wise men from the East, or the shepherds from the area around Bethlehem. Grecchio had become the modern Bethlehem and the Nativity scene became the most significant part of our Christmas celebration, even until today. The more we appreciate the stable, the manger (called *Presepio* in Italian) the more we are able to celebrate Christmas [-] the birth of Our Lord and Savior, Jesus Who will become, through His earthly journey, the Glorified Christ. As long as I can remember, the Nativity scene is the major part of our Christmas scene, and should be. In introducing a visual significance to the birth of Our Lord, St. Francis gave us a more wonderful opportunity to reflect on the meaning of the Nativity event and the entire Christmas message. When my bride and I visited Assisi a few years ago, all the images of the first visual reenactment of Bethlehem at Grecchio were very much a part of what makes that place so important in the life of Christians and indeed, and hopefully, of others who visit.

Thanks to St. Francis, the joyful aspect of the Christmas scene reminds us to continue the festivities which the season acknowledges by including our own decorations which invite us to focus on what is most important: the celebrating. To celebrate is to publicly express our joy, our happiness. To enjoy means to embrace those for whom we care. We all know that the birth of any baby should be a joyous event. Christmas is a time to celebrate, to enjoy. It is a time to remember that the most significant friendship that we human persons enjoy is that of being related to the God Who rejoices in giving us life. It reminds us of the Genesis creation accounts and tells us that God is with us *more intimately* now than even in Genesis. No matter what has happened in the past hundreds and thousands of years, the covenant between God and us is alive and well. St. Francis must have been so aware of God's love for us that he wanted to make sure we would remember in this very special way, the crèche of love. No wonder he is associated with peace;

the peace of mind, the inner peace, that lets us know that we are God's children and He will care for us as completely as any loving parents care for their children. Since our present Pope chose the name Francis, he has certainly lived up to the life and preaching of St. Francis of Assisi. He is a "Christmas" pope, a pope of peace and hope and joy.

Christmas decorations are ways of celebrating the birth of Jesus as a very special event. Decorations draw our attention to the person who is being acknowledged. The birthday cake and candles point us to the person whose birthday we are celebrating. The wedding toast helps us to celebrate the couple who are starting their married life together. A Christmas tree, lights, ornaments, help us to focus not simply on the scene but rather on what the scene celebrates. What Christmas celebrates: the birth of God become Man, is not found in the decorations, but rather in what the decorations point us towards [-] the birth of Our Savior, and the joy that this event should entail. *God loves us so much that He became like us.* He identified with us as the lover identifies with the one loved. There is no "love fest" like Christmas. Maybe the reason that an increasing number of people seem to have difficulty in celebrating this occasion, or maybe the reason that there seems to be an increasing number of people who object to public displays of joy at this time of year is because there is an increasing number of people who are afraid to love. Maybe some people think that love is illusory or some think that they are unlovable despite being created *in the image and likeness of God*. Or maybe they are people who haven't been loved as they should be by the people who are closely related to them in their journey. That is truly sad.

Matthew's account of the Good News begins with a genealogy, which is not like the kind that we try to trace on the internet today. Ours depends on available documents which link offspring to those who preceded us in life. Birth certificates and ships' manifests help us in the ancestral quest. We traced our parents' emigration from Ireland and Italy through birth certificates found in our travels and through passport information.

The genealogy in Matthew's gospel is more a literary device than one which relies on the record keeping of legal documents. His is a theological tracing of Jesus back through David and eventually to Abraham, the father of the Jewish people. As Abraham wandered far to seek a place to begin the growth of the God's chosen people, so Mary and Joseph wandered from their home to Bethlehem, a winter's journey of some eighty miles. Did they travel by caravan to avoid being attacked by one of the many roving bands of robbers? It certainly had to be a difficult week's journey with Mary nine months pregnant. Matthew's gospel is aimed at an audience of people raised in the Old Testament traditions. He will focus on Jesus as the new Moses, and one greater than Moses, because Jesus is the Messiah promised of old. We read of Him and identify Him with the passage from the prophet Isaiah…"Therefore the Lord himself will give you this sign: the virgin shall be with child, and bear a son, and shall call him Immanuel…"

Luke's version also has a genealogy, which strangely enough appears not at the beginning of the gospel, where we would expect to find it. It is strategically placed in chapter three after John baptizes Jesus. His is a baptismal genealogy tracing Jesus back to Adam. As Adam was tempted and failed to keep the covenant; so Jesus will be tempted, but will overcome whatever obstacles in life could possibly keep us away from returning God's love. The audience to whom Luke is writing consists of Gentiles, people not familiar with the Old Testament tradition. He will not use the number of Old Testament references that Matthew will use, because of the different audiences. His approach is to divide his writings into *the Old Testament period* linking Jesus to his Israelite roots. This includes the parallel Infancy Narratives of John the Baptist and Jesus, John's preaching and baptizing of Jesus, ending with his genealogy. What Luke refers to as *The Center of Time period* will focus on words and actions of Jesus' public ministry beginning with the temptation scene in chapter four and continuing through His Ascension into heaven at the conclusion of chapter twenty-four. It includes His praying, teaching and preaching, healing, and the passion story of His suffering and death. Finally there is *The Time of the Church period* which is covered in Luke's companion volume, "Acts of the Apostles." The followers of Jesus, Messianites, or Jewish coverts, and Gentile Christians, will continue Jesus' proclamation of the Father's love for all His children, and they will journey throughout the world spreading the message that lets us know there is Good News. Luke's gospel ends with the Ascension of Jesus into heaven, and the Acts of the Apostles begins with the Ascension of Jesus into heaven. This is why I think that the Acts of the Apostles is part two of Luke's gospel. What Jesus does in the gospel, the church, consisting of His followers, is called to do in the Acts.

In each infancy narrative there is an angelic, or heavenly announcement, that the child to be born will be called Jesus meaning "Yahweh saves" and He is coming to fulfill the Old Testament prophecies of a saving Messiah. The Messiah, the anointed One, has been promised by God going far back into the Old Testament. This also helps us to understand the purpose of the genealogy in each account. It shows God's concern for His people. The Old Testament people through whom Jesus is traced are people who have served God by caring for His creation. I suspect that some of them were more consistently faithful than others, but, in a real sense, they all responded to the covenant call to take care of the world. It is similar to our response to God's word. Some of us are more consistently faithful than others. Thank God, he loves us all! Jesus is traced through His earthly ancestors. There will be no descendants of Jesus in any contemporary sense. This is primarily a theological genealogy. Jesus is the One Promised of old. He is the Messiah. He is the Savior. He will save us from condemnation and He will save us for everlasting life with the God of all creation. He will heal what was broken in the Garden of Eden.

This is a birth announcement unlike any other before or since. This is truly a new beginning for humankind. It is not simply God's gift [-] a token or offering from one person to another [-] rather it is God's personal involving with and intimate embrace of each of us. God so loved the world that he embraced our humanity. God's gift to us is Himself. He so loves us that He identifies with us like the lover identifies with the one loved. How does a lover identify with the one loved? The lover wants to appreciate and share the thoughts, the hopes, the lives of the ones loved. The lover listens and watches so that he or she can enter gradually and then more deeply into the lives of the one or the ones loved. Not only does the lover seek to understand, but the lover wants to experience both the joys and the pains of the one loved. The lover's committing to the one loved involves easing the burden of suffering and increasing the enjoyment of life in all its expressions. This is true whether the lover is parent or spouse, child or sibling, friend or

161

neighbor, caretaker or teacher or sponsor. In sharing our humanity with us, Jesus will ultimately develop the intimacy of friendship that makes Him not only our creator, but also our brother and our friend, and eventually our savior. By embracing our humanity He renews the covenant relationship that was born in the Garden of Eden, because He is with us again, but as one of us. This embracing of our humanity by God becoming man deepens the significance of the covenant as well as acknowledging humanity's special role in the caretaking of the incredible gift of creation. This gives us a sense of why Christmas is meant to be such a joy-filled reminder of our relationship with God, and signals a new and revived beginning, no matter what we have experienced previously.

In each of the written gospel accounts, the audience does play a significant role. The authors focus on different characters to bring out the theological importance of the nativity scene. In Matthew, the angel appears to Joseph, while in Luke, the angel appears to Mary. The Christological focus on Jesus in the Matthean account is the Promised Messiah, the new Moses and one greater than Moses. It emerges in a very patriarchal cultural. Joseph, who is the husband of Mary, will remind the gospel audience of the patriarch Joseph in the Book of Genesis. He also had dreams, or visions, which led him to save his people from famine and ensure the continuance of the patriarchal line which began with Abraham.

Those who enjoy theatre will recall the wonderful music production of "Joseph and the Amazing Technicolor Dream Coat." It portrays in very upbeat musical numbers, the story of the youngest son of the patriarch, Jacob, who went from brother to slave to Pharaoh's advisor to savior of the family. Joseph is portrayed as a dreamer and his dream involves being leader of the family. His eleven older brothers did not particularly care for the fact that their father favored Joseph. Their selling him to itinerant desert traders, intent on enslaving him is much harsher to read in scripture than is seen on the Broadway stage. Sometimes it might be better to appreciate life as if it were a musical production rather than everyday reality. The music is meant to be uplifting to the human spirit and this joyous musical is a tribute to the covenant as Joseph shows God's love for His people. The show reminds us that God wants us, His people, to dance, to celebrate and to sing out with loud voices, rather than to mumble incoherently and to "pass the buck." He wants us to be actors on this stage of life, rather than simply being spectators watching others perform [-] watching those who not only are supporters of life, but also watching too many others who are destroyers of life. The musical and the infancy narratives cry out that Jesus wants us to participate with Him in this wonderful Garden of Eden, in Bethlehem, in wherever we find ourselves today. Only the time and place, and the characters, like us, change. By the way, Dona and I love musicals.

God stays the same enthusiastic creator He has always been. He could have appeared more dramatically...like a column of fire...or some sort of "Godzilla" or other apocalyptically frightening presence...but as it says in Genesis...*And so it happened, God looked at everything He had made, and found it very good.* (Chapter 1, verse 31) So Jesus comes, just like us. Being human is good; so good that God embraces our humanity. If God is for us, then why do so many of us reject His gift of our life? The angel's appearance to Joseph in the New Testament is accepted by him as a sign of God's presence in his marriage. He will protect his wife and his infant son in much the same manner that Joseph protected his people in the Old Testament days.

The Christological focus in Luke's account is on Jesus as the Champion of the outcasts of society. These outcasts, or disenfranchised men and women will play important roles in responding to Jesus. Women were universally considered social and political outcasts. While many barriers to feminine participation in social and political life have fortunately been overturned and corrected, there still exist too many barriers in too many areas of the world today. There are still too many women and children, and men, used and abused by pornographic and sexually warped people. Physical, emotional, political, economic and religious abuses are plagues that are still prevalent in too many of our contemporary societies. There is still much work to be done to break the chains that harmfully bind too many people. When people are imprisoned by their own lack of self worth, or are enslaved to the selfish wants of other people, it becomes so difficult to experience the joy for which God created us. Maybe that means that our contemporary choices involve either addressing and resolving these issues in the name of fairness or justice, or giving up and saying there is no use in doing anything. If we choose the former, then we would be caring for God's creation and if we choose the latter, then we are not fulfilling our purpose as God's greatest creation. We may not be unanimous in agreeing how to resolve issues, but we must be unanimous on the need for dialog and action if God's creation is to realize His loving purpose. We are social by nature, our sister and our brother's keeper. The role of Mary, a social outcast in Luke's gospel underscores her significance as the first of Jesus' faithful disciples.

There are different devotions in every religious tradition. Praying the rosary is a Catholic devotion which recalls the significant mysteries of our faith. The Joyful Mysteries are rooted in the Lucan Infancy Narrative. There are also the Sorrowful Mysteries rooted in the Passion Narrative, and the Glorious Mysteries arising out of the Resurrection of Jesus. Each rosary consists of five decades, or remembrances of events in the life of Jesus and Mary.

The first Joyful Mystery is the *Annunciation* of Jesus' birth by the angel who appears to Mary, acknowledging her fidelity to God and proclaiming that she is called to be the mother of the Messiah promised of old. She accepts because it is God's will and God's call. She is a religious person, and without raising a barrage of questions, she trusts God's messenger and accepts being the earthly mother of Jesus, whatever that will involve. The *Visitation* by Mary to her cousin, Elizabeth to help her during her pregnancy, is an act of service, an act of compassion and caring. Elizabeth has conceived late in life which acknowledges one of the often stated prophetic themes of the Old Testament; namely, with God all is possible. Mary's presence is another sign of God's caring for His people. It is in this visit to her cousin that Mary receives the first human sign that her own pregnancy will be so significant. Elizabeth says that the infant in her womb leapt for joy when Mary approached. This is the initial public acknowledging of Jesus as the Messianic hope promised of old. Mary's response is the beautiful hymn of praise called the "Magnificat" in which she thanks God for having acknowledged her as a humble servant and for keeping His promise to Israel. "...He has come to the help of Israel his servant, mindful of his mercy—according to the promise He made to our ancestors—of his mercy to Abraham and to his descendants forever..." Mary's spoken prayer acknowledges her faith in the Old Testament prophecies that God cares for His chosen people. After a long and obviously painful trip, as any pregnant woman in her final trimester will acknowledge, the *Nativity or Birth* of Jesus in the humble surroundings of the manger in Bethlehem is an act of universal love that binds us to God in way never before imagined. God embraces our humanity in the most intimate of ways. He becomes like us. The *Presentation* of Jesus in the Temple, shortly after His birth, is a requirement of the Mosaic Law. Simon and Anna, rejoicing that God has allowed them to witness the promised Messiah, prophesied to Mary that "a sword of sorrow will pierce her heart." This is a reminder that life is not without its roadblocks and that in the human condition, in our life's journey, joy is not simply the absence of sorrow, but the always presence of God. Finally the *Finding of the (twelve year old) Child Jesus in the Temple* gives Mary a foreshadowing of her Son's ministry in life, an act which emphasizes the importance of teaching and learning. This last mystery dramatically foreshadows Jesus' vocation or calling in life. All of these devotional exercises are rooted in the opening section of Luke's account of the Good News. Mary leads the "outcast" followers of Jesus in Luke's gospel and in today's world. She is clearly not only mother of Jesus but His first Christian disciple.

When most of us put together the Christmas crib and decorate it with the nativity figures, we include the shepherds and the magi, or wise men from the East. I am not sure how many of us realize that they don't appear in both infancy narratives. The shepherds appear only in Luke's account, while the magi appear only in Matthew's account. Clearly, shepherds were outcasts in times past. They took care of the "dirty" sheep. In many cases, the shepherds weren't even allowed to come into the town limits, because they were considered unclean and their job was considered to be unsanitary. Health concerns especially with respect to the taking care of animals, was not a particularly high priority at the time. Isn't it ironic that in today's age, health care is such a politically explosive issue and there are still so many "shepherds" that are not adequately provided for by public health care. Maybe these contemporary shepherds don't have everything they need in life because of their age, or their economic situation, or their nationality, or their race, or perhaps their immigration status, but many of them are considered "outcasts." One wonders sometimes how far we have progressed in some areas of life. Shepherds, therefore, were not usually considered to be clean people, either physically or spiritually. It was different in situations in which the family owners participated in the shepherding of the flock, but primarily shepherds were "hired hands." The public shepherds smelled terribly because they were charged with taking care of the community's sheep and the goats. They were the epitome of social outcasts. Because of this, often their food would be left at the town outposts and many of them were "personae non gratae" within many town limits. They were not welcomed within the "normal" social confines of life. And yet it was because of their care and concern for the sheep entrusted to them, that merchants and farmers were able to live as well as possible. It is ironic that the "outcast" shepherd was the "caretaker" of the flock which he didn't own, but protected anyway. They didn't brand the sheep in those days, everything was done by sound. The sheep "knew" the voice of the shepherd and responded only to his call. It is no wonder then, that they are the first visitors to the Infant Jesus in the stable at Bethlehem. Jesus was born not according to the social and economic boundaries of civilized society of that time, or of our time. Yet the purpose of Luke's gospel is clear. The shepherds represent the reality that Jesus came for all people, even those who are the social outcasts of every civilized culture and society. Jesus' love is universal. He came to show His concern for *all* of us. An interesting question for us: if Jesus were to be born today, who would be the first people to show up to acknowledge him? I suspect it wouldn't include too many people whom modern society idolizes because of their looks, or positions, or artistic abilities, or athletic prowess. He would not be a celebrity baby. It is more likely He would be born in a "cardboard" city under a highway surrounded by the homeless, than in a suite in an expensive hospital natal center. I sometimes wonder if our Christmas decorating which is clearly meant to celebrate the joy of this wonderful event, doesn't sometimes divert our attention from the reality that – Emmanuel – God became man primarily to acknowledge and empower, as much as that is possible – the poor and the downtrodden of society. I do think that many of us are aware of that and contribute what we can – but this still remains the focus of God becoming man. When we are celebrating, as we ought, we need to be nudged a bit to remember this aspect of Christmas. Saint Francis of Assisi did.

When we look at Matthew's account, instead of shepherds, there are visitors from the East. Whether they are astrologers or kings is of minor importance in this theological author's account. If you want to appreciate a more scholarly account of the birth of Jesus, I recommend "The Birth of the Messiah" by Raymond Brown. It is far more thoughtfully researched and developed than I intend to write, and certainly one of the more influential books I have ever read. We know very little about those visitors historically, so we have to try to understand their theological significance within the infancy narrative. They are clearly "gentiles", non-Jews, and they have come from a long distance. Certainly, they are learned men. They have, using their own explanation, "followed the star." Astrologers, wise men, whatever title they deserve, they have come over a thousand miles to acknowledge, to worship, to give homage to one whom they believe is and will be very, very important. Are they fools? Are they chasing rainbows? Whatever the reason, they believe that their traveling has been rewarded in finding someone who will greatly influence what happens to humankind. How many of us would give up many months or even a year to pursue that which we are not completely certain of, and yet rejoice in what we have found, even when we are not fully aware of what we have found?

In this day and age, far too many of us want to know the next three detailed steps we have to take to find some kind of immediate (earthly) fulfillment. And how many of us are disappointed? Fulfillment depends not on the steps one takes but on the person one becomes. Aristotle said that "all philosophy begins in wonder..." I am not too sure there are enough of us in life who still wonder. The magi did. Was Bethlehem worth their wonder? We never hear from them again, but then how many of us will be remembered after we die? They gave very precious gifts, which, of course, is what Christmas is about [-] the giving of gifts [-] precious gifts. We remember Gaspar, who brought frankincense. We remember Malchior, who gifted Jesus with gold. And we remember Balthazar, whose present was myrrh. The gold suggests a kingly gift and Jesus is acknowledged as Christ the King. Frankincense is associated with liturgical celebrations and Jesus is revered as the High Priest. Myrrh is essentially embalming ointment to be used at someone's death and burial and so as we will see in Chapter Six, the women brought it to the tomb of Jesus after His death, but it was not necessary because Jesus, the Suffering Servant, had already risen from the dead.

The magi were simply preparing Jesus for His ministry. The gifts acknowledge Emmanuel as the messianic hope who will rescue all of us from the death of loneliness, from the death of being unloved. As far as I am concerned, I admire the fact that they took a risk in traveling a great distance and yet were not sure of what they would find. Now they are recognized annually as we decorate our Christmas scene [-] not too shabby for "guys" who lived a long time ago and still encourage us today to travel through the unknown in search of what or who is most important in life.

In the literary world, we appreciate O. Henry's story of the "Gift of the Magi." A young married couple, Della and Jim, very poor and very deeply in love, realizing that Christmas is upon them, give to each other the most precious gifts they have. Della, realizing she has less than two dollars for a gift, cuts off her beautiful long hair to raise money to buy Jim a watch fob for his most precious possession, his grandfather's watch. Jim hocks his most valuable possession, his grandfather's watch, to buy her a jeweled comb to care for her beautiful hair. The gifts are clearly the most unselfish ones the poor couple could give to each other. Theologically or secularly, Christmas is the most significant time of the year for gift-giving. The gift of God to us confirms this is so. Like Della and Jim, God's gift of Himself to us is the most generous one He could offer. Were Della and Jim foolish? Were the magi? Is Emmanuel? What they have in common is unselfish and sacrificial love…nothing foolish there!

In the art world, "The Adoration of the Magi" is a dramatic rendition of the reality of Jesus touching the lives of all people, even those whose regal robes are so out of place in the poorly lit cave-stable at Bethlehem. A number of very famous artists have captured this visitation, each with his personal dramatic perspective. Among them are Rembrandt, Giotto, and Ruebens. In the Uffizi Gallery in Florence, Italy, alone there are eight paintings of this scene, including Leonardo da Vinci, Botticelli,

Filippino Lippi, and Albrecht Durer. These artistic expressions capture the theological role played by the magi in the gospel. They give us a visual glimpse of the most miraculous birth in human history. Artistically, the "Adoration of the Shepherds" has also been captured by such artists as Bronzino and El Greco who include the angelic hosts in their paintings. Carvaggio, on the other hand, focuses only on the shepherds and the awe which they portray upon encountering the infant and his mother. The splendidly robed magi and poorly clad shepherds represent the reality that Jesus' love is universal. He came for all of humankind, no one is overlooked. Thanks to the concern of St. Francis of Assisi and the expression of the God-given talents of so many wonderful artists, we have imprinted in our imaginations visions of the Nativity scene to help us more fully appreciate God's love for us throughout our earthly existence. I think that sending religiously inspired Christmas cards to friends and family is a beautiful expression of the significance of this Christian celebration.

The infancy narratives are theology; so they involve the responses of acceptance and rejection. Clearly the Annunciation to Mary in each gospel results in her faith response to God's invitation. She said "yes" to God's call to be the mother of Jesus. Her acceptance is not quite like ours because, unlike Mary, we have thousands of years of scriptural understanding and traditional practices to help us to make our decision. Our decision to accept Jesus is as freely made as is Mary's, yet she had much less in the way of learning and understanding than we have. Perhaps this is what makes her acceptance so amazing. She was engaged to Joseph and this was not out of the ordinary for the time; so she was preparing to marry, a very usual cultural event. In reading the gospels, the angelic vision must make Mary realize that God is making Himself known to her in an unusual way. This is not simply part of a religious or liturgical event. It is deeply personal. Mary seems to appreciate this immediately, even though it gives her cause for concern. She recognizes God's presence which indicates she is a person of religious conviction. It is God's request that causes her concern. God wants her to be the mother of the Messiah, the One promised of old who will be the savior of all humankind. Her hesitation is not based on misunderstanding or fear. She asks how this can be because she has not had any sexual relationships with a man. The messenger of the Lord, the angel, replies by describing the Virgin birth, and the presence of the Holy Spirit. She doesn't ask for detailed instructions or raise a lot of questions. She believes in God. She appreciates that scripture has promised a Messiah and she answers: "Behold the handmaid of the Lord...be it done unto *me* according to *Your Word*..." She said "yes" to God without an explanation that I am sure most of us, both past and present believers, would have wanted. Mary simply realized that God wants this and God wants me involved; so I am. For any believer, the one question that has to be answered is: do I really believe what Christ said and did? Mary shows us the way to answer...even before Christ said what He said and did what He did. No wonder she is the first of all the disciples. Mary's humility is what Father Daniel Lord SJ spoke of in a prayer he wrote years ago. In part it states "...Let me realize that when I am most humble, I am most human, most truthful, and most worthy of your most serious consideration..." Mary's "yes" is her faith response to God Who "seriously considered her." She is simultaneously so powerful and so humble, as well as being so wonderful a model for each of us. Make no mistake about this: each of us will have to respond to God's call to us. Let us pray for Mary's simplicity and humility so we can answer as we ought.

I was engaged once. And now, after more than fifty-nine years of marriage, five boys who married five great girls, and eight wonderful grandchildren, my bride and I are still on our honeymoon. But if Dona had come to me before we were married and said she was pregnant and I knew that I was not involved, would we have married? If she added, that it is God's will and not another man, that she is pregnant, I am not sure that I would have been as faithful to her as Joseph was to Mary. Maybe I would. I don't know. In any event it was certainly a difficult decision for Joseph to make. His fiancée is pregnant and he is not the biological father. I wonder if any of his friends knew, and if they did what advice would they have given him. Did they laugh at him? Scripture tells us that instead of taking some drastic legal action which would be damaging to Mary's reputation (and given the social status of a man and a woman at that time, Joseph could easily have hurt Mary legally), he decides to end the relationship quietly without bringing attention to the situation. It speaks of a compassionate and caring man. He is willing to be kind to Mary even though he has to feel some hurt, some confusion, some apprehension. An angelic appearance to Joseph announces that this is indeed God's will and it is okay for Joseph to marry Mary and raise his family. His acceptance, his "yes" confirms that he too is a religious person. He believes in the promises God has made to His people. He doesn't waste time on what, why, how, where, when; he responds and fulfills his obligation as husband to Mary and earthly father to Jesus. He loves her. He loves God. That is the strength of this humble man, of whom we know little in terms of his life long pursuits. We can simply admire, appreciate, and try to imitate his marital and covenantal love. Not only did he hear God's voice, but he listened to His message and acted as he was called. He fulfilled his vocation as Jesus' earthly father. How many times have we failed to hear God's voice, whether through listening or seeing? While Joseph has but a short appearance in the gospels, he is a role model for everyone's lifetime, at least everyone who is a person of faith, a person of hope, a loving person.

In a real sense, Mary's "yes" and Joseph's "yes" overcame Adam's and Eve's "no" in the Garden of Eden. The Garden of Eden was God's plan, God's hope, God's way of celebrating life. When Adam and Eve turned away from God, their decision affected how our relationship with God would play out. He never abandoned us, nor did He ever stop loving us, but like so many other times in life, when things don't emerge as expected, it is time for Plan B. I think that God become man is Plan B for us. Some Plan B approaches are used because the initial plan is a failure. Some Plan B approaches are developed to help one or both parties to more fully appreciate what could be. The covenant is certainly not a failure because we still live in the Garden of Eden. But God's plan B, Christmas, is meant to be eye-opening for us. It is God's very personal response to our rejection of Him. His love never is withdrawn because of our fears, faults, and failings. His love is unconditional. It would never have happened without Adam and Eve saying "no" and without Mary and Joseph saying "yes" to God. At least, it wouldn't have happened in the way it did. So Thanks to them!

Mary and Joseph were both religious persons. To me, that means that God is important, significant, essential and influential in their lives. Religion, from the Latin, re-ligare, means to tie one's self back to God (our English word "ligament" comes from this.) We are meant to be tied to God. The religious person consciously admits that God is important in one's life today, that God is acknowledged as being life and love, that God takes us and everyone we know as individually and personally special, and that when we can see others as important to God, we can respond as we ought. When we can't see others as important to God, because of what they do and say, we have to call upon Him, to tie ourselves back to Him so that we can try to reach out and embrace them.

The Holy Family is the focus of Christmas, the focus of the Nativity scene. What makes them holy is that Jesus, Mary and Joseph, are consciously doing God's will. They are living the words of the Our Father...*may your kingdom come on earth as it is in heaven*...a kingdom which acknowledges God's loving creation and God's concern for each one whom He has created. As previously mentioned, there is a wonderful play that appeared on Broadway for years, and it is our most favorite musical of all time. *Les Miserables* is a musical based on Victor Hugo's book about a man, Jean Valjean, who steals a loaf of bread to feed his sister's family. He is caught and imprisoned for twenty years. He is freed and then hounded for more years by his original jailer, Inspector Javier, who operates on the principle that "once a criminal always a criminal." Unlike Emmanuel, forgiveness is not in Inspector Javier's makeup. The music is wonderful. The lyrics are moving. The turning point for his conversion is that a bishop, a religious person, gives him a gift. The gift is something Jean had stolen from the bishop. The Bishop gave the homeless man, Jean Valjean, food and lodging, just like God had given Adam and Eve the Garden of Eden. As our original parents refused God's gift, so Jean Valjean abuses the bishop's hospitality by stealing silverware and sneaking away in the middle of the night. When captured with the property in his possession, the bishop tells the police that he gave these priceless objects to Valjean as a gift. He is thus freed from any legal obligations which would have sent him back to prison. The bishop's gift liberates Jean from the bonds of a life of civil punishment as certainly as the Exodus in the Old Testament liberated God's people from a life of unjust punishment. A gift! The gift of Joseph and Mary to each other transcends any legalistic practices. The gift of God to Mary and Joseph transcends human boundaries. The gift to Jean Valjean goes beyond any social or legal consideration. Christmas celebrates all these gifts!

Hugo's story plot focuses upon human injustice and suffering and despite the chronological difference (the setting for "Les Miserables" is France of the 1830's) the character portrayals are so moving that it is easy to identify with the pain and suffering, and with the compassion and the care which is dramatized. It is the timeless story of the abuse of authority and the injustice suffered by the innocent victims. What happens in the drama is what we play out in our everyday lives with the people who come in and out of our earthly journey. In one of the songs, Jean Val Jean sings this line: "...to love another person is to see the face of God." I think that this is such an incredibly powerful insight into the human condition. What makes the holy family, holy, is precisely this insight. God becoming man, Emmanuel - God with us - is the meaning of Christmas. Jesus has come among us so that we may love one another as fully and completely as is possible. Mary's "yes" and Joseph's "yes" are expressions of love which bring the face of God into their lives, and consequently into our lives in a way we never thought imaginable. The birth of Jesus brings His face vividly and intimately into our lives. He is not a God to be acknowledged or worshipped from afar, but He is Emmanuel – God Who is with us. This is how special we human beings are. Why can we not more obviously appreciate God's gift to us – Himself!

The artists' expressions of the adoration of the shepherds and the magi are responses to the "face of God" Who has come among us to manifest God's unconditional love. The shepherds and the magi are all of us [-] rich and poor [-] gentile and Jew [-] learned and unlearned, and when we love, we encounter the "face of God." When we love, we make holy the relationships between us, because we are imaging what God is doing in Genesis one, creating, creating freely and developing a special relationship with humankind, whose free choice is to accept or reject God's love offered in the covenant friendship. Christmas brings us the joy of loving reflected in the acceptance of Mary and Joseph for each other and for Jesus, and in Jesus' accepting of the shepherds and magi who represent the universality of humankind; that is, all of us. Among our choices in life is to be counted among the shepherds or the magi. Jesus embraces our humanity which makes our being woman and man so much more significant. The birth of Jesus allows us to experience literally "the face of God." God is "madly in love" with us. What Christmas celebrates, in Mary's "yes" and in Joseph's "yes" is the return to "holiness" which was lost through Adam and Eve's failure to love God. Jesus, the Holy One, has renewed the holiness of the human condition by being born as one of us. His divinity has touched our humanity in a way that not even our original parents were touched in the creation of the covenant relationship. We are human. We are loved by God. We are called to be holy people.

As we know, not everyone handles "good news" well. Not everyone accepts God's desire to be involved in our lives. In the infancy narratives there were those who rejected Jesus' coming. One was a violent rejection and one was a subtle rejection. In Matthew's account, Herod appears as the political and military leader in Israel, although a puppet of the real rulers, the Roman Empire. The appearance of the magi looking for "… the newborn king of the Jews…" raised more than eyebrows at Herod's court." A "newborn king", real or imagined, could pose a threat to the political power, however limited, that Herod desired. As we read in Matthew's account, Herod authorizes the "slaughter of the innocents" in the attempt to eliminate any possible "royal" competition. Historically, the massacre confirms the notion that "life is cheap" especially if one's allegiance is not on the "right" side, which is the side of the one who massacres, or enslaves, or tries to reduce the importance of others. In Machiavellian terms, you have to be on the side of "The Prince" because "might is right." A purging of a captive people was a rather usual way of keeping the population under control; so this is a more ordinary event for that time. Some recent events unfortunately have given us a dramatic reminder of the slaughtering of innocent people. The destruction of the twin towers in New York on September11, 2001 resulted in the merciless killing of almost three thousand people, whose only reason for being murdered was that they were in the buildings. It was both traumatic and dramatic to stand at "Ground Zero" and realize you are standing on the graves of innocents. The numbers of innocents is not the only concern, but the fact that it happens at all [-] that some of God's creatures kill others simply for [-] who knows what?

At an elementary school in Connecticut, a few years ago, twenty first graders were murdered by an obviously disturbed young man who had access to weaponry designed to be used in military combat. The innocent were six and seven year old children who will never have the opportunity to reach out to others in this world. This was not a military conflict, and the military type weaponry used had nothing to do with war, and yet innocent blood was shed, just like the slaughter of the innocents recorded in Matthew's account of the "Good News." The political outrage that has emerged since pits people who want the sale of guns to be severely controlled versus those who want more people to have guns; so they can "protect" themselves. Overlooked in the venomous argument between the opposing groups is the reality that innocent people have been slaughtered. Have we come very far from the time of Herod and the occupation of the Roman Empire? For the readers of Matthew's gospel, it is a theological reminder of Moses who was saved from the massacre of innocent children in the Book of Exodus. He was rescued by the Pharaoh's daughter and raised in Egypt. In the aftermath of the Newton, Connecticut, massacre of the innocents, there was no political salvation by the United States Congress, regarding gun law prohibition, as there was for Moses by the intervention of the political Pharaoh's daughter. Jesus is also a reminder of Israel, God's beloved people in the Old Testament. It is the Exodus that is the great religious liberation experience, the freeing of the people from enslavement to human institutions of bondage in order to be with the God of their covenant experience. The God of the covenant is He whose love is unconditional, no matter what our earthly condition happens to be. In the book of Exodus, the Chosen People flee from the oppression of Egypt and in Matthew's gospel the Holy Family flees from their own land into Egypt. Ironic! Evil is evil [-] only the names of the persecutors and the persecuted change.

Just like the patriarch Joseph in the Old Testament who saved his people from famine; so Joseph the husband of Mary will save his family from the murderous Herod. He will lead them back to Nazareth just as Moses and Joshua led the Israelites out of Egyptian slavery into the Promised Land. It is also a liberating religious experience and one that so many of us must go through in life if we are to focus on the significance of God's love for us so that we can love one another. Each of us must be liberated from whatever bonds hold us back from loving as completely and as openly as possible. This is why, in the Catholic tradition, the sacrament of Penance precedes the sacrament of the Eucharist. In order to receive Our Lord into our bodies and into our hearts, it is so important to be freed from whatever might hold us back from receiving Him graciously and openly; so that we can do "His will" which is to love others as fully and completely as we can.

The rejection of Jesus in the Lucan account is not as violent, but it is real. After Mary and Joseph had traveled a great distance to get to Bethlehem, they were refused a room in the inn. Mary is pregnant and about to give birth. She is a person in need of help, of assistance. Giving birth is painful and it is only in the joy of accepting the gift of a son or daughter that allows the mother to accept the pain and suffering she undergoes. The need for assistance is real, whether that comes in the form of a midwife or doctors and nurses. To turn Mary and Joseph away is a refusal to help those in need. One may argue that legally the innkeeper is not obligated, which, I guess, is why not everything legal is necessarily moral or ethical. (Reminder: in times past and present, slavery has been considered legal, but it never has been, nor ever will be moral, no matter what form the slavery takes.) This innkeeper is the opposite of a character he foreshadows later on in Luke's gospel; namely, the Good Samaritan. The Good Samaritan will be the unlikely person (because the Samaritans and the Jews were enemies) who will go out of his way to help the Jewish man who was beaten by bandits and left to die (chapter 10.) He took care of the violated and injured Jewish man who was ignored by his "own kind." A priest and a Levite (those who served the priests) saw him and kept on walking; they didn't want to get "involved." The human person is social by nature; therefore, we are our brothers' and our sisters' keepers. We are responsible for those who enter into our life's adventures whether or not they have been invited. Maybe the innkeeper "felt badly" about his hopeful guests and their welfare, but that does not excuse him from ignoring or dismissing those in need. We must remember that actions speak louder than words. Herod and the innkeeper are reminders that they also represent choices we can make in responding to the Nativity story in our own lives. Do

I welcome Emmanuel, or do I oppose Him, or do I choose not to get "involved"?

I wrote that Christmas is a time of joy and it is. Joy, in the human condition, or on our earthly journey, does not necessarily mean the absence of sorrow or hurt. Human happiness coexists with human hurt. We live in a world that is in process and because it is in process it is not yet completed. Our joy, at times, hopefully for long periods of time, doesn't mean that difficulties and pain and suffering are missing, but it does mean that God is present, and therefore involved in the suffering. A compassionate Creator! The joy experienced by Mary and Joseph, by the shepherds and the magi is real because they accepted that Jesus is God become man – Emmanuel - God with us. God loves us so much that He becomes like us. That is the most incredible reason for celebrating. Yet, the rejections by Herod and by the innkeeper are reminders that hatred and abandonment, fear and ignorance, pain and suffering are part and parcel of life's journey. The joy of Christmas is neither make-believe nor false. It is real because it recognizes that God loves us. Why else would He identify with us? He said it in Genesis. He showed His concern for His people throughout the Old Testament, whether they, (or we in this day and age) reciprocated or not. Now He's fulfilling His promise to all of us which is to save us because He loves us [-] and to save us for loving ourselves and others, including God, whether we actually return His love or not.

Every January, a friend of mine journeys to Washington, DC, to participate in the "March for Life" event. It is, and had been held annually for forty years as a protest against the United States Supreme Court decision to allow legalized abortion in the United States. It is entitled the "Roe vs. Wade Decision" which basically states that "pro-choice" (the woman's choice) is more important than "pro-life"; so that the fetus can be put to death by the decision of someone other than the fetus. By the way, the fetus can only become a child and "nothing" or "no one" else. According to a man-made law, the decision to end a human life is apparently more important than our covenantal responsibility to allow a human life to begin. The fetus has no choice to decide to come into existence. The fetus had no choice to be conceived, and now no choice to be born. I certainly understand that for some, the choice to deny a child life is a very difficult and painful one. But it should be apparent that understanding choices isn't more important than making the choices.

Maybe the real challenge of Christmas is wondering how convinced I am that God really embraced our humanity in the person of Jesus and how does this event make me more significant because Jesus embraced my humanity. Let's explore some contemporary Christmas stories to see if they can shed light on the Infancy Narratives, and offer some support to the religious story that God embraced our humanity because He loves us unconditionally and that, indeed, human life is so important, and such a gift, that human nature's primary concern should be caring, not destroying.

A Christmas gift or a birthday gift can be freely offered by one person to another, and the other person may immediately, or ultimately, accept or reject the gift. I may appreciate a gift given by another, or discard it. I may cherish the gift because of the giver, or I may treat it with disrespect because I have no respect for the giver. The gift may be something or someone that gladdens me, or the gift may be something or someone who saddens me. For most of us, as children, a birthday or Christmas present was always special. The happiness it brought was measured by the smiles on our faces, and by how long one wanted to play with it or wear it. It wasn't important how expensive the gift, but rather how much it meant to the one receiving the gift. One of the greatest pleasures I have had in life was to buy toys for our boys at Christmas. I could select items that did not exist when I was a child. Since expense was one of the criteria for choosing toys, I always tried to avoid anything requiring batteries. When we became grandparents, the world had changed again and the toys are different. Nowadays I have to go to a store with a note explaining what I want to purchase. I am never sure whether it would be sixty pounds or six ounces. My wonder was gone, replaced by modern marvels of digital and expensive visual and audio marvels. They were and are beyond my simple understanding of playing with toys. But the grandchildren enjoy them; so the Christmas spirit has not been lost. Gift giving continues to be such an important part of Christmas because it is born of the gift of Jesus to each of us. It is most important to remember that it is not only the gift giving, but who the gift giving celebrates.

As a teacher, I always enjoyed the Christmas season. I would share Christmas stories with my classes at Xavier. Whether cartoons or movies, books or real life stories, the purpose of sharing them was to point to what we usually refer to as "the Christmas spirit." Christmas stories are conversion stories. They are stories about the heart, about love, about being happy, and about the call to share with others. They are stories which call people to change what is important in their own lives. They are stories about how to respond to life whether that is in wonder like the shepherds, or in appreciation like the magi, or in joy like the angels who sang the "Gloria." They are stories which highlight the reality that people are more important than things. They are stories which tell us that God loves us so much He wants to be like us; so God became human. The "things" of Christmas are meant to help us appreciate what the "Christmas spirit" is. Life begins to have rich meaning when we appreciate those around us. The spirit of Christmas is truly a spirit of giving, of sharing, of trying to make others happy. Christmas involves stories of thanksgiving and hope and joy [-] not always easy to embrace in a world that harbors both people of good faith and people whose selfishness or fear or mistrust builds walls rather than bridges. Unfortunately, cynicism is unhealthily thriving in our contemporary culture. The cynicism is probably related to the overly commercial aspect of the season, but Jesus was born in the midst of a time of political oppression and social and religious unrest. It was not a great scene for rejoicing then, and often it is not so great a scene for rejoicing now. But the contemporary scene can never extinguish our joy as long as we do not allow that to happen. All is not favorable for the universal enjoying of Christmas; so we seek meaning where we can. There are books and movies and cartoons rooted in the commerce of everyday life, so let's see how we can discover the Christmas spirit in them.

The "Grinch" is one of my favorite Christmas characters. This green bodied slimy Dr. Seuss character was mean spirited and uncaring. His bitterness was so deeply rooted that he didn't want anyone else to enjoy life; especially at a joyful occasion like Christmas. Can you think of someone you have met in life who shows Grinch-like characteristics? He tried to ruin the Christmas celebrating of the Whos in Whoville by stealing their trees and decorations, their food and drink, and all the gifts hanging by the chimney with care. But it was Cindy Lou Who and the rest of the people of Whoville who influenced the conversion process of the Grinch. The people of Whoville sang joyfully because they were together. Their singing and welcoming of the Grinch led to his conversion. Their happiness was simply in being together, even though all their "stuff" had been stolen. The great revelation in the story was that the Grinch's heart was too small. He couldn't begin to appreciate that people are more significant and lovable than things. Because of their response, the Grinch realized that the gift of Christmas is personal; it has to do with those who share life with you. Did the shepherds have the same experience when they heard the angelic hosts proclaim, in song, the wonder of the birth of Jesus? Maybe this is why the singing and humming of Christmas carols and hymns is so enjoyed around this time of the year. It deals more with the gift of life than the gifts of toys and clothes and jewelry which are "stuff." The gifts or presents simply represent, or symbolize, what the relationship between people is, but they are not the essence of the relationship.

The cartoon claims that his heart grew three sizes that day. To me this is the great gift of Christmas. Jesus allows our hearts to grow. He became like us, how great is that? The way He does that is by letting us enter into the lives of others. Hope springs in the human heart when we begin to realize that others care for us. The Grinch brought everything back to the people of Whoville; so they could celebrate together. They sat at the table and shared the "roast beast." Christmas is a time to allow the heart to grow so that we can begin to appreciate the gift of Jesus in our lives and to allow our hearts and the hearts of others to grow in affection, in joy and hope, in concern for those who share the wonder of our humanity. The best way to fill the stockings hung by the chimney is care-fully. I wonder how much the hearts of the shepherds and the magi grew when they met Jesus. Some of us are shepherds and some of us are magi. What would it take for us to appreciate that God loves us so much that He is willing to welcome us to His birth-day? There are no financial or class distinctions at the stable in Bethlehem. There is no need for reservations in advance, or for special credit or debit card holders. The Grinch was welcomed by the people of Whoville, not unlike we are welcomed by the people of God in the sacrament of Baptism. All the sacraments are communal celebrations. Christmas is a communal celebration during which families strive to share with one another. For some it is hard to share, to celebrate. It was for the Grinch because his heart was too small. His conversion, his growth of heartfelt thanks came about when he knew he was accepted. He belonged with others. Christmas calls for the conversion of each of our hearts, because we belong to God Who cares so much for us that He became like us. He embraced our humanity, and we belong to Him. I wonder how the shepherds and the magi were converted, how they changed their hearts after they had met Jesus? Are our hearts changed at every Christmas celebration, or has Christmas become such a routine that we are concerned more with buying presents than being a presence to the most wonderful miracle of all time, Emmanuel - God is with us?

I have come a little later in life to appreciate the Christmas season cartoon, "Rudolph, the Red-Nosed Reindeer. The book appeared on the scene in the 1930's and the television presentation in the 1960's. It does have elements of the Christmas story. Rudolph is different than other reindeer in that he possesses a red blinking nose. Rather than simply being a facial characteristic, it results in his being ridiculed and alienated from his peers.

It is the perennial sad story of the differences among people which separate us rather than our similarities bringing us together. We appear to be different; therefore one of us is superior to the other, and since only Rudolph differs, the others shun him. It is called prejudice, judging another without knowledge of the other's personality. Your appearance or my appearance is enough to signal one of us is "better" than the other. Rudolph's nose is viewed by others as a sign of weakness and he doesn't feel like he can fit into his surroundings. No wonder he wanders away from home only to hook up with Hermey who is also "on the run." Hermey is an elf who would rather study dentistry than make toys. Neither "fits in to" what is expected of them as seen by their peers. How often this happens in families and among peers. You are different than I am or than we are, and therefore we prejudge that you should be an outcast.

This is often exacerbated by the "bullying" factor among groups of people. Peer pressure often leads to group alienation. How sad and how true! How many people run away from home or give up on their gifts and hopes because they are avoided by others for no other reason than they are "different." Rudolph's family and Clarice, a young doe who is "sweet" on him (which tells us that not everyone is alienated from Rudolph) venture out to find him, but are captured by the Abominable Snow Monster. After some harrowing adventures which include Hermey's knowledge of dentistry leading to the "untoothing" of the monster, everyone returns to the North Pole. Apologies and forgiveness follow and on a cloudy Christmas Eve, Rudolph's "weakness" become his and Santa's "strength" as they are able to bring gifts and toys to children all over the world. What had initially made him an object of scorn among his peers, eventually led to the coming together of the whole community. In our weakness, there is strength. Jesus came in the fragileness and vulnerability of human infancy, not as a mighty, demanding, or powerful Deity. He did not come as we might have expected, but He came as one of us. He came so that we could more fully appreciate what it means for the human person to be created "in the image of God." He came for the shepherds and magi in life. How can our weaknesses strengthen ourselves and others?

During the story, Rudolph and Hermey are instrumental in freeing broken and unused toys from the Island of Misfit Toys. These are gifts and presents which were rejected by children to whom they were freely offered. Sometimes we don't accept the gifts we are given or we are careless or thoughtless in playing with them. We don't always accept others because there is something different. They are not the same color, or don't wear the same clothes, or speak the same language. Are Rudolph and Hermey "Christ" figures? They have gifts or talents that differ from others. They are rejected by others, though not by all. They care for those less fortunate and liberate them from the chains that bind them. They help others by using their gifts. Their actions lead to others being joyful. This is "good news." This is what Christmas heralds!

The birth of Jesus does not seem to be an earth shattering event in terms of the time in which it happened. A Jewish boy is born to wandering parents who had to settle for a hollowed out animal stable situation because they did not make reservations in advance. This is hardly an endorsement for a celebrity personality, or even for a gifted personality. And yet, what a difference Jesus makes! He did all the things that Rudolph and Hermey mimicked in their story. The "Good News" is that God became like us because He loves us. The "Good News" continues when we share this love with others, whether as real persons or as reel personalities.

When we start to get to "serious secular" Christmas inspired stories, we turn to Charles Dickens' "A Christmas Carol." This is a must read if we want to more fully appreciate the Christmas spirit generated by Jesus' birth. There are some interesting background notes to the writing of this book in 1843. Among the factors leading to the publishing of the book is that Dickens was attempting to champion the poor who were being punished by the "progress" of the Industrial Revolution in England. While making the few very wealthy, it was alienating the poor who were being pushed into menial and repetitive work with little pay. (Remember, this happens during the 1840's, not the 21st century. Maybe technological "progress" isn't as liberating as we think. And sometimes we have to think how far we have come in our treatment of people who serve and are served. There are still too many outcasts among us, courtesy of the events following most recently from the 2008 immoral recession brought about by financial practices which should never have happened, as well as the terrible worldwide conflicts which include murdering innocents and uprooting people from their homes.) "Peace on earth" is not as widely present as hopefully it can be in time, but it certainly is a universal goal worth pursuing. Ask God. He became like us to help us to pursue it.

Dickens was also influenced by his own background. His father had been sent to prison and he had to leave school to work in a "blacking" factory. He had the lowly and degrading job of putting labels on boot polishing bottles. This was a far cry from the world of a gentleman to which he aspired, and to which he had hoped his educational pursuits would lead. Fortunately, Dickens did not play the blame game because of his father's activities. He did not ignore his moral obligations and it was at this time in his life that he began to develop a social conscience. The developing of social consciousness leads one to care for others and for what is happening to others rather than simply focusing upon one's self. Now that would be a major Christmas gift for people. Finally, it was only a few years previously when Christmas celebrations began again in England after one hundred and fifty years or so of puritanical censorship. For many years in England, Christmas was, at best, a day of fasting. Prince Albert, the German husband of Queen Victoria had only recently reintroduced the Christmas tree, and Christmas celebrating was once again beginning to be part of the scene in the Great Britain of the mid nineteenth century.

The central character in "A Christmas Carol" is Ebenezer Scrooge who is described as a ...*a wrenching, grasping, squeezing, clutching, covetous old sinner...* He must have been the model for the Grinch, who looks like a pet poodle compared to Scrooge. The very word "Scrooge" has an immediate understanding in the vocabulary of most contemporaries. He is a businessman who should appear in every Business Ethics book as the epitome of the stingiest, the meanest, and the most immoral of unjust capitalist owners. They not only see the purpose of business as lining ONLY their own pockets, but are angered at the thought or mention of employee benefits, product safety, or consumer expectations. The environment is meant to be plundered and the idea of the "common good" is not to be found in his vocabulary. "Look out for number one... and only number one!" The poor deserve all the abuse they get, socially, economically, and politically. He is the Gordon Gecko of the movie "Wall Street" infamy who tries to live out the motto "greed is good."

The book opens with Ebenezer refusing an invitation from his nephew and only living relative, Fred, to visit for Christmas dinner because it is a waste of time. The nephew pleads, that Christmas is, of all times, the opportunity to lay aside hurts and embrace the joy that only family and friends can bring. Ebenezer is angry that he must give his overworked and underpaid clerk, Bob Cratchit, the day off, with pay, because it is a local custom. Christmas had long been uncelebrated as a festive occasion, but acknowledged as a legalistically "religious" observation only. The Crachitt family includes four children. The youngest is Tiny Tim, a sickly little boy who will probably die soon because there isn't enough money to afford him the medical assistance he needs. Scrooge's response to all of this is "Bah Humbug!" He dismisses his nephew's invitation to celebrate dinner and he expresses his objection to having to give his clerk a paid holiday for Christmas. On his way home, Scrooge encounters two gentlemen collecting for the widows and orphans at Christmas as a way of acknowledging the need for people to be generous, and he refuses them outright, contending, as a self righteous legalist, that he contributes taxes for housing the poor in prisons and in orphanages. All in all, Ebenezer Scrooge is a person who cares "nothing" for others. He has no gift to give to others, and he certainly doesn't see his life as a gift.

I think that Dickens' imagination in setting up the story is not unlike that of the author of the Book of Job. The essential difference between Job and Scrooge is that Job wrestles with spiritual bankruptcy while Ebenezer's spiritual life has been extinguished. He is a spiritual shell; there is no life in him. Job is upset with God and Scrooge is upset with all life, other than his own. Yahweh confronted Job as we have seen. Well, God will confront Ebenezer Scrooge, because unless God is involved in our lives, there can be no significant change in the way we respond to ourselves and to others. We would simply wallow in our self pity unless we become aware that we are social by nature. The world is not mine. It's ours!

Scrooge's partner, Jacob Marley, died seven years ago on Christmas Eve. This particular Christmas Eve, he appears, as a ghost or spirit, to Ebenezer to show him how miserable he is since he died. He tells Ebenezer that it is the consequences of the miserly life he lived on earth. His is the chained existence of one who never cared for others in life. He ignored his obligations to humankind during his life and consequently he goes through the afterlife dragging the burdensome chains which doom him to the terrible pain of being alone. Marley says to Scrooge *"... mankind was my business...The common welfare was my business; charity, mercy, forbearance, and benevolence...the dealings of my trade were but a drop of water in the comprehensive ocean of my business"* and Marley failed to carry out the obligations of his human condition. From the book of Deuteronomy through the gospels and the epistles, the Old and the New Testaments speak eloquently of our responsibility to *Love one another as God loves us.* God is not kidding around here. We are **obliged,** to love one another! Another word for "obliged" is **"commanded."** We may not be comfortable at times with being commanded or obliged but the point

185

is: we are our brother's and sister's keeper whether we like it or not. The prophets of the Old Testament reiterated certain themes. One of the themes is that God's ways are not always our ways. Using Marley as His means of grace (and only God would consider Marley as a channel of grace, we wouldn't), God tells Scrooge that He will send three "spirits" to visit him that night. Marley's presence has (to all appearances) nothing to do with helping Marley, but depending upon how Ebenezer responds, it has everything to do with Ebenezer's outcome. Marley says the spirits will appear beginning at one o'clock in the morning.

The first of the spiritual beings, (were they like the angels who appeared to Mary and to Joseph in the Infancy Narratives?) The Spirit of Christmas Past arrived on time, taking Ebenezer on a spiritual journey to his past. The spirit showed Ebenezer his youth, which included being ignored by his father probably because Ebenezer's mother died giving birth to him. He was a lonely child and in boarding school for much of his youth until there was a family reconciliation thanks to his sister, Fan. (She is the mother of Scrooge's nephew, Fred, who had invited him to Christmas dinner.) His early job opportunities included being accepted in an employer's family and a courtship with a young lady, named Belle, whom he loved. However, his early employment led to a concentration on trying to accumulate wealth and an ignoring of social considerations, including the possibility of very intimate personal relationships. He prioritized things over people. How much did his earlier loneliness led to selfishness, to alienating himself from others? There is obviously a connection for which Ebenezer bears some responsibility.

Later, the Spirit of Christmas Present appears showing him where his "aloneness" has led him. He has no relationship with his nephew, who pities him. He has no relationship with his clerk, Bob Cratchitt and his family who actually pray for him. And He has no concern for the poor who need him as is evidenced in the scene with the two men seeking alms for the poor. They make a plea to Ebenezer who gives one of the all time "cop out" answers the rich give for not contributing to the poor ...*are there no prisons, are there no workshops to house these people*...after all, my taxes provide for them. There is a clear disconnect between Ebenezer and people in need. He is also shown the home and family life of his clerk and how, despite the economic difficulties they experience, (thanks in large part to his unfair employer-employee package), they appreciate what they possess, and they toast Ebenezer's health and pray for him, who has done little for them, but whom they see as a child of God.

The Spirit of Christmas Future is the last of the spiritual beings, or angels, sent to Ebenezer. Briefly, he is shown two very sad scenes. One is the home of Bob Cratchit and his family after Tiny Tim has died because there are no medical resources available to help him. The family's pain is shared by all of them as they comfort one another with memories of his time shared with them. The other scene is Ebenezer's tombstone, which highlights the reality that there is no one to mourn for him. No one cares, but then he hasn't cared for anyone. How sad Ebenezer must feel that there is no one to care what happens to him. The spiritual beings have taken him on a journey that begins with loneliness, leads to rejection of others and by others, and ends with abandonment. Can you seriously reflect on yourself and realize that no-one cares for you... or least that is what you think? Now that is very sad. When we speak of salvation, we speak of God saving us from ever being alone, **and** saving us to be with others. Salvation is not just "liberation" nor is it only "reaching a goal." It involves a pathway, a journeying. It is not a private concern, because others are involved, both those who need to be cared for and those who can care for others. As a Eucharistic minister, I am amazed by how much "shut-ins" appreciate Our Lord coming to them in Communion. They welcome God's presence because it means they are not forgotten. They have a relation with the community, a sense of still belonging. They know they are not alone. God seeks them in their own limited surroundings. Yet they also realize that their current, somewhat infirmed reality, involves them praying for others, who are in similar situations to their own. Their community involves other unseen "shut-ins" and their shared companion is the God Who made them and is always with them. They have a sense of being saved from loneliness and being saved to continue loving through their praying for others.

Ebenezer's revelation that night is that while he thinks he is alone, well maybe, he is not alone. Whatever else Christmas is, it includes that we are never alone, but that God is with us. The clanging of the church bells on Christmas morning awaken Ebenezer from his self imposed alienation from people, to the realization that he is still alive and he is not alone. That is what Scrooge came to believe as a result of his interacting with the spirits on Christmas Eve. He experienced a *metanoia,* a change of heart, a spiritual awakening, a liberation. How did he respond? He was giddy. He was so happy that life was different and he could enjoy life. He responded by repenting of his previous life, and in his converting, he looked to caring for others. He became a generous person. He sent a fatted turkey to the Crachits without announcing who sent it. He went to Church. He was appreciative. He spent Christmas dinner with his nephew, Fred, and the family. Generosity, acknowledging God, sharing with family are earmarks of his conversion, and characteristics of Christmas celebration. He gave Bob Cratchit a raise and told him to light the coals to warm the office. People, you have to see this movie. Whether it is Alastair Sim, George C Scott, or Patrick Stewart as Ebenezer Scrooge, it is wonder-filled. Each actor has a certain individual gift or talent to contribute to the performance, but the story shouts out the coming of Christ to bring life and love to our communities. God embraces our humanity and our response should change us forever.

Certainly "A Christmas Carol" reminds us to prioritize what makes life important. Bethlehem is more important religiously than it is geographically. The shepherds are more important theologically than they are occupationally. The magi are more important as religious figures than they are as foreign visitors. Scrooge is more important existentially than he is as a literary character. The Grinch is more important in his conversion than in his cartoon costuming. Rudolph is more important in what he accomplished rather than in how he looked. There is one more movie that I would like to reflect upon in trying to appreciate how "wonderful" the Christmas Story is.

The first date my bride and I shared was January 19, 1957. We went to an Italian restaurant and to a movie. The movie was "Wings of Eagles" with John Wayne. Now I really like John Wayne, but this was probably the worst movie in which he ever appeared. But since we are still on the honeymoon fifty-nine years later, it was only a "blip." And every January 19th we go out on a date to see a movie and go to an Italian restaurant. The Italian restaurant is never a problem, but sometimes picking a movie is. Many of our contemporary movies substitute mocking for comedy, horror and carnage for reality, and using and degrading people for "adult" entertainment; so it does become a challenge to look for movies we could enjoy. Every Christmas season, however, we do take time to watch one of the all-time great movies ever screened, "It's a Wonderful Life."

This movie focuses upon the marriage between George and Mary Bailey, played by Jimmy Stewart and Donna Reed. After a series of events in which George is unable to "follow his dream" of traveling the world, he winds up being the chief officer for the Bailey Building and Loan Company of Bedford Falls, NY. It was his father's business, born of a desire to help the people who were so often under the dominion of the town bully and chief slumlord, Mr. Potter, who is not unlike Ebenezer Scrooge, except that Mr. Potter does not convert. The movie opens on Christmas Eve with absent-minded Uncle Billy Bailey misplacing an $8,000 bank deposit, which is recovered by the evil Mr. Potter, who hides the money. His intention is to get George (Jimmy Stewart) in deep trouble with the law. This is a situation which will land poor George in disgrace and in jail. Like the book of Job where the opening takes place in heaven, so does this movie. Clarence Oddbody is an angel who has not yet earned his wings and also happens to be George's guardian angel. He reviews George's life and finds many wonderful characteristics about him. He saved his younger brother, Harry, from drowning when he was nine years old. As a boy, George worked at the Gower Pharmacy as a messenger and soda fountain "jerk." He saved a patient of Mr. Gower's, the pharmacist, from being poisoned by a mistaken prescription. He forfeited his chance at college by taking over his father's business and let his brother attend in his place. Instead of following his desire to travel, he marries Mary Hatch and they raise four beautiful children. They never get a chance to go on a honeymoon, but rather use the money to revive the shaky business and loan association during a Depression era "run on the bank." In short, he is a caring person, whose generosity and concern for others marks him as a "really good guy." As a teacher in a Jesuit high school and in a Jesuit college, I embraced that one of our gospel concerns was to develop in our students a moral and religious awareness. Part of the mission of Jesuit education is to prepare our students to become "men and women for others." George Bailey certainly qualified to be a "man for others." He would have been a great Jesuit school student.

The Christmas Eve crisis is the background for this great story of "good will to men and women." Clarence's challenge, as his guardian angel, is how to help George Bailey, whose current problems include meeting his financial and legal obligations and caring for his family. He would not be able to fulfill them if he landed in jail. In desperation, George asks Mr. Potter for help and is rejected. George, in his own burdened reasoning, begins to think that he is "worth more dead than alive" because there is a small insurance policy. This underscores the terrible pull of temptation in our lives. Not knowing what else to do, he wishes, and prays that he had never been born. This was Job's wish also. Clarence imaginatively uses this and tells George that his wish is granted. Since George had never been born, his brother Harry died when he was nine years old, and never became a war hero saving hundreds of sailors on an aircraft carrier under attack by the enemy. Mr. Gower, the pharmacist, went to prison in disgrace for prescribing the wrong medicine to an innocent victim. The Bailey Building and Loan Association never provided money for decent housing to so many people and Potter's bank policies (like a number of recent bank policies) led to so many people leading economically unfulfilling and poverty ridden lives. Mary Hatch never married and there were no Bailey children. Bedford Falls became Pottersville where many people led lives of oppression, depression and despair. After a "suicide" conversation and a rescue involving his Guardian Angel, Clarence, George begins to realize how much he has been allowed to serve others and how much they have benefited by his concern. He is willing to "face the music" because he realizes the love of family and friends which he has experienced throughout his life trumps any adversity experienced on life's journey. Eventually he is rescued from being held legally accountable for the "stolen" bank deposit by the generosity of scores of people he has served and befriended over the years. It is a wonderful story because he realizes his "wonderful life" emerges thanks to all the people he has touched and been touched by throughout life. The "good news" expressions of the generosity of others rescued George and his family on that Christmas Eve. You know, there is nothing "corny" about this story, because so many of our lives have been rescued and redeemed, by others whom we have touched and have responded to us. Just think about it.

Actions have consequences and the consequences of George Bailey's actions over the years taught him (like it taught the Grinch) that "stuff" will never be as important as people, especially family and friends. That is why he was able to celebrate Christmas. He came to realize that his own significance as a human person has to do with being loved by and loving those with whom one is in contact, beginning obviously with his wife and children, family and friends. The Grinch had the people of Whoville. Rudolph had all the characters at the North Pole. Scrooge had his nephew and family, the Crachitts, the people of London, both poor and rich. Jesus, on that first Christmas night had Mary and Joseph, the shepherds and, later on, the magi. Christmas is, above all, a feast of family and friends. It is a feast of loving support and recognition of how significant each one of us is as a human person. It is characterized by gift giving, but the genuineness of the gift giving deals with how one answers the following two questions:

> *How does the gift of Emmanuel...God is with us as a child...change the way I **should** look at the human condition?*

Hint: surprise and wonder

> *What do I change in my response to others...especially family and friends...so that I can consistently be a gift to those who come in and out of my life?*

Hint: resolution: internal and external

I believe that most people who celebrate Christmas enjoy the company and the festivities, at least, eventually. There is the shopping for gifts. Will the presents be appreciated? Is the present appropriate? How much should I spend? There are days of preparing and wondering if there is enough food for all invited, and whether all who are invited will come. There is the journeying which can have its share of anxieties. Then there are those unexpected events which often threaten to turn a planned celebration into an uncertainty, if not a nightmare. Mary and Joseph had neither credit cards nor Amtrak reservations as they prepared for a long and difficult journey. They weren't even sure where they would stay when they arrived. They certainly did not expect to share the miracle of birth with animals, shepherds, and foreigners from the East. They did not expect their first crib to be a trough to feed cattle and sheep. Yet they had made preparations. They had both said "yes" to God and had confirmed their "yes" to each other. Their faith that God was the author of all life was their source. They knew that their lives would be forever changed with the birth of this child (as it should be with anyone who becomes a parent); so it was in hope they faced an uncharted future. But no matter what they would face, their religious conviction and their marital love strengthened their resolve to follow

The Great Commandment articulated in the Book of Deuteronomy (6:4) "Hear, O Israel! The Lord is our God, the Lord alone! Therefore, you shall love the Lord, your God, will all your heart, and with all your soul, and with all your strength." Mary and Joseph were raised to appreciate that God cares for them. They were prepared because of their commitment to God and to each other and yet, I am sure, their joy in giving birth must have been deepened by the surprise visit of shepherds repeating the joy of the angelic host who directed them to Jesus' nursery. Just think how nice it is to hear strangers say how wonderful your child is. Their joy must have been multiplied by the visit and the gift giving of the Eastern foreigners who journeyed from afar simply to be able to gaze upon the Infant Jesus. Just think how appreciative you are for the gifts bestowed upon you and your child by people who you don't know well, but who are so generous.

Thousands of years of accumulated knowledge of God and humanity, of the covenant relationship, has given me, and all of us, an understanding of the divine and the human, that neither the Holy Family, nor the shepherds, nor the magi possessed during that first Christmas season. Yet, in addressing the first question above: do I have anything like the joy of the shepherds in entering the stable at Bethlehem? Is there a sense of spontaneity to my celebrating Christmas? Does Christmas allow me to appreciate God's wonderful surprise? Being a human person is great. It is so great that God became like us. How can we not celebrate God's gift of Himself to us? He embraced my, our, humanity. My relationship with God has entered a stage of intimacy because we share human nature. Oh, I know that I am still in the "image" of God, but Emmanuel, God is with us, has deepened the relationship in a way none of us could have imagined. Is Christmas only a day set aside, once a year, to reflect and rejoice? Or is Christmas an ongoing, existential, part of my very significant and responsible everyday experience?

In prioritizing the importance of Christmas, how much time and effort have I given to prayer and reflection? Am I capable of making the same act of faith that the shepherds and the magi made? Or am I too distracted by the rest of the "stuff" involved with the Christmas festivities? It is mind-boggling how much individuals and families can ruin the celebrating for themselves and others. Instead of "Glory to God," too often we live out "Bah humbugs!" I think the main reason we get distracted during this season is dwelling upon how much *I* am obligated to do as a family member or as a friend. *I* get in the way of *my* celebrating. The Grinch, Ebenezer and George Bailey were all distracted too. When they began to focus on others, on the significance of life, they worked through their distractions. If we focus on the reason for Christmas [-] Emmanuel [-] we too can put everything in its proper place. The author of all life has embraced the form of our humanity, truly giving us a significance we didn't previously realize that we had. He entered our image. He became one of us. To honor another person is to become like that person [-] in the way he or she acts and in the principles he or she upholds (which we will explore in the next chapter) and in the care and concern he or she shows towards others (which we will explore in the last chapter.) God became us. In his first letter John writes

> "...let us love one another because love is of God; everyone who loves is begotten by God and knows God. Whoever is without love does not know God, for God is love. In this way the love of God was revealed to us: God sent his only son into the world so that we might have life through him. In this is love: not that we have loved God, but that he loved us and sent his Son as expiation for our sins..."

193

Christmas confirms the Genesis covenant relationship between God and us and becomes a daily reminder that what is necessary for us to live with some degree of significance is that we love. Love is primarily a relationship; so naturally and necessarily this involves others, including God as an Other Person. How can anyone of us treat our own humanity or the humanity of anyone else with less than the same respect God bestowed on us that first Christmas night? And yet, war and injustice, poverty and ignorance, selfishness and envy, deceit and disrespect and fear indicate that the vicious Herods of life, as well as the care-less innkeepers are still alive and harming and ignoring the innocents.

He was born into the fragileness of infancy, to be cared for by others, by family, to be nourished and nurtured physically and spiritually. To hold an infant in one's arms is to realize the fragility of life. He wasn't marked by a "lightening bolt" like Harry Potter as an infant, but the reason Harry, or Jesus, or anyone of us survives infancy is because of the love and care of those around us. To abandon an infant is among the most terrible of human offenses. To raise and care for an infant is among the most burdensome of responsibilities and among the most wonderful of joys (a mystery). Just as human freedom is both a burden and a blessing (a mystery), so is human life a mystery in which Jesus honors us by embracing both the joys and the difficulties of humanity.

Our initial response to Christmas ought to be *surprise and wonder.* It should be like the joyful surprise of the audience of children of all ages at a Christmas showing of the seasonal favorite, "The Nutcracker." It should be like the wide-eyed amazement as the Christmas Tree, on the stage, grows up to the ceiling. It should be exciting as the Nutcracker prince leading the gingerbread soldiers against the Mouse King and his army. It should be as awesome as the unfolding of the dream sequences which continue to burst upon the stage during the second act. Of all God's creations, He chose to become like us. This is a sort of inversion of Genesis one in which we are created "in God's image." If God chooses to come into the world in the same manner as each of us comes into the world, then there is "something" that shouts out that human nature is so significant that even God chose to embrace it! What a surprise! We love surprises and yet we so often overlook the most significant of surprises. Emmanuel [-] God is with us. He became like us. He embraced our humanity as an infant, the most fragile and helpless of human persons, dependent on others for living. God did not choose to enter into time and space as some sort of colossal heavenly star or asteroid, some supernova, or incredibly sized chimpanzee or gigantic cactus plant that demanded attention and fear from all mortals.

Christmas is a time to *wonder* about the greatness of human nature which gives rise to our personal relationship with God. Why do we war against each other? Why do we intentionally hurt each other? Why do we ignore each other? Why do our physical differences cause us to be suspicious of each other? No other created being has a personal relationship with the Creator, with God Who made everything and Who is the cause of all that is. And yet, human nature is so often taken for granted or worse, abused, betrayed, denied, tortured and abandoned. We look at the calendar and know that every year Christmas is December 25th. There are three weeks before the day arrives, then two, then one. It is expected, taken for granted. There is no surprise. There is no wonder. How terribly sad that is for us! The "Good News" begins with: God loves us SO much, He became like us [-] Emmanuel. How can this not be such wonderful news? Maybe this is what Nietzsche meant when the madman in the market place cried that "...the event itself is much too great, too distant, too far from the comprehension of many even for the tidings of it to be thought of as having arrived yet, not to speak of the idea that many people might know what has *really* happened here..." Until we wonder, until Emmanuel becomes personal, we will not realize the significance of Christmas.

Christmas is an event, but not one that is simply a date on a calendar. It is an event which changes the significance of human nature by relating us to God in a way never seriously imagined, a miracle. Instead of God being "up there" and us being "down here", He is "with us" in a manner in which He is not with any other of His creations. How should we respond to this insight, this "turn of events"? It should be with a resolve, both internally and externally. *Internally*, we should appreciate more obviously my gift of life as a reflection of God's creative nature towards us. To appreciate the gift of life means to be thankful that we have come into the world and be aware that God is with us in a very intimate way. He does not dictate to us, but rather He accompanies us.

It doesn't mean there aren't hurts and pain. It doesn't mean that there aren't cruelties and injustice. But it does mean that each one of us is never alone, because God is with us. *Externally*, we should be aware that we have the power to help and to heal as well as the ability to distort that power by harassing and hurting others. That is a serious power. It is not to be used lightly because the people whom we will encounter on our life's journey also possess these powers, and they are also reflective of God's creative nature, whether or not they appreciate that God is with them.

My favorite Christmas hymn is "O Holy Night." The words of that joyous song summarize the magnificence of Christmas...

> *Long lay the world in sin and error pining*
> *Till He appeared*
> *And the world felt its worth....*

And the world felt its worth. We are the world, and Christmas gives us significance, worth, that we would never have imagined, until Christ embraced our humanity. My philosopher buddy Socrates' words now become prophetic "...life is worth living...." I wonder: what am I going to do about this relationship? Hopefully, my response will echo that of the reborn Grinch, the reclaimed Rudolph, the repentant Scrooge, and the renewed George Bailey. They share in common a realization that love is a gift no one of us should refuse to appreciate, to nurture, and to share with those who come in and out of one's life. God offered this relational gift in creation and more intimately personalized His gift in Christmas by being with us [-] Emmanuel. The gift is real. Mary and Joseph, the shepherds and the magi, Herod and the innkeeper all really responded, with differing consequences.

Gifts just don't happen. They don't materialize out of nothing. There is much in the way of preparation that goes into the activity of gift giving. You have to know the individual whom you want to gift. To gift another person follows from coming to love him or her. You want to individualize the gift; so you must think about what would be of interest to this person. What would make him or her happy? What would he or she embrace, care for, and share? The Old Testament prepares us for the

New Testament but the gift of the Messiah is still a surprise. The season of Advent prepares us for Christmas and the surprise is Emmanuel. The season of Lent prepares us for the Cross and for Easter and the surprise is that torture and death do not end life. Life prepares us for death which is either the fullness of life or the failure of life. What is the surprise that awaits us as we prepare for eternity by the way we live our daily lives?

"O Holy Night" has become a wonderfully traditional Christmas carol. In chapter one, I suggested that what Adam and Eve lost was our sense of holiness. Jesus at Bethlehem recovers for us the meaning of holiness. Life has been more clearly and deeply identified with a realization that God continues to care for us without reservation. How important is our humanity? God became man. That's really Good News! What Christmas celebrates is that the friendship created in the Garden of Eden has become more intimate in the stable at Bethlehem. What was created as holy has been renewed. Emmanuel [-] God is with us. O Holy Night…and Day! Holy is not about what is distant or untouchable. Holy has to do with the relationship I have with my Creator God, Who thought so much of me that He became like me. Holy has to do with the realization that those with whom I come into contact through life are, like me, called to be holy. Holy has to do with what makes life and living an ongoing Christmas gift. Let us leave this chapter with this question *because actions speak louder than words…especially my actions:*

> **To what degree, or depth, can I appreciate that the birth of Jesus has restored to me that being holy is worthwhile…and that becoming holy is a real possibility for me? How can I embrace this gift and share it with my fellow travelers on this life's journey to God's holy kingdom?**

CHAPTER FIVE

Getting to Know You

There is a wonderful Broadway musical entitled "The King and I." It came to the stage in the late 1940's or early 1950's, and was eventually made into a movie. The original book entitled "Anna and the King of Siam" is based on the memoirs of a British widow, Anna Leonowen, who becomes a governess and teacher to the fifteen children of the King of Siam in the 1860's. There are many memorable songs from the show, but one of them is entitled, "Getting to Know You." It captures the desire of this English teacher to understand and appreciate the young people of a very different culture. As a teacher, I agree with her that getting to know your students can be as important as the knowledge and values you invite them to learn. If you don't get to know them, it becomes more difficult to help them accept your invitation to learn. I know that some people, including educators, speak of value-free learning experiences. If a teacher is enthusiastic about what he or she is teaching, and/or has a concern for his and her students, then I find it very difficult to speak of a "value-free" education. Maybe this is because I consider teaching a ministry, or a vocation, much more than a job. It fills a need in life far more than simply filling a position. And perhaps, as students get to know their teacher (assuming the teacher reveals himself or herself) then they can better appreciate what is being taught. What we are attempting in this essay, however, is to get to know the Teacher; so we can better appreciate the meaning of His ministry, and hopefully, more fully embrace His teachings. The Teacher is the historical Jesus Who becomes the Risen Christ.

In the late 1970's I was part of a group of four Jesuit priests and four lay teachers in New York Province high schools who developed a program for Jesuit secondary educators. Father Bill Wood SJ was our leader. It was called the "Colloquium on the Ministry of Teaching" and it aimed at inviting, encouraging, and supporting Jesuit secondary educators to envision and embrace teaching as a ministry, as a calling, a vocation, rather than as a job, or a quest for personal fulfillment. It incorporated social and spiritual elements, and was designed to include time for individual reflection as well as interaction between teachers and administrators from different schools. Primarily, the focus was on one's own school and how we could plan to see more clearly and express more obviously the "Ignatian vision" for the faculty and students of each particular school. This "vision" aims at developing not simply the student's intellectual abilities, but the whole person as a compassionate and socially aware individual. This "vision" strives to challenge young students to become "men and women for others" in a world which too often focuses upon "me." The motivation for this Ignation vision" (the vision of Ignatius of Loyola, founder of the Jesuits) is "for the greater glory of God ("ad majorem dei gloriam".) It is a Christian calling, a Catholic calling. It is a call to find God in all aspects of life. It was designed to see our teaching ministry as a call to share, to heal, and to be responsible for enlightening those entrusted to us. The man who hired me to teach at Xavier High School, Father Vincent Duminuco SJ, described this vision beautifully, when he explained that our purpose, as teachers, is to develop people who are intellectually prepared for a life long journey, socially aware of the need for justice to be practiced in our world in which it is too often absent, and to exercise compassion in reaching out to serve others. The "key words" used are competent, conscientious, and compassionate. ["The Jesuit Ratio Studiorum" edited by V. Duminuco S.J.] Teaching is ultimately a call to be a servant. A Christian teacher is called to be a servant of Christ, Who happens to be a servant to all humankind, everywhere.

In the last chapter we read that the Good News means "God loves us so much that He becomes like us, shares life with us, and gives all

He is for us, Himself on the Cross; so that we may be with Him now and forever." In this essay, I would like to concentrate on the second part…"…*He shares life with us…*" We discover Jesus sharing life with us primarily through the gospel stories. Hopefully we get to know Him more intimately through prayer and practice, which are both a challenge and an invitation to us. The gospels are life giving stories. I have chosen stories with which I believe most of us are able to relate. My purpose is to reveal more obviously the concern of the Teacher, Jesus, for us, His students, His followers, His witnesses, His servants…His creation.

To prepare us to more fully appreciate these stories I would like to offer some additional background on the "Good News" according to Saints Mark, Matthew, Luke, and John. Getting a sense of the audience and the focus of each of these followers of Christ should help us to better appreciate the "sharing of Jesus with us." The better we come to know our Teacher, Jesus Christ, hopefully our understanding of His teachings will be clearer, and our motivation "to love others as He loves us" will become a deeper practice in our lives.

Saint Mark's Gospel, according to scholars, is the first written account of the Good News, sometime around 65 AD. Trying to locate it chronologically is important because authors write to specific audiences at specific times. For example, I could not include the economic breakdown of the United States and the effects of the super storm "Sandy" unless my audience had lived, and are living, through these events; this is also true of the gospel authors. The time of Mark's gospel is during a Roman persecution. It is a time when the people in power are abusing their authority, their power, by persecuting those who are "different" from them. The Romans are persecuting the Jews. Since the Romans make no distinction between the Israelites and the Messianites, or Christians, the persecution includes those in the early Church. We are familiar with this expression of persecution. If you are different than us, you are the enemy. It is similar to any type of persecution in which difference is the reason for the persecutor to assail the persecuted. Women in the United States overcame a form of political persecution when they won the right to vote in presidential elections through the 19th amendment to the constitution in 1920. Black people were enslaved because they were a different color and the racial persecution was prolonged economically and educationally for many years after the US Civil War (1861-1865) for emancipation of slaves was fought. In some areas of our country, the war is still being waged. Catholics were religiously persecuted in Northern Ireland for years and Muslims were persecuted in Kosovo as late as the 1990s. Sadly, persecution is a constant companion for far too many people in today's world. The Holocaust is probably the most historically infamous of persecutions perpetrated by the Nazis upon the Jewish people of Germany, Austria, Poland and other European countries during the Second World War. There are many other past and, unfortunately, contemporary examples of persecution based only on the reality that somehow you are different from me. Our difference might be because of color, or sexuality, or religious conviction, or nationality, or political affiliation. It is rooted in the fear that because you differ from me, you are a threat. It flies in the face of trying to focus on what connects us as human persons by emphasizing that our differences are obviously more threatening than the reality that we share human nature.

The focus on Jesus in Mark's gospel is that of the "Suffering Servant." Just as Jesus suffered and died that we might have life and have it to the fullest, His followers are also suffering unjustly. Jesus as "Suffering Servant" is a reminder of the Old Testament theme of the "suffering servant" in Deutero-Isaiah (written during the Babylonian captivity). Deutero-Isaiah (or the second author of the Book of Isaiah) is trying to console the captive Israelites whose land has been conquered by the Babylonians and who are imprisoned in a foreign land. Mark's focus on Jesus has the same purpose as that of the Old Testament prophet, that is, to give hope to those who are currently being persecuted. They share in Jesus' ministry; therefore they are given hope that they will overcome death as He did. Mark's primary focus on Jesus is His death on the Cross, the ultimate sacrifice. The author prepares us by showing the rejection of Jesus and His teachings throughout the gospel. There are a series of miracles, including healings in the second chapter which threaten the synagogue leaders that Jesus might be gaining popularity and jeopardizing their cherished positions of leadership in the community. Their rejection of Jesus comes in chapter 3:6 where we read "The Pharisees went out and at once began to plot with the

Herodians against Him, discussing how to destroy Him." Their fear led them to plan sinister action. After the healing of a woman and the raising of Jairus' daughter (see below), His own townspeople reject Jesus (6:1-6) because He won't perform miracles for them. Who does He think He is? They simply refused to listen. Jesus is only the carpenter's son. There's nothing special about Him, so there is no need to pay attention to Him. They are blind. They didn't plot against Him as the leaders did, but they simply rejected Him as "too good to be true" because He won't put on a miracle "show" for them. They simply dismissed Jesus as not worth hearing because He did not dance to their tune. The third rejection of Jesus is by His own disciples (8:14-21) when they fail to understand that the miracle of the loaves of bread and the feeding of the 4,000 people refers more to the need for spiritual feeding of the people rather than this particular miraculous feeding of huge group of people. Their rejection is temporary, a bump in their road to become genuine witnesses to Jesus' love for all of us.

There were different motivations for the rejections of Jesus. The disciples simply misunderstood what Jesus had done. The townspeople really wanted Jesus to be a performer of miracles, because of what He had done in other places. They wanted to be entertained. The Pharisees, or leaders, were afraid because they recognized the good works Jesus had done and worried that the people would turn against them. They sought to protect their own positions and saw Jesus as a serious threat to that. As we read this gospel today, do we who suffer, or who know others who are suffering, draw the same hope that the audience of Mark did? Do we find meaning in our suffering and therefore experience the hope that our suffering is not our final chapter in life? Or are we more likely to reject Jesus? Why?

Suffering is tough and I don't think that any reasonable person seeks to suffer. In my service as parish Eucharistic Minister, I have been bringing Our Lord in communion to those who are suffering, or simply elderly, and are not able to attend Church services. I have met some in forty years of serving who aren't afraid of suffering, as well as some who are afraid that that they are not worthy of their suffering. But whether they are fearful or resigned, they are brave people who know they need help in order to deal with their difficulties in life. They are happy to receive this help through the Eucharist, confident that Our Lord is present to them in their pain and suffering. Their concern is usually not focused so much are "getting better" but on reconciling themselves with their suffering and attempting to accept their burden with the conviction that God is always with them [-] they are not alone.

Remember that the gospels are not biographies of Jesus. They are theology and theology is the study of God revealed in time and or history, and the *human response* which is yes or no, acceptance or rejection, faith or disbelief. How do we respond to Jesus as the "Suffering Servant", to the one who took upon Himself our sins, our "no's", our rejections, our disbelief, our fears, our failures to love, in order to strengthen us with the hope that we are significant in the Father's eyes? How do we accept that the "Suffering Servant" shares our pain? The Gospel of Mark, like the other gospels, calls for us to reflect, not simply to read. It calls for us to respond, not simply to analyze.

Saint Matthew's gospel, around 80 AD, is directed to a different audience, composed of Jewish-Christians (or Messianites) and Jews "on the fence." Jewish-Christians are those raised in the Old Testament tradition who came to accept Jesus as the Messiah (the Anointed One) promised of old. Those "on the fence" refer to people raised in the Jewish tradition who are trying to decide whether or not to accept Jesus as the promised Messiah. For many of them, it would involve being ostracized by their families and friends. It is not simply a question of crossing the street to a different place of worship. The move would involve sociological and economic implications for their choice. They might lose friendships they have fostered over the years because of their decision to follow Jesus. Their families might no longer accept them into the households in which they were born and raised. The author of Matthew's gospel makes the most references to the Old Testament in his effort to be supportive of faith in Jesus for the Jewish-Christians as well as offering encouragement to those "on the fence" to make the "leap of faith."

In this gospel, Jesus is presented as the "new Moses" and one "greater than Moses." This gospel author is conscious of the inner conflicts and struggles which many people in his audience are undergoing. A faith decision is one that affects not only the individual and his or her direction in life, but will touch those whom he has known or will come to know. It may alienate many with whom they have shared lifelong friendships. We all know that in developing priorities in life for ourselves, we sometimes have to leave behind some convictions we held and change others. We might have to sever ties with some people with whom we were friends and neighbors. That can be very difficult.

There are many references to the Old Testament in this gospel as the author focuses on Jesus as God's promise to send the Messiah. For our contemporary Church, do we see Jesus as fulfilling God's covenant promise to care for us? Do we accept Jesus as the Messiah promised of old, even if our initial expectations of "messiah" are different from the "Suffering Servant"? Many had hoped that the messiah would be a political leader whose primary task would be to lead the Jewish people out from under the yoke of the Romans. After all, at this time it is clear that the oppressive Romans are the enemy. Many, probably with good reasons, hoped the Messiah would vanquish the Roman enemy and restore the "glory days" of David and Solomon's empire.

What happens when our expectations in life are not met? We either drop all our expectations, or we change them, because now we know what we didn't realize before, and we accept what we had previously ignored or rejected. It happens because human judgment is always subject to change based on developing human knowledge. Getting to know what you embrace and proclaim is a process. Getting to accept others is a major part of our human process of growth. We come to believe when before we did not, or we come to believe more deeply than we ever did because our experiences are supported by a developing or broadening of knowledge regarding life and life's journey. Our new revelation is that Matthew's Christological focus is directed to the same person as Mark's. The *promised Messiah*, instead of a Davidic warrior king turns out to be the *Suffering Servant*. This is how deeply Jesus immerses Himself into our humanity. He suffers and dies so that we might have the fullness of life both here and hereafter, and somehow that "fullness" involves loving and being loved, and fulfilling the covenant call expressed in Genesis. The Messiah comes to "lead" by immersing Himself in our human condition, which involves suffering, sometimes brought about by our having to make painful decisions, or by the decision of others which deny our own freely made choices.

St. Luke's gospel, while written around the same time as St. Matthew's, is directed to a Gentile audience. The broad term "gentile" basically means a non-Jewish audience. Gentiles are people who are not raised in the Old Testament traditions. From the perspective of the Mosaic Law followers, gentiles were essentially outcasts, because of their lack of the religious traditions of the Israelites. The Christological focus on Jesus is the "Champion of the outcasts." In this account of the Good News, people who were treated as social, religious, and political outcasts are very important to Jesus Who has come among all of us. His message of love, of the Father's concern, of the Spirit's assistance is universal. Women, shepherds, soldiers are important people in God's plan of salvation. It is the only gospel that has the story of the Good Samaritan. Sociologically, the Jews and the Samaritans were not neighbors, but harbored deep resentments against each other. This is not unlike so many past and present situations which we witness in our own lifetimes. As previously mentioned, some people won't accept others because they are different. They oppose others based on differences of color, sex, creed, nationality, economic class, political parties, rather than identifying with what unites us, our human nature and using that as a basis for interrelating. Luke's message clearly focuses on God's *universal* love. His love is directed not only to the Jewish people, or Christians, or Muslims, or Hindus, but to *everybody*. It is called the covenant, which is God's unconditional and universal care and concern for each of us, believer as well as non-believer, a love that can only be as alive as possible to the extent to which we respond. Remember, love is a primarily a relationship. The *promised Messiah* is the *Suffering Servant* and the *Champion of the outcasts*. The *Glorified Christ* will lead His people, not as the head of a conquering army, but from the throne of the Cross, and victory will emerge when "we love one another as He has loved us."

The gospels written by Mark, Matthew and Luke comprise what we refer to as the "synoptic tradition." "Syn" means "with" and "optic" refers to being "seen" by the "eye' of the soul as much as the bodily organ. These gospels can be placed side by side and "seen" as following a similar sequence of events. Mark's account has about 660 verses, Matthew's has about 1,050 verses and Luke's contains about 1,200 verses. The basic synoptic sequence involves Jesus' baptism and temptation scenes which are His preparation for His public ministry; His public ministry consisting of what He said (His teachings) and what He did (His miracles). Finally, there are the Passion narratives which include His betrayal, His unjust sentencing, His suffering, His death on the Cross, and His resurrection. Both Matthew and Luke develop Mark's account beginning with an Infancy Narrative account in each gospel, and incorporating stories which basically give more significance to the disciples and the roles they will play in the church. Perhaps, it is important to remember that when Mark wrote his account of the "Good News", many of Jesus' early followers thought that the second coming of Christ in the final worldly judgment would be immanent. The Roman persecutions and the destruction of the Temple at Jerusalem in 70 AD were thought by some, perhaps by many, that the end of time was close at hand. There would be little need of an earthly church. When Matthew, Luke and John wrote, there was a realization that the second coming of Christ in judgment was not to happen in the near future, and Jesus' ministry was to be continued by His disciples, both those who walked with Him then and us, who walk with Him today.

If I could make a distinction for the purposes of trying to appreciate the gospels, I would say that the synoptic tradition focuses more on the humanity of Jesus without ignoring His divinity, while the Johannine tradition focuses more on the divinity of Jesus without ignoring His humanity. The Johannine tradition consists of the Gospel according to John, the three letters of John, and the Book of Revelation. There are probably at least three authors involved.

Let me comment on authorship. We live in a very litigious society. The law is usually very clear with respect to ownership, to what someone owns and the obligations which follow as owner. This is true of one's material property or possessions, and in this day and age with the issues and concerns of intellectual property, or creations of the mind, both individual and corporate. If I sign a document, or write an article, or accept a debt, then I become responsible for its contents, especially if there is legal action that might follow. And now with "Facebook" and "tweeting", the ramifications of what people say are as public as it gets, and authors are held responsible for what they say or for how other people interpret what has been said. I think it is ironic that this social networking is done through mechanical devices without face to face (social) contact. Maybe that is why I don't tweet. I would rather speak face to face with people than contact them through a mechanical device, no matter how convenient. You are certainly worth more of my attention that can be gained in a mechanically forwarded message of 140 characters even if accompanied by emogis. Judgment, whether in the form of acceptance or condemnation, is swift and unfortunately very often enacted without much reflection. We live in a world in which people seem all too often to expect immediate actions and instant results. Wisdom involves a reflective understanding of messages, not a glance at characters on a screen. This is accompanied with little or no thought on what is said or done. After all, we should remember that the one who reads the tweets doesn't always take time to listen to what tweeter intends. Maybe that is why one of the most common questions is: "What did you mean by that?" The answer to this question is what can lead to conversation.

To get back to the gospels, authorship in ancient times was identified not necessarily with the writer of some piece, but rather with an influential person in the community. The Book of Deuteronomy in the Old Testament is referred to as Moses' farewell address to his people. Having been written about five hundred years after his death would make it very difficult for him to be the actual author of the book. The person we identify as the actual writer is called the Deuteronomist author. A "farewell address" is a literary device which attempts to acknowledge the significance of a particular individual. Moses, in this case, is the leading figure in the history of the Israelite people and very influential for many centuries after his death. The dialogue "Phaedo" in Greek philosophy is Socrates' farewell address written years after his death by his student, Plato, as an acknowledgement of the lasting importance of his teacher in Western thought. So authorship does not necessarily refer to the actual writer of the work, but, at times, to an influential communal figure. In John's gospel story, the "Last Supper" scene (chapters thirteen through seventeen) is also referred to as Jesus' farewell address to His apostles.

The audience of John's gospel is similar to that of Matthew's. They are early believers in accepting Jesus as the Messiah promised of old and those who are wrestling with whether or not to accept Jesus as this promised Messiah. He focuses on Jesus as the "Glorified Christ," the Divine Son of God Who is always in charge of what He is about. This gospel, unlike the synoptic accounts, begins with a prologue that links Jesus clearly with the Divine Creating Father and Who graciously comes among His Father's followers, the Israelites, and is rejected by many of them. He then reaches out to others, the Gentiles, and is accepted by many. The theological point of the prologue is that the Father's love is universal and Jesus has come among us to proclaim that to all people. It is as philosophic a portion as will be found in any of the gospels, but it still remains theological, which is the consistent content of all scripture. Among the ideas in the prologue is that God is not always accepted by those who claim to be believers or followers. Perhaps it is an acknowledgement that "actions speak louder than words." "Hypocrite" is a word in the vocabulary of any religious group that most people understand, but rarely accept that it applies to them. The primary opposition to Jesus in this gospel seems to come from the synagogue leaders. Sometimes religious leaders in their zeal (or desire for power or fear of the loss of power or prestige, or hypocrisy) can create situations in which people are turned away from expressing their allegiance to God. It gives rise, I think, to the difference between the letter of the law and the spirit of the law. (And as an aside, it is not limited to religious leadership, but is evident in other aspects of life as well; examples include political, social, educational, and familial leadership. How many of us have been judged by the following authority; "you will do this because I am your father...no other explanation." As a father, I think it can occasionally be an acceptable explanation, but never as a model to follow in every instance, especially as children grow in knowledge and wisdom.)

If I follow the letter of the law, I measure my religious conviction only by my attendance at church or synagogues functions, by my contributions to a parish or a community, by not getting into any situation that might challenge what I believe, by not questioning any religious authority; in short, by appearances. I go through the motions. Many of us, who live by the letter of the law, whether religious or civil, can be decent, law abiding people. But never to question, never to reflect, never to wonder leads to a passion-less or pro forma expression of one's spiritual life, and ultimately, a failing to respond to the covenant invitation to love one another as God loves us. The root of "spiritual" is spirit or aliveness. How alive am I to the presence of God in my life; so that I can enter into what my religious conviction calls me to be; namely, a caretaker, a shepherd. How can I do what God wants me to do unless I reflect upon what it means to care and act with the depth and breadth of compassion for those who come in and out of my life? Throughout John's gospel the people who respond to Jesus' call to love are not usually the church or synagogue attending legalists, but those who are touched by Jesus to live out the Good News [-] the Samaritan woman at the well, the Samaritan villagers, the Roman official and his sick child, the man born blind, Mary and Martha and eventually Peter and the other apostles, as well as the Centurion on Calvary's hill.

Returning to the synoptic gospels, we do not know who the author of Mark's gospel is. There is one tradition that suggests it might have been the disciple who fled the Garden of Gethsemane when Jesus was arrested. He left behind his robe and fled naked. He was scared out of his clothes, and to "save" his own skin, couldn't wait to abandon Jesus. The fragile basis for this is that this scene only appears in Mark's Gospel. It is the briefest and most succinct of the gospels. It becomes clear that it is written during a time of great upheaval.

Matthew was a tax collector. Historically, when the Romans conquered a territory they would assign taxes which the people would have to pay. Usually a family, or group of people, would pay all the taxes for the community to the Roman officials and with the protection of the Roman army would be able to collect from the people as much as they could. This meant they could collect a far greater amount than paid to the Romans. This would be equivalent to today's financial fees collected for handling the community's money. Because they had the support of the Roman guards (which, of course, means that they know how to "work the system") they took advantage of the people to line their own pockets with wealth. They were despised by their own people; hence, they were often ostracized from Jewish society. At times they were not allowed to be educated in Jewish schools or to socialize in Jewish circles. They were banned from the temple. The gospel according to Matthew is a teacher's delight. It is wonderfully constructed and I think the clearest of the gospels to teach. It is most likely written by a former rabbi or rabbinical student who became a Messianite. Matthew is the apostle who proclaimed in word the Risen Christ. It is a reasonable assumption that the author of the gospel was converted through the apostle, Matthew, and put his God given talents to work to produce the written account of the gospel at the behest of the Matthean community.

There does seem to be some evidence that the author of Luke's gospel is a physician. He is the only author to describe "hematidrosa", the sweat of blood in the Garden of Gethsemane. Dr. Pierre Barbet, a French physician, was one of a number of scientists who examined the Shroud of Turin, the cloth in which many now think the body of Jesus was wrapped after His death. Dr. Barbet writes of his scientific examination, but what really caught my attention is a section he appended to the end of his treatise. He describes, as a physician, the bodily, or corporal, passion of Jesus from the time He entered Gethsemane until His death on the Cross. It is a most powerful meditation which focuses upon the tremendous pain and suffering of Jesus over His last less than twenty-four hours preceding death on the Cross. He describes the medical phenomenon of "hematidrosa"...*a microscopic hemorrhage following from intense emotional anxiety and resulting in a mixture of sweat and blood pouring from the affected individual...rare...but medically documented.* This is the beginning of the painful experience Jesus has from Holy Thursday evening until Good Friday afternoon. I used to share this meditation in classes at Xavier High School just before our Easter break each year. It was then, and remains for me today, a very moving Holy Week prayer. But my point here is to identify Luke as a physician because he is the only evangelist to describe this "medical" phenomenon.

John is a fisherman when Jesus calls him to be a fisher of men, to become His disciple. Chances are that the beloved disciple John did not have the educational background to be able to write the gospel attributed to him. As in Matthew's account, I suspect that the author heard John proclaim the Good News and upon conversion used his talents to put into writing the fourth gospel. This is what makes the gospels an expression of the early Christian community rather than a "best seller" written by an individual. What makes the Gospel a "best seller" is the messenger, Jesus, and His message that God loves us. Thanks to the evangelists, we have the original "Good News."

To get to know who Jesus is, I have chosen two passages from each gospel. There are others which could have been used. I think these will offer a fair, though incomplete, introduction to getting to know Jesus as a person. The passages are:

Jesus' vision of His ministry, or calling............Luke (chapter) 4, (verses) 16-21
Jesus' storytelling......................................Mark 4: 1-20
Jesus' friendship is for everyone ....John 4: 4-42
Jesus' expectations of His friends......................Matthew 5: 3-16
Jesus' notion of the religious person ....Mark 5: 21-43
Jesus' actions which speak louder than words....... John 13: 1-20
Jesus as a beacon of hope..................................... Matthew 17:1-9
Jesus' friendly advice...Luke 16: 19-31

In the synoptic gospels, Jesus prepares for His public ministry through the baptism and temptation scenes. Baptism welcomes us into the community of God's people by forgiving our sinful human condition (Genesis 3), and preparing us for God's saving love. Jesus didn't need to be forgiven, but since He came among us as God's saving gift, His baptism by John shows how deeply He identifies with us both through our very humanity as in His birth, and in the temptations we face regularly in life, especially the temptation to be less than we could be [-] to be less than loving people. For the Cross to become the means of our redemption, then Jesus chose to identify with our sinful condition, with our humanity, because we are the ones He will ransom. We are the ones for whom He will pay the price of His life and love; so that we may love as He loves us.

The temptation scene is a very significant expression of Jesus identifying with the frailty of our humanity. While Mark simply mentions the temptations, both Matthew and Luke elaborate upon them. Jesus' temptations are our temptations. Using the Matthean sequence, the first temptation follows upon Jesus fasting in the desert. He is hungry and the temptation is to use His power to take care of Himself first by turning stones into bread in order to feed Himself. It is our temptation so often described as "look out for number one" or "you owe it to yourself." The temptation is real to all human persons, especially, I think, when we have been misunderstood, or even ignored, or we are hurting because of some experience which we have initiated or of which we are a victim. We all have some gifts or talents or abilities, and at times instead of using them to share with others, we are tempted to serve only ourselves, or primarily ourselves. It is the temptation to be *selfish*, and if we are feeling physically or emotionally weak, the temptation seems to increase. Jesus identifies with us in this situation. His temptation is our temptation, but He overcomes it by having His priorities straight. He says, in effect, that taking care of our bodily needs is necessary for our physical well-being, but following God's word is more important because it is necessary for our spiritual well-being. Working out is good for the body, but spiritual working out involves the developing of our response to the covenant with God. Perhaps our contemporary health concerns for our bodies have led many of us to make the gym more important than the Church. Being physically "buffed" is certainly an admirable goal, but being spiritually "buffed" is necessary for our well-being (our "eudaemonia.", our happiness or fulfilling as a human person.)

The next temptation has Jesus upon on the ledge of the temple and the temptation is posed to Him by Satan (the personification of evil): "If you are the Son of God, throw yourself down. For it is written: 'He will command His angels concerning you and with their hands they will support you, lest you dash your foot upon a stone'" The temptation here is to place restrictions on our relationship with God, and by extension, on our relationship with others. Do something and then place the burden on God to deliver what you want. In each temptation scene, it begins with the conditional "if" [-] if you are who you say you are, then, it should be okay if you go ahead and tempt fate, or tempt your Father. It would be similar to our praying to God to deliver "something" for us (a job, a person, or a passing grade) and we will do whatever he wants. I will be your friend if you do this for me or as long as you do this for me or when you do this for me. It is the temptation to *place conditions on our relationships with others*, and God is an Other Person to us. It is the temptation to "bypass" the covenant, which is unconditional. God loves us. He has shown this through the Trinitarian love expressions of creation, redemption, and being present to us in our thoughts, words, and actions. We probably give in to this temptation because we want to have some control in a relationship. Being vulnerable is not easy and looking for "guarantees" from the other person in the relationship might make us "feel" a little better, even if the relationship is with God. Maybe it is trying to make God in "our image." No doubt, this is what I was thinking, when I mentioned (in Chapter Three) the time I thought my father had a heart attack, and I prayed to God promising all sorts of stuff if my Dad could be okay. I was trying to place conditions on God's love because I thought His love had more to do with my desires than His unconditional concern. In my fear for my father's health, I forgot that the God who created us out of love and for loving, "has our back" through every event in life. My trust in God at that time had been replaced by my being afraid to lose my father.

In the third temptation, Satan claims that he will give Jesus the world if He would simply fall down and worship him. Jesus tells him that it is not going to happen because the world is not Satan's to give. God is the creator and Satan is a creature, the fallen angel. Satan obviously thinks he has a chance because so often we are tempted to give up hoping there is any goodness in life. The temptation is to *despair, to give up hope in the fundamental goodness of life*. God created this world and as created it is good and He has created us to be caretakers. We read headlines in newspapers and watch television and there certainly are temptations at times to say "what's the use?" "What can I do?" The present day newspaper headlines include different countries threats of military conflict, Sunnis and Shiites killing each other in the Middle East, politicians betraying their constituencies and either being jailed or escaping the consequences of their actions, fake news being manufactured by hackers to mislead and misrepresent, the rich getting richer and the poor getting poorer while consumer prices rise, the stock market rises, and millions are spent by the few to control the political, economic and social situations of so many throughout the world. The temptation to despair is real.

There are people who betray us at times, and people whom we trust who don't live up to our expectations. There are temptations to surrender, but temptations, as we have said, are part of the power of free will and the ability to choose from alternatives, which are, to succumb to temptation, or to overcome temptation. Jesus faced them and we face them, and that's the reality. The choices we make, given the temptations we experience, will result in either a strengthening of our character or a weakening of our character, whether as individuals, as a community, a society, or a world. When will we realize we are all visitors in life? We journey through a life created for us by God [-] Who invites us to take care of His creation, not to try to make it our own, because the world is not ours to own, or to possess in any way. We are called into this world to care for it and to conduct ourselves as guests who can appreciate the invitation to share life with each other.

What also ties the baptismal and temptation scenes together is the presence of the Holy Spirit. The spirit of God is present in wonderful times of celebration (baptism) and in times when we must make difficult choices (temptation.) From the beginning the Holy Spirit is with Jesus as He begins His public ministry, just as the spirit of God is with us in everything we do. Are we spiritual people? Are we people consistently alive to the presence of God in our lives? Or are we essentially selfish people? Are we continually placing conditions on our relationships with others? Do we choose frequently to "pass the buck" by giving up hope that God has created a good world, no matter how many human flaws we can identify? After all, the world is still in process. Let's get to know Jesus.

Getting to know Jesus through His vision of His ministry, or calling, or vocation
Luke 4:16-21

At the beginning of His public ministry in Luke's account, Jesus reads from the Old Testament Book of Trito-Isaiah (the third author of this book) and uses this passage as the vision for His own New Testament ministry, His own service to God's people. He announces His goals and how He proposes to accomplish them. As a teacher, you announce to your students what your course aims are and how you plan to accomplish them. Jesus begins by acknowledging that God is with Him and He identifies five aspects of His vocation. The first is to *bring glad tidings to the poor.* Today, there are far many more poor than there should be owing to unscrupulous and unethical financial people and violent and prejudiced warlords and terrorists whose motivation is to serve only their own greedy and selfish interests. There are too many outcasts, who live fearfully in their own countries or as unwanted refugees in foreign territories. Remember that the focus in Luke's gospel is on Jesus as the Champion of outcasts. Jesus is proclaiming that God's love is universal, that His Father has a very special concern for the poor, the outcasts, those whom society is much more inclined to overlook. Let us recall that the shepherds are the first ones invited to witness to Emmanuel, God is with us. There is no one who is outside the scope of God's care and concern. There is no one whom He overlooks. There is no one without value in God's eyes, no matter what his or her earthly status might be. Jesus' purpose in life is to bring joy through the Good News that each of us is loved by the God Who brought us into life, especially those who experience little earthly joy in life's struggles.

The second articulation of his vision is *to proclaim liberty to captives.* There is no prison, whether a state run penal institution, a political, social or religious ostracizing of someone, or our own self-inflicted fears and phobias that cannot be liberated by God's willingness to ransom us. There is no sin that cannot be forgiven, nor earthly judgment that can interfere with God's concern for each one of His people. Perhaps the worst of prisons are the ones in which we choose to confine ourselves out of fear, or insecurity, or self-loathing. These are the toughest to penetrate because we build them ourselves out of false images of self and of others. There are terrible temptations to surrender to frustration or despair and yet Jesus shows us that there is nothing which can prevent us from leaning on Him [-] not nature, not injustice, not evil, not sickness nor even death.

His third vision is give *recovery of sight to the blind.* The focus here is on our spiritual blindness which so many of us adopt because we don't think we are worth God's concern, or the concern of others. Too often we see only what we want to see because we do not dare to acknowledge any caring relation with God. Why don't we listen to the words of the hymn, "If God is for us, who can be against?" Jesus is shouting out that He is for us. We have eyes to see; so let us see that our relation to God is personal. He is the divine person and we are the human persons. In being persons we relate, we interact. Why do we turn a blind eye or a deaf ear to our significance as "imago dei"? We are made in the image of God. We have the power to create love relationships. God is not threatened by our love, nor should anyone else be threatened. Jesus comes among us to open our eyes to the wonder of life, which is, to love one another as He loves us.

His next vision includes *letting the oppressed go free*. What is it that burdens us in life so much that we can't enjoy life without artificial stimulants or material possessions? Why do we seem so often to love things and use people instead of loving people and using things? Why do we become so enslaved to the gadgets around us in life? Why do we become so concerned with the "stuff" we can't have or shouldn't have or can't afford to buy? To be oppressed is to be weighed down by earthly concerns that blind us to thinking that we have to solve everything on our own. Being oppressed means to feel isolated, and to think one is alone, while Jesus' vision includes letting us know that we are never alone. Love is a relationship and God's claim is to love us. Why don't we believe Him? Why don't we take Him at His word? Why are we afraid to identify our vision of life with His' vision?

Finally, Jesus announces *a year acceptable to the Lord*. The "year" means that the present is the time of salvation. What we do today, how we act, will reflect our willingness to accept God's invitation to be with Him forever...or not. Our earthly journey is made with Emmanuel [-] the God Who is with us. We are not alone throughout our earthly adventure, but the God Who made us in His image and likeness is and will always be with us. After all, we are social by nature which means we are interrelated with others, and since God is an "other" to us, He is constantly in touch with us as we live out our lives. Each one of our years is a time during which God is with us.

In articulating this vision, Jesus draws on the Old Testament. This is important because He said that He had come not to destroy the Old (Mosaic) Law but to fulfill it. This shows that His vision of life, like our

216

vision, is rooted in what preceded us, not as a finished product which we are meant to blindly follow, but as a preparation or guide for us to go beyond, to evolve. The concern of Jesus is for the here and now, the present. In a real sense, the here and now is all we have. The past is present to us through memory and the future is present to us through anticipation, desire, planning and hoping. The present acknowledges the past and foreshadows the future. The scope of Jesus' ministry is universal. His vision includes those who agree with Him and those who do not. Jesus' ministry involves each and every one of us. He walks with us and we accept His vision if we are willing to walk with Him, no matter where that will lead, but confident, as the old Irish blessing says, that He holds us in the palm of His hand. Today and tomorrow are always more important than yesterday.

Visions allow us to imagine, to formulate ideas and plans, and to prioritize values. How do I envision the journey I have been invited to take by being born? Is my vision of life hope-full or hope-less? The answer, I think, depends on how closely my vision of life, as an activity to be practiced, corresponds to Jesus' vision of life, a vision that begins with the covenant and ends in the glory of sharing the banquet table of the Father. My vision is that of a Christian in a real world fraught with victories and setbacks. I am optimistic. If God is for us, who can be against us?

In the synoptic gospels, there is an episode at Caesara Philippi, (Mk 8:27; Mt 16:13; and Lk 9:18) in which Jesus asks Peter: *And you, who do you say that I am?* Peter answered: *You are the Christ.* He didn't fully understand what Jesus' concerns were then, but he came to understand in time and through trial and suffering. Will I, in time, come to respond convincingly to Jesus or not? Will I believe that He lived out His vision? Will I embrace His vision through what I say and do in my life's journey? Do I really believe that His vision of how life should be lived is the same vision that I should accept? How I live life will answer these questions; and there will be consequences.

Getting to know Jesus through His storytelling
Mark 4:1-20

The genuine storyteller, as distinct from the gossip or the news reporter, always reveals his or her understanding of the significance of life. Each of our lives is a story in the making and the final chapter is death, and, at this point, we can't guarantee what the sequel to our life's story will be. However, there are signposts along our life's journey, and following a keen vision can lead us to what we should do. The concern is, however, what kind of story we tell by who we are and especially through what we try to teach others, because others are always learning from us. All of us can learn what is good and should be followed as well as what is not good and should be avoided. One of the ways in which we reveal ourselves is through what we say and how we say it. The story of Jesus is revealed to a great extent in what He taught through the parables. A parable is a story which has an important message to teach. It focuses on ordinary situations and invites us to look differently at life, to see life more deeply than we usually do. Maybe Jesus' parables are trying to show us that the ordinary is really extraordinary because we can find ourselves in the story. I think that one of the great stories Jesus told is found in each of the synoptic gospels. I have chosen Mark's version.

It is the story of the sower who went out to plant seeds in the fields, in the places we frequent in life. In this story, the seed is the Word of God, His vision, which is scattered around by the sower, or farmer, who really is Jesus. The story reveals great insights into the human condition especially as it shows how different people respond to the same teaching or insight into life. *Some seed fell on the path and the birds devoured it.* These are people so distracted they are barely conscious of what is happening around them. They rarely stop to wonder about anything and life becomes little more than unquestioned occasions with no seeming significance. Life passes some people by and they aren't even aware of it. *Some seed fell on rocky ground and never took root.* These are people who initially get excited, but without reflection or study, never take to heart the significance of what they are experiencing. They felt good at first, but they did nothing to encourage seeking further understanding. Perhaps they are like people who fail to form visions about life, or fail to prioritize values for living life. They are people who make decisions based on feelings, which are fleeting, rather than on thoughtful reflection which leads to understanding. *Some fell among the thorns which choked them and allowed no growth.* These were people who wanted to get involved in trying to appreciate the Word of God, but who were distracted either by passing or by misleading concerns of life around them. For them, God is not as important as what they do or what they want. Perhaps these are well-intentioned people, overcome by events and disparities in life which blind them to the goodness of people and creation. Could they be Elipahaz, Bildad, and Zophar, Job's "friends?" (Chapter 3) They tend to live life from one distraction to the next. They are primarily spectators in the arena, or drama, we know as life. And finally *some seed fell on rich soil and produced varying degrees of fruit…some a little and some more…and some much more.* These are the people who pray, who reflect, who acknowledge that God is part of their lives and whose actions are aimed at trying to love others as they realize how unconditionally God loves them. Anyone who has planted a garden in the backyard knows that plants don't grow without preparing the soil and helping it to be receptive to whatever the weather might bring. This means being able to withstand the effects of bad weather and to take advantage of the benefits of good weather. Children, also, need to be nurtured and nourished physically, psychologically, emotionally, socially and religiously to be able to prepare them to eventually become adults, capable of understanding and nourishing themselves and others. How we prepare for life involves developing priorities as to what is important to consider during our life's journey. The sower knows what the priorities are for allowing growth to have the greatest possibility to happen in life, whether that involves the backyard where plant life blossoms or one's background where human life begins to grow. This is a great story about the different people with whom we will interact while traveling through life's journey and it reveals Jesus' understanding and appreciation about our shared human journey.

Father John Shea wrote a number of books, one of which was entitled "Stories of God." The premise was that God created us because He loves stories and each of us is a story in the making. One aspect of the story of the sower is that Jesus recognizes and acknowledges that we are at different levels of understanding our relationship with the Father. But perhaps the greatest insight the story offers states that the Word of God (the seed) which fell on good ground *yielded fruit thirty, sixty, or hundred fold.* Jesus is certainly not saying that the importance of people lies in the quantity of their production, but rather that some people are by nature, or effort, or position, more productive than others. The greater our gifts and talents and opportunities are, the greater the responsibility to reap what has been sown for us. The importance is not quantitative, but qualitative. He is saying that those of us who hear the Word of God and try our best to put into practice in our lives (that is, nourishing the Word of God), will produce, with God's help, whatever our varying talents and gifts can contribute. Some of us have greater audiences to whom we contribute. Others have smaller audiences with whom we serve. The one who produces a hundredfold is not a better person than the one who produces thirty fold, but the insight is that we are responsible for using whatever our gifts are and they are not the same for everyone. There are no gold, silver and bronze medals with Jesus. There is the invitation to tell our story by how we minister to those who come in and out of our lives. In finishing the race, we all become winners in God's eyes. What is the old saying? "Quitters never win, and winners never quit!" Maybe there is some significant religious insight in that statement.

A dear friend, Sister Liz Kelly CSJ, a great storyteller in her own right, gifted me once with a tiny book entitled "The Gift of Story: A wise tale about what is enough." The author is Clarissa Pinkola Estes. It is only thirty pages long, but so powerful. It begins with reference to the tale of Bal Shem Tov, a Jewish rabbi, who on his deathbed, passes along the gift of keeping the covenant with God to those who follow. (Father Shea makes the same reference in his book: so the story is old and revered. He quotes a passage from a book by Elie Wiesel; so there are many great story tellers who relate to the tale of Bal Shem Tov.) The story tells the people where to go and how to address God and what liturgical expressions should be followed and God will come. Over time the comforting story of God coming to His people is told, but the details are forgotten. Where is the exact place? What are the particular rituals to be followed? What is the specific wording to be used? Even when these aspects of the tale are lost or forgotten, the story is the same: call on God and He will come. Dr Estes' conclusion, Father Shea's conclusion, Sister Liz' conclusion, and Elie Wiesel's conclusion are the same. As long as there is someone to tell the story, no matter how many details are forgotten, the meaning is the same: God is with us, whether we fail to reap as well as we sow, or if we reap only some of what we sow (God's word). He is with us. Jesus always tells the same story.

What stories in life influence us? Whose stories do I believe? Which stories do I pass along to children, to family, to students, to friends, to fellow pilgrims on my life's journey? Which stories inspire me? In Chapter Two I referred to the four great "No's" in life. No one makes you learn. No one makes you forgive. No one makes you believe. No one makes you love. Our learning, forgiving, believing and loving genuinely are our own responses [-] our own expressions. They are our gifts to others. They stamp us with the mark of "self" or "individual." I think that our responses to life are reflections of the stories we tell by what we say and what we do. We are social by nature; so we are influenced by what we see and hear, and feel and touch. We are influenced, touched by the stories we have read. We are also, each one of us, a story in the making, which isn't finished until our final chapter, and then others will continue to read us through memory. How will my life's story read? Will others know I am a Christian by the way I lived my story? Do the stories that Jesus tells show His concern for everyone He meets? Is He a Teacher Who is genuinely concerned about those whom he serves? Do His stories reflect His vision? Will mine?

Getting to know Jesus through His friends
John 4:4-42

Do you have any friends? So who are they? Are they people who share your lifestyle? Your interests? Your community? Your educational background? Your comfort zone? I think that most of us are not prejudiced people, but there probably are some people we would tend to avoid rather than attempt to befriend, which we might do if we had met them under different circumstances. But in many cases, the first move would have to be up to them. In the fourth chapter of John's account of the Good News, Jesus comes into contact with a Samaritan woman, which, at that time, would be considered as an inappropriate gender, social, or religious encounter. At that time, this meeting would not be expected to become a conversation, but this is what happens between them. Socially, politically, religiously, the Jewish people and the Samaritans would not be conversing about "anything" because enemy would be a more accurate description than would neighborly. The "ice breaker" in the conversation is Jesus asking for a drink of water from the well because He is thirsty. In the course of their lengthy conversation, she comes to see Jesus not as a cultural outsider, but as a prophet and finally she acknowledges Him as the promised Messiah.

As the scene changes she is thirsting after the "living water" that will nourish her relationship with the living God. She goes off to tell the townspeople whom she has met as the disciples return to the well. They can't believe that Jesus was speaking with a woman in public, and even more "politically incorrect," a Samaritan woman. Eventually the topic turns to food, which gives Jesus the opportunity to speak to His followers, His friends, about feeding the world with spiritual food. Jesus says "My food is to do the will of the One Who sent me and to complete His work." He is foreshadowing the "Bread of Life" or the Eucharistic discourse in chapter six of this gospel. The next scene in this section has the woman returning with the Samaritan townsfolk to hear the word of God and to welcome the God not only of the Jews, but of the Samaritans, and every one of us, into their hearts and lives. While the townspeople came to hear Jesus initially because of the witnessing of the woman, they departed believing on their own and acknowledging Jesus as the "savior of the world." Jesus made many friends in that "unfriendly" Samaritan place revealing that friendship transcends all cultural boundaries. God's love is universal. Who are the Samaritans in my own life? Am I willing to share my story with them in the hopes of developing a friendship?

The inverse of this story is found in Luke's account of the "Good Samaritan" who took care of the Jewish man who was beaten by robbers and left for dead. When the man's fellow Jews, or fellow Christians, or fellow countrymen left him on the side of the road, because they did not want to get involved, the foreigner, the outsider, the stranger took care of him simply because he was someone who was in need of help. The point of that story is that each one of us is called to be a "good Samaritan." It doesn't matter who is hurt. If someone is hurting, then I should be helping. Actions speak louder than words.

I don't think it is terribly surprising that Jesus would reach out to others who did not belong to His own "earthly" cultural or religious enclave. At His birth there were the polar social opposites of the shepherds and the magi. He called a tax collector to be an apostle. And certainly, His own band of apostles would defy any kind of categorizing as a socially and intellectually focused organization called together for a universal mission. Today there would not be any corporate "head hunters" looking at the apostle's resumes to consider them for a position which would touch the lives of everyone for the life of the world to come. Were they the "best men" for the position? Of course, they were. They are saints. They accepted Jesus' friendship. They willed the best for Jesus through their service to Him, by teaching what Jesus taught. They committed themselves to Him even accepting death. They were martyrs. And He was always with them.

It's the twenty-first century. Do I consider myself Jesus' friend? What does that mean? I've been baptized; so I do think my parents cared enough about me to ensure that I could respond to Christ. Have I? Has my work and my play reflected His friendship, His vision? Do I, by the way I live my life, tell His stories? Are my friends taken from a select and narrow band of people who share my comfort zone, or have I gone out into the highways and byways in an effort to love the people whom God has made, even if, at times, some of them make me really uncomfortable? In life, I suspect that most people develop many acquaintances, but nourish relatively few friendships. The developing of friendships involves time, concern, and effort and there are varying degrees of companionship because of the differing experiences that are shared. My wife is my best friend on our earthly journey and she is the one person who allows me the greatest expression of human freedom while being the one person who could most seriously hurt me, because of the intimacy of our journeying together. This is the mystery of the human condition. We are simultaneously powerful and fragile. What about God? He created me and will acknowledge at the end of my journey whether or not I befriended Him. We both know that He considers me as friend because I am here. This is the mystery of the covenant. His friendship (covenant) is with Jews and Christians, Samaritans and

Romans, and even the Foleys. We are all called to friendship with Him. What stops some of us from saying "Yes"?

Getting to know Jesus through His expectations
Matthew 5: 3-16

All of us have expectations in life. They are part of our being free to choose from alternative courses of action what it is we want to do in life and the type of person we decide to become. As a teacher, I have expectations of my students. These expectations aren't the same for everyone, because they have differing talents, abilities, work habits and opportunities. They have expectations of me as their teacher. Some may have greater expectations than others for a variety of reasons. We have expectations of our friends which differ regarding who they are and how well we know them. I have always thought that the idea of a "good" friend doesn't make much sense. What is the alternative [-] a "bad" friend? To be a friend is good. Depending on shared life experiences, some are closer than others. I believe there are degrees of friendship, but if I am befriended by someone or if I develop a friendship with another person, that is, by definition, "good." After all, human knowledge involves a learning process which is always subject to change based on our shared experiences in life. They have expectations of us. I have expectations of myself and sometimes I am happily surprised by what I do and what I have accomplished, and sometimes I am very disappointed by what I have failed to do. But as a sinner, I have been offered forgiveness which includes changing expectations, and hopefully, living them out more consciously and conscientiously.

Jesus has expectations of us otherwise His friendship would not mean much. I think His expectations of us are clearly expressed in the Sermon on the Mount which we find in chapters five through seven of Matthew's account of the Good News. More particularly, His expectations are identified in the opening section of this discourse, which we refer as "the Beatitudes." These are the *attitudes* we should *be* developing, or nurturing, as we journey through life. One doesn't simply become a friend, or an enemy, by making a statement, or a declaration, or by tweeting, or by the proximity of our cubicles in the workplace. One develops positions, or approaches, or builds up certain ways of consistently responding to others. Some attitudes, or positions, encourage one to be friendly, and others do not. The developing of attitudes involves not only the influence of those around us, but also the choices one makes in creating his or her position towards others.

Jesus' expectations are that we will be *happy as people who are poor in spirit...the anawim...*He expects us to rely on Him. After all, He created us and He redeemed us, because, as He said in John's gospel "I call you friends. You did not choose me, I chose you..." (John 15:15) The *anawim* is a Jewish word referring to those among us who know that we need God in our lives. We are spiritually wounded if He is not a part of our lives. We rely on Him to help us on our journey. We lean on Him as a friend leans on another for support, for encouragement, for companionship. He expects us *to be gentle,* to be care-full in our dealings with others as well as with ourselves. To be gentle in a world that too often mocks and ridicules requires strength, which is not a given, but a choice. Being gentle, or kind, is always admirable, but not always encouraged or appreciated by the actions of others. Too often the social context rewards life's bullies who take what is not theirs, and ridicule and reject those who are willing to give of themselves. It takes a strong willed person to be gentle.

Jesus continues the beatitudes. He expects us *to mourn...*to be people who comfort others in their sorrow and hurt and to reach out as compassionately as possible to be healers of those who are hurting. The revered Dutch priest, Henri Nouwen, taught, preached, and wrote about Christian Spirituality. I think that his most penetrating understanding of the spiritual Christian man or woman is the willingness of one to enter into the suffering of another. The wonderful description he offers is that we answer Jesus' call to be "wounded healers of the wounded." He calls us to be compassionate to others. He calls us to be people who acknowledge our own wounds in life and the need to be healed and yet are ourselves willing to recognize and to attend to others who are also in need of healing. Our willingness to be comforters in life should be directed more towards others than towards ourselves.

Jesus encourages us *to hunger and thirst for what should be done in life* no matter what anyone's "station" in life is. Justice is not simply for a select few, but for everyone, but not all people can or are willing to help themselves. We will be happy, fulfilled, blessed, when we act as we ought, without prejudice toward whomever we meet, whether we think they are deserving, or not. He expects us *to be merciful...*to be forgiving. I often think that the most important part of the "Our Father" prayer is when we say "forgive us our trespasses as we forgive those who trespass against us..." because in this part of the prayer we are called to enter into the redeeming of the world with Jesus. We are called to be active members in salvation history. The call involves acting as Christ does in the lives of people. It would be ludicrous if we were expected to do this on our own, but as He says to the apostles at the end of Matthew's gospel "...Go...and behold I am with you always, even until the end of time." We are called to do Christ's work with His assurance that He is with us. It becomes possible for us to do His work and act as the "Bride of Christ," the Church, the people of God, because He has promised we are not alone. Our relationship with Him should model the intimacy of friendship between married spouses. We can live up to His expectations of us as covenant partners. Sadly, as we know, this is not always the case, but there is still time because today and tomorrow are always more important than yesterday.

The beatitudes or expectations continue with being called to be *pure of heart,* people of integrity, people who aren't "phonies." Sincerity is difficult to express in a world that is often cynical. People have been disappointed by those who were in trusted positions of authority. Greedy bankers, dishonest politicians, pedophile priests, irresponsible parents, or careless peers have all contributed to an atmosphere which makes people who are genuinely concerned with others suspect to many observers. And yet Jesus calls us to be sincere and ...*to be peacemakers...* not simply people opposed to violence, but people who seriously try to "love thy enemy" which we know is difficult. Sometimes it is difficult to love a person whom you really care for, let alone for an enemy, but this is possible because the power of choice includes forgiveness. His expectations include that we... *be people who are willing to suffer injustice in doing God's will rather than seek revenge because their love is rejected by others.* There is nothing in Jesus' expectations about "an eye for an eye, and a tooth for a tooth." If God is for us, who can be against

226

us? Unfortunately, there are some who are vengeful and we have met them, and sometimes they are even us!

We spoke in the first chapter about the A, B, C's of friendship [-] acceptance, benevolence, and committing. In addition, another of the significant aspects of friendship is that, it is a gift; an ongoing act of fidelity on the part of one person to another person. It is the activity of loving through which one person is willing to acknowledge the other person as more significant than he or she is no matter what situation arises. It is not only about feelings, though they are often very strong, and sometimes confusing. Feelings come and go but friendship involves obligations and responsibilities, which need to be understood and practiced. It takes time and effort to develop and to sustain. While the intention and goal of friendship is a joyful union, we know that does not always evolve, because one party may not fully appreciate what is happening at a particular time or whether the relationship is growing. Expectations may not always be met, but there is always hope which includes the courage and the strength never to give up. Are Jesus' beatitudes reasonable? If they can be put into practice with consistency by reasoning people, then the answer is "yes." Reasonable doesn't necessarily translate into easy to do, but it does translate into possible to do.

I think I understand Jesus' expectations of me, as humanly as I can. By the way, I am using "humanly" in this context not as an excuse for not knowing Jesus' expectations of me as His friend. Rather, I am using "humanly" to acknowledge my inability to know and to appreciate how unconditionally God wants me as His friend and therefore might miss the depth of meaning in some of His "be-attitude" expectations. I don't waste time on wondering why God loves me. He brought me into life and that means I am loveable, even when I fail to express that as I should. After all, in Luke's gospel He says "When a man has had a great deal given him, a great deal will be demanded of him; when a man has had a great deal given him on trust, even more will be expected of him." (12:48) I am still trying to figure how much is expected of me. My only question then is: is His friendship worth the expectations as identified in the Sermon on the Mount? Please God, I have tried to answer "yes" to this question as faithfully and consistently as possible and will continue to try to repeat the same answer as I grow in wisdom and knowledge, or not. What I do know is I want to serve and the Beatitudes, as expectations on how to act and as positions to take in my own earthly journey, help me to understand and appreciate what is involved.

The Beatitudes are characteristics of love, and love is clearly identified in the Sermon on the Mount with ways of acting, not simply emotions or feelings, or nice sounding phrases. They begin with a change of heart on the part of the individual and they become invitations to others to recognize not only the significance of the covenant, but also to realize that God embraced our humanity because of His love for each of us.

Getting to know Jesus through His idea of the "religious person"
Mark 5:21 - 43

When we talk about God, about the covenant, about the Old and the New Testaments, about Jesus, we are talking about and reflecting upon "religious" ideas and "religious" qualities and characteristics. If I asked my senior high school students: would you want your yearbook picture to identify you as the most "religious" student in the class? I suspect that, good people though they are, no one would be very enthusiastic or comfortable with that description. That's too bad, because some of them, even in their teen years, are religious people. But to be advertised as "religious" [-] I am sure relatively few would be able to handle that. I know that language can sometimes be inadequate to explain terminology and relationships, but this is my understanding of what constitutes a "religious" person. A religious person is an individual who consciously relates to God through a communal, or social, expression. He or she belongs to a group of people who worship together in a church, a synagogue, or a mosque. The object of their worshipping is a personal Being whom we call God.

A spiritual person is one who is alive to the presence of God in his or her journeying through life. God means "something" to them in their pursuit of meaning in life. He or she prays, reflects, and looks to God for ways of appreciating and living out their earthly existence. A "spiritual" person may see himself or herself as someone whose "religious" worship or understanding is a private practice and does not worship in and with a community. Ideally, the religious person is a spiritual person. As an individual I make choices to return God's love for me and as a social being I draw strength from and offer support to others both within and outside of my religious community, because I need others in order to be myself. God means "something" necessary and valuable in the daily life of religious people. Unfortunately this is not always acknowledged and so we distinguish "religious" persons as those who live by the "letter of the law" and religious persons (without the "quotation" marks) who live by the "spirit of the law." The former are primarily religious spectators. They attend services regularly or frequently or as convenience allows. They support the religious community, usually financially, but also in other well meaning ways. They are more passive than active because they don't tend to search for religious wisdom on their own. They are satisfied with the role of spectator. Please don't misunderstand, these people, whether Christian or Jew or Muslim, or with whatever group they are affiliated, are usually decent people who seek to "do no harm." Those who live by the "spirit of the law" are those who pursue religious understanding through participating more personally and with more conviction in what their communal expression involves. For Christians, it means that the Beatitudes are meant to be expressions of daily living rather than inspirations to be admired, or slogans that sound "good." I believe that the religious person [-] a person who lives in accordance with the "spirit of the law" [-] is a spiritual person, conscious of God's presence in his or her life, and who is a doer, an actor, and not simply a spectator in life.

In Mark's gospel, there are two stories linked together in which I think we are given examples of the religious person. A synagogue official named Jairus pleads with Jesus to come and save his daughter who is "desperately sick." (It would be curious to know what other synagogue officials thought of Jairus' request for Jesus' help.) Jesus goes with him, and a huge crowd accompanies them. A woman who has been sick for many years, suffering from some serious medical complications and without any hope of being cured is in the crowd. Because of her illness, it is very possible that she is considered religiously "impure" and could have been ostracized from communal worship. She thinks "If I can but

229

touch His cloak, I will be well again." And as she does, Jesus immediately asks "Who touched me?" The disciples cannot believe He felt anyone's touch in this crushing sea of humanity, but He did. He was sensitive, aware, of her touch. She acknowledges her presence and He tells her that her faith has saved her. She is cured of her illness because she believed in Jesus' ability to heal and in His concern for those who are hurting. They continue to Jairus' home, but the little twelve year old girl is dead and the mourning has already begun. Jesus says that she is simply asleep and they mock Him. He touches and calls to her to "arise." She does. She is brought back from death, which is not only miraculous, but a foreshadowing, no doubt, of resurrection of both Lazarus, who later dies a natural death, and of Jesus Who overcomes death to live in eternal glory.

The stories are certainly about faith in Jesus and the consequences of faith. But, I think, there is more. What makes this story a description of the religious person? Jesus is on a life and death mission at the request of the young girl's father. Along the way He stops to heal the woman who has been hurting. He pays attention to her and reaches out to cure her in response to her faith, to her belief that Jesus can do "something good" for her. Jesus is modeling what it means to be a religious person in this story. He is showing how a religious person should respond on his or her life's journey. Any religious person knows that his or her existence is ultimately a life or death situation, and the individual person is *primarily* responsible for how his or her own life is lived through the choices one makes. At death, each of us will experience the consequences of the way we lived our lives. We will be judged because there are consequences to our freely chosen actions throughout life. The religious person is one who consciously ties himself or herself to others along the way, because God wants us to be attentive to others and to care for them. Yet, I think it is fair to say that both the woman and Jairus act in such a way that they could be called religious persons also. They sought God's help and by doing this, they acknowledged their need for Him. Maybe their seeking God's presence will eventually be evident to others by the way they care for their fellow travelers in life. Thanking God involves how one responds intentionally and compassionately to others. Thanksgiving involves actions, not simply words.

Heaven and hell are terms which describe the consequences of our earthly existence. Heaven is the fulfillment of the human person and hell is the failure of the human person to express what it means to be "made in the image and likeness of God." They are the results of whether we have graciously accepted the gift of life, both our own and others, or whether we have squandered the treasure of life either in ourselves and/ or in others. The religious person is aware of the significance of one's own life, and its significance as a God given gift. However, in each of our journeys, the individual is not the only concern. Each of us must be attuned and sensitive to those who will touch our lives throughout our journey. We will encounter others, not necessarily when we are prepared, but when they are hurting or in need, and it is our obligation to "heal the sick, and clothe the naked, and comfort those who are hurting." We simply cannot ignore them because we are responsible for ourselves. The individual recognizes not only the responsibility to "tend to one's own soul" (to acknowledge the wording of Socrates and Plato), but also the obligation to care for those whose lives touch him or her along the way, because he or she is "her brother and sister's keeper." It is not a matter of convenience but it is a matter of care taking. We are distinctly individual and naturally social simultaneously. This is the mystery of human existence and the most important response is to be a religious person. Our journey ends in eternal life or eternal damnation depending upon how we lived life. The religious person is conscious of his or her intimate friendship with the creating God, Who has ransomed us, saved us, from being unloved, and is always present to us. The religious person, then, is conscious also of others who are supportive on this journey, as well as those who are not supportive. Whether people care for us or don't, they are God's children and consequently become the obligation of the religious person. Towards the end of the "Sermon on the Mount" in Matthew's Gospel, Jesus says, "It is not those who say to me, Lord, Lord, who will enter the Kingdom of Heaven, but the person who does the will of My Father in heaven." (7:21)

A religious person is primarily a doer. A religious person does the will of the Father, which is to love one another as He loves us. In order to love others, I must love myself as well. Was the woman's appealing to Jesus and Jairus' imploring of Jesus rooted in their realizations that God created them and loves them? I think that this is the case. Essentially they acted because they knew God loved them. In Luke, chapter 19, we read the story of the chief tax collector Zaccheus who, literally, went out on a limb simply to see Jesus, of Whom he had heard so much. Jesus stops to dine with him. Is Zaccheus showing signs of being a religious person by his interest in Jesus? Are seeking to know God and what God wants signs of the religious novice? They are a necessary beginning. Characteristic of the religious person is the recognition that actions speak louder than words. The religious person's concern becomes: to what extent does one's understanding of God result in actions of covenant love for self and others on life's journey? The religious person is a doer, a lover.

Ultimately, my significance as a human person is not going to be judged by my physical stature, my mental abilities, my social standing, my economic achievements [-] but am I a religious person? Am I alive to the presence of God in my life? And what did I do about this relationship? Maybe the most important question Jesus ever asked was addressed first to Peter and the apostles, and is addressed today to you and to me, and to everyone we meet...*And you, who do you say that I am?* (Mt 16:15; Mk 8:29; Lk 9:20) How I live my life is the answer to this question. The consequence of my answer is ultimately *eternal* life or death. Remember that the root of the word *religion, re-ligare,* means to tie oneself back consciously to a creating, redeeming, ever present God. Am I conscious of God's people who touch my life as I journey? How do I respond to them? How do I touch them, without compromising the gift, including its responsibility, of my own God-given life? Am I a religious person?

Getting to know Jesus whose actions speak louder than words
John 13:1 - 20

We have already seen Jesus in action. He embraces the nature of the religious person through being baptized by John. As the Son of God, he doesn't need to be forgiven of His sins because He is sinless. The sacrament of baptism is both a purging of the sinful condition of being part of the "fallen" human race, but also a welcoming into the community of God's people [-] a reunion with our covenantal God. Baptism recognizes both the identifying with the sinful condition of humanity and the "exodus" or religious liberation, or Passover, from the effects of the world's sinful condition. Jesus embraces our humanity and consequently He identifies with our weaknesses and with our need for salvation. We fast from bodily nourishment in order to acknowledge our need for forgiveness and because He has identified with our human nature, Jesus also fasts, in the desert, to prepare for His public ministry, which is to redeem us, ransom us, from our sinful inclinations. He is tempted to surrender His allegiance and give up hope in the goodness of creation, but He responds in fidelity to the Father. He envisions a calling that involves ministering to others. He teaches, always with an aim of letting us know God's concern, and God's expectations of us, His chosen people. The baptism and temptation scenes are not simply interesting and imaginatively well told stories but they are also challenges to the listener to act. But Jesus is not only a compassionate teacher or an inspirational preacher. He is a servant, who will ultimately become **the servant** who suffers for us and through His suffering will heal the relationship between God and man.

Jesus teaches throughout the gospels preparing us, His followers, to teach others, and not simply by words, but by deeds. However, in each of the gospels, there is one particular section in which He concentrates more specifically on teaching His disciples to become servants, to become disciples, to become religious people and not simply followers. Chapter 8:22 in Mark's account begins with the healing of the blind man at Bethsaida, and ends with the healing of the blind man, Bartimaeus (10:52.) Jesus is instructing the disciples to be concerned primarily about the spiritual blindness of people. The disciples had misunderstood the feeding of the 4,000 with loaves and fish thinking that physical nourishment was what they needed. Jesus is teaching them that His way and His words and actions are primarily for their spiritual needs. Jesus predicts His passion three times; therefore, they must be ready to suffer. He teaches that they must become like little children, open to wonder and to a sense of belonging. He offers them hope through the Transfiguration scene. (9:2-8) Earthly riches wouldn't help them. He challenges them to declare who He is and corrects their misunderstandings. He emphasizes their call to ministry by saying, "... the Son of Man, Himself, did not come to be served, but to serve, and to give His life as a ransom for many." (10:45) He invites them to follow.

I think that the major teaching section on discipleship in Matthew's gospel is the Sermon on the Mount (chapters 5 – 7), which as we have seen begins with the "beatitudes", the attitudes which He calls on His followers to develop and express. The mission of the disciple is to be the "salt of the earth" and the "light of the world." How do we make life tasteful instead of tasteless? Irreverence, ridicule and mockery, vulgar speech and violent action which are so carelessly expressed in so many areas of life today certainly encourages being "tasteless" in our interacting with others. Whether on television shows or in the movies, in political and social interacting, there is no question that "tasteless" conduct has become very public, and rarely challenged. How should we respond; so that personal and communal dignity is tastefully restored to the people God has created? How do we "enlighten" the world by what we say and by what we do? Jesus says that He has "not come to abolish the law and the prophets, but to fulfill them"...to fulfill the covenant promise of God's friendship. He contrasts the "true" disciple from the "false" disciple [-] the person who follows the "spirit of the law (of God)," as opposed to the one who follows the "letter of the law." He ends with the wonderful parable of the one who builds a house on sand and the one who builds a house on rock. A house built on sand, is blown away with the first storm, with the first temptation. A house built on rock is constructed on a strong foundation. It takes time and effort to become a follower [-] to become one who loves as Jesus loves. It is a process, not a statement and not a wish.

The section in Luke's account, which concentrates on discipleship, is called the "travel narrative" (9:51 -19:28). Jesus is traveling to Jerusalem, on a life and death mission, where He will embrace the Cross; so that "we might have life and have it to the fullest." The beginning of this journey is tough. A disciple wants to bury his father and Jesus says "let the dead bury the dead." Another follower wants to say "goodbye" to friends before following Jesus Who essentially says that He won't wait for him. This does not seem like the Jesus Who came "not to be served, but to serve." What does this introduction mean? He is emphasizing the urgency to discipleship. The time is always now, not later. "You know not the time, nor the hour." Discipleship is concerned with loving service, not with convenience, nor even with real or perceived social obligations. It deals with God's work, and His work is here and now. Only Luke's journey narrative includes the stories of the "Good Samaritan" and the "Prodigal Son." The point of the "Good Samaritan" is that we are the unlikely person who is called to minister to those whom we don't even know or of whom we might be suspicious. In the "prodigal son" story, the response called for is forgiveness, not simply on the part of the father, but also of the elder son. Unfortunately the elder son's response is focused entirely on himself and he sees no joy in his brother's return. I call it a "family" parable because it is played out in so many families, when, because of a real or a supposed slight by one member, friction is created throughout the family. People choose different sides and differing ways of responding. Some will condemn the one member, while others will seek to embrace the return of the "sinner." The merciful father forgave the prodigal son, but the elder brother's envy prevented him from rejoicing over the brother who was lost, but is found, and has returned. There is the story of Zacchaeus, whom Jesus acknowledges and shares his table. Zacchaeus is a "chief" tax collector which makes him "persona not grata" with many of the people in the area. Jesus is always the model of the "religious person" and therefore always welcoming not only to followers, but to outcasts like the Good Samaritan, the prodigal son and Zacchaeus as well." Being Jesus' follower is neither always comfortable nor convenient, but it is always concerned with "loving these, the least of my brethren."

The teachings on discipleship in the synoptic accounts seem, I think, to focus on what the disciple (each of us) should do; so that we remain faithful to Jesus, to the Teacher. Jesus models for us how to become disciples, how to act so that we can bring the Father's love to those who are in need. While discipleship continues to be primarily involved with actions, there is a long discourse in John's gospel which occurs during the Last Supper scene, and focuses on the nature of Our Lord's concern for and relationship with His disciples.

As this is the final teaching episode in the public ministry of Jesus in John's gospel, it is also referred to as Jesus' farewell address to the disciples. Beginning at chapter 13:33, it continues through the next four chapters. Unlike the synoptic accounts of the Last Supper the words of blessing and thanksgiving for the Passover meal are not included. We will consider these in our next chapter. In this farewell address, Jesus focuses on the nature of discipleship and the relationship between Jesus and those whom He has called to "Come, follow Me!" Jesus reveals, in His earthly journey, the love of the Father for all He has created. He tells the disciples He is "going away" but He will not abandon them. He will send the "Paraclete", the counselor, the Holy Spirit, who will teach them by enlightening them on what Jesus has revealed. We all know that the learning process, while easier for some of us than others, always requires reflection and ongoing effort to more fully appreciate what we have learned. So it is with the disciples. They have learned from Jesus, but as we will see in the Garden of Gethsemane (next chapter), they haven't yet appreciated everything they have learned. I am always encouraged by the disciples. In a real sense they are my heroes, because, like me, it took longer than it should have for me, and I suspect for many of us, to appreciate what Jesus is trying to do by loving us. The disciples were with Jesus for some three years and it wasn't until His death, His resurrection, and the arrival of the Holy Spirit to figure out what they should have, but didn't. They should have figured out that God's ways are not our ways. I believe they thought He was indeed the promised Messiah, but they never suspected He would also be the Suffering Servant. I am guessing this is where the phrase "better late than never" arose. So Jesus tells them He is leaving (they don't quite understand), but that He will be sending "Help." Then He describes what the nature of their relationship should be. He is the vine, they (we) are the branches and the Father is the vine dresser. In chapter fifteen Jesus says...

"...I am the vine, you are the branches. He who abides in me and I in him, he it is that bears much fruit, for apart from me you can do nothing...If you abide in me, and my words abide in you, ask whatever you will, and it shall be done for you. By this my Father is glorified, that you bear much fruit, and so prove to be my disciples. As the Father have loved me, so have I loved you; abide in my love. If you keep my commandments, you will abide in my love, just as I have kept my Father's commandments and abide in His love...

"These things I have spoken to you, that my joy may be in you, and that your joy may be full...This is my commandment, that you love one another as I have loved you. Greater love has no man than that a man lay down his life for his friends. You are my friends if you do what I command you....I have called you friends, for all that I have heard from my Father I have made known to you. You did not choose me, I chose and appointed you that you should go and bear fruit and that your fruit should abide; so that whatever you ask the Father in my name, he may give it to you. This I command you: Love one another..."

So the nature of discipleship is friendship with God and the practice of discipleship involves service to others. Friendship involves the A, B, Cs [-] acceptance, benevolence, and committing and is necessarily mutual if it is to embrace the love it seeks. To practice the covenant, friendship with God, there is a "twist." To return God's love the practice of discipleship involves our obligation, our commandment to serve our fellow man and woman. It goes beyond choice to obligation. This is what Jesus models before teaching about discipleship in the Johannine "farewell address."

Beautiful and moving and educational as the words of His teaching on discipleship are, Jesus begins the Last Supper scene in John's account with a parable in action and this is really the focal point of this section. Parables are essentially spoken stories which have a purpose or challenge. Jesus acts out this story, but the purpose and the challenge is clear [-] to serve, because, for Jesus and for His disciples, actions speak louder than words.

Jesus "...got up from the table, removed His outer garment and taking a towel wrapped it around His waist; He then poured water into a basin and began to wash the disciples feet and to wipe them with the towel He was wearing....When He had washed their feet...He went back to the table. 'Do you understand what I have done to you? You call me Lord and Master and rightly; so I am. If I, then, the Lord and Master, have washed your feet, you should wash each other's feet. I have given you an example so that you may copy what I have done to you....'"

"I tell you most solemnly, no servant is greater than his master; no messenger is greater than the one who sent him...whoever welcomes the one I send welcomes me, and whoever welcomes me welcomes the one who sent me..."

"I have given you an example." I have once again modeled the role of the disciple. The real meaning of the washing of the feet will be revealed tomorrow when Jesus "...lays down His life for His friends..." on the Cross on Calvary's hill. And his friends include those gathered at the table that night as well as us, both those of us who gather around the table of the Lord today, and those of us who don't. He washed Judas' feet that night, but then Judas went out and betrayed Him. When He came to wash Peter's feet, Peter protested. When Jesus said if He didn't then Peter wouldn't be associated with Him. The blustering Peter then asked Jesus to clean him from head to foot, because if there is anyone prepared to be with and defend Jesus, it's me says Peter. It isn't necessary replies Jesus, just the washing of the feet. Clearly this is a baptismal symbol, suggesting the dying to sin and the rising to the fullness of life in Christ, which will begin with the events of Good Friday and be fulfilled in the Easter Resurrection.

It is interesting to reflect on this scene which precedes the "farewell address." Judas is a disciple, a companion of Jesus. But when he calls Jesus, "friend", his words are false and his freely chosen actions are despicable. His actions don't speak louder than his words. In a few hours, Peter's bravado will disappear in denying three times that he has any knowledge of this Jesus. His actions initially will fail to carry out his companionship with Jesus, but there will be time for grief and for reconciliation. Jesus' actions speak louder than His words, because tomorrow He will "...lay down His life for His friends..." So if I protest that I am not worthy of Jesus' love and passion, I am only kidding myself. He has already answered the question: I, Judas, Peter, and everyone else is worthy of His love, because it is ultimately His choice to accept the Cross. All that is left is to answer whether or not I believe what He says and does by the way I live my life. Will I take the path of the unrepentant Judas or the repentant Peter? At least the odds are in our favor, as long as we cling to the vine.

Getting to know Jesus as a beacon of hope
Matthew 17:1-8

Saint Augustine (354 – 430) is a Doctor of the Church. The honorary title "Doctor" is given to a saint, man or woman, whose life, teaching and preaching, has contributed greatly to understanding what it means to follow Christ. Augustine's "Confessions" tell of his struggle to appreciate God in his life and the temptations he faced and overcame in reconciling himself with his Creator. His "City of God" is a masterpiece of Christian Philosophy in answering the struggle between good and evil, between man's wants and man's needs, between the significance of the temporal and the eternal. It is rooted in the fall of Rome to the barbarian hordes, and the blame that was heaped on Christianity for this event. After all, the Romans had called Rome, "the eternal city", which was never supposed to fall. What I would like to focus upon briefly here is "The Enchiridon" which means "manual" and was written by Augustine to someone named Laurentius. It describes faith, hope and love as essential virtues to embrace in worshipping Christ, in seeking happiness. We don't know how well Laurentius was served by this handbook, but we do know it has been influential in serving Christians throughout the ages.

The philosophers, Plato and Aristotle, spoke of *eudaemonia,* the pursuit of happiness, or well-being, or fulfillment of the human person. They spoke of achieving happiness through virtuous living. They spoke primarily of the cardinal, or pivotal, virtues the human person had to practice in the pursuit of happiness. These traditional or philosophic human virtues are prudence, justice, fortitude, and temperance. The "Catechism of the Catholic Church" states that "The human virtues are rooted in the theological virtues (which) relate directly to God...they are faith, hope, and charity..." Jesus speaks of our pursuit of happiness when teaching the Beatitudes. He is speaking about being faithful, hopeful, and charitable, or loving, as necessary for pursuing happiness.

When most of us reflect upon faith, or belief, or committing, we have a reasonable understanding of what is intended and how it may develop. A person of faith understands another person, or a movement, whether political, social, economic, moral or religious and sees the potential benefits that are offered by this person or movement. The particular person or movement gives evidence of being credible, believable. Then one freely chooses to involve oneself in associating with the person or movement. There is a realization that understanding "something" and involving oneself in moving "something" forward weds theory and practice. Understanding is put into practice with consistency.

I am attracted to another person for any number of reasons. He or she is funny, intelligent, sincere, caring, and we develop a friendship. We commit ourselves to each other. We go further than attraction or being acquaintances. We become friends, which is a faith relationship. I understand how a political or social movement is helping people to "better" themselves educationally, politically, or financially, and I use my talents or abilities to further the movement. I commit myself to joining and furthering a cause that benefits others. I become associated with the movement. I become part of it. Being a faithful person seems reasonable to me. I can understand what fidelity, or being faithful, means. It becomes a particular existential question when I ask: to whom or to what specifically will I pledge my fidelity?

Nana Mouskouri (my second favorite female singer, after Lena Horne) sings a song entitled "Only Love." Among the lyrics are: "love changes everything...how you live and how you die...Nothing in the world will ever be the same..." These words speak of the power of love between people. There are many insights into understanding love and many aspects of a love relationship that we can understand. There is attraction which can be physical, emotional, social, moral, and/or intellectual. These are important attractions without which very few relationships could grow. There are also the lesser attractions. We root for the same team, enjoy the same kind of shows, like the same movies, or cook the same foods. There is acceptance, in varying degrees, by each party. There is a comfortableness that develops between lovers which results in a deepening trust, or faith, in each other. Love and fidelity seem to be reasonable companions. Communication becomes something that is not only easy to do, but the parties involved look forward to conversation, to relating to each other. All the above is confirmed by sharing experiences of being together. The intimacy differs depending on the nature of the relationship. Of course, we might eventually end up saying, "Well, why did you believe him in the first place? Regarding credibility, he doesn't have a very good track record." Or one might say, "How could you love her? What is the matter with you?" Faith and love relationships can be fleeting experiences or can be the experience of a lifetime. Dona and

I are still on the honeymoon primarily because we play at marriage rather than trying to work at it. Work involves waiting for problems to develop and then confront and attempt to solve them. Playing involves continually enjoying what you are doing by balancing life. They both require planning and execution, as well as effort. So we play!

I think it is reasonable to say that one can appreciate an experience of fidelity or love through what is shared with others. When it comes to understanding hope, the situation is not the same because what we hope for has not yet happened, or, at least, has not been fully realized. We know that hoping is not wishing, because when you wish for anything, there is not much you can do. I want to win the lottery; so I buy a ticket. That's all I can do. This is wishing. The result is not something we can control, or influence. What we hope for is, in a sense, beyond our control, but includes an element of our involvement; so let's look at an event in Jesus' life in which I believe He was offering hope to the disciples.

In each of the synoptic gospels, the Transfiguration scene occurs shortly after Peter's answer to Jesus' question: who do people say that I am? Peter answers "You are the Christ, the Son of the living God." Jesus responds by saying that Peter's belief in Him has moved him to realize that he is the Messiah, the promised one. Do I think that Peter also believed that Jesus is Emmanuel, God become man? It will take the Resurrection, the Ascension, and the Descent of the Holy Spirit upon the apostles before their faith matures enough to live and proclaim the Good News. Shortly after this revelation to Peter, Jesus predicts His passion, death and resurrection. They are journeying to Jerusalem where Jesus will suffer and die. Peter protests that this will not happen while he is around to defend Jesus. Peter made the connection between Jesus and the Old Testament promise of the Messiah, but he overlooked, or forgot, or didn't want to accept the Old Testament notion of the Suffering Servant. His Messiah would not be a Suffering Servant. His faith in Jesus was sincere, but inadequate. How do you respond to one who is faithful to you, to one who returns your love? You offer this person hope, even if, initially, he or she is unable to recognize it.

On the way to Jerusalem, Jesus takes Peter, James and John up a mountain path where He is transfigured before them. "...His face shone like the sun, and his garments became white as light. And behold, there appeared to them Moses and Elijah talking with him." The apostles' initial response is that this is indeed a sacred place, let's build a monument. They didn't realize at the time that this event is a foreshadowing of the Resurrection. They might have been thinking that perhaps indeed Jesus is divine, is Emmanuel, but they still had to have been wondering how the passion prediction fits into all of this. The appearance of Moses and Elijah confirms the messianic fulfilling for them. The Mosaic Law begins on Mount Sinai with Yahweh saying to His people through Moses, the mediator, "I, the Lord, am your God, who brought you out of the land of Egypt, that place of slavery." (Exodus 20:2) The Ten Commandments are given as concrete examples of how the Israelites should respond to their saving God. Throughout the rest of the Pentateuch, or Torah, the Mosaic Law is refined and developed to underscore the need for acting in accordance with God's will for His people. This covenant with the Israelites is reemphasized with the words in Deuteronomy 6:4-6, "Hear, O Israel! The Lord is our God, the Lord alone! Therefore, you shall love the Lord, your God, with all your heart, and with all your soul, and with all your strength. Take to heart these words which I enjoin on you today." The prophets, like Elijah, spent many ages encouraging and challenging the people to live out these words, but not everyone, then or now, responds.

A voice came from the clouds saying, "This is my beloved Son with whom I am well pleased, listen to Him." The disciples dropped to the ground in fear. Jesus gently pulls them up telling them not to be afraid. Jesus has come not only to fulfill what Moses and the prophets proclaimed, but came as Emmanuel, God with us. The Messiah, promised of old, is the Suffering Servant, whose care is primarily, then and today, for the outcasts in life.

In Section VIII of "The Enchiridion" which is entitled "The Distinction between Faith and Hope, and Mutual Dependence of Faith, Hope, and Love, Augustine writes: *There is no love without hope, no hope without love, and neither love nor hope without faith.* Language conveys meaning. Faith, hope, and love are terms, words, which we use to communicate meaning. Faith is a term of origin [-] I believe in God; I commit myself as husband to Dona and as father to our boys;

I bind myself, as a teacher, to the Jesuit educational principle of *cura personalis,* the care of the individual student. Love is an expressive term referring to continuity, to ongoing activity [-] I love God by keeping the commandments and trying to live out the Beatitudes; I love my bride through caring for her and supporting her and encouraging our children to grow in "wisdom and knowledge" through example; I show my love for teaching by preparing, by listening, by bothering my students to think. Hope involves that which has not yet happened, but incorporates my concern, my desire, and my action. Hope is my motivation, my strength, my spiritedness for continuing my faithful committing to other persons AND for finding ways to express this continuity through ever caring and loving actions and activity. Saint Paul wrote in his letter to the Corinthians (1Cor 13:13) "So faith, hope, love remain, these three; but the greatest of these is love." I think that *love* is the outward and persistent expression of those who are mutually committed to each other and are willing to embrace new ways of caring for each other in the *hope* of keeping alive their *fidelity.* "Greater love than this no one has than to lay down one's life for a friend." (John 15:13)

Jesus showed His faith in the disciples by calling them to follow Him. He showed His love by teaching them, by praying for and with them, by leading them. The Transfiguration is Jesus' attempt to prepare them for the passion and death by giving them a glimpse, a foreshadowing of the glory. The whiteness of Jesus' garments is a sign of the apocalyptic victory of good over evil. The cloud indicates the presence of God. The conversation with Moses and Elijah (who foreshadows John the Baptist) confirm Jesus as the Messianic hope. The apostles do not yet fully appreciate what has happened, but they will. I would love to have been present at their post Resurrection conversation when they said to each other, "So this is what the Transfiguration is all about." Gabriel Marcel, the Catholic Existentialist philosopher wrote in "Homo Viator" that hope is prophetic. The hope that Jesus manifested in the Transfiguration was clearly prophetic. The hope that I try to offer anyone stems from my committing to that person, or persons, and how I lovingly express that committing with persistence.

Getting to know Jesus' through His Friendly Advice
Luke 16:19-31

I think it is safe to say that Jesus' earthly visit revealed Him as a teacher who, along with many invitations to learn, dispensed much beneficial advice. He was also not shy about expressing "tough love" and our need to search for answers rather than waiting for someone to tell us what to do. This final parable, that I have chosen, is only found in Luke's gospel as part of the teaching section called the "Travel Narrative." Jesus is on His way to Jerusalem to embrace the Cross; so there is a purpose to this trip. In the preceding chapter (15) of Luke's gospel, there are three parables about rejoicing over finding what was lost. The first is the story of the lost sheep, where the shepherd leaves the flock to search for the one sheep that was lost. The next story deals with the poor woman who frantically combs the whole house looking for a lost coin. The third and most memorable story is that of the prodigal son (15:11-32) who leaves his father's house, squanders his inheritance, and returns seeking forgiveness. The father's joy is so overwhelming that his welcoming of the son overshadows any hurt or pain suffered when the child left. The jealous elder brother refuses to reconcile with him. There is joy to be experienced in the recovery of things that are lost, whether inanimate or animate. But the greatest joy is in the return of someone who had strayed but has "come home." These are the stories that are the basis for the sacrament of Penance, the sacrament of reconciliation.

In the sixteenth chapter, Luke deals with another theme which is very much in keeping with the focus on Jesus as the "Champion of outcasts." It is clear that there were people, perhaps many people, who believed that the possession of large amounts of wealth meant that they were favored by God. One's material possessions or social, political, or "religious" standing indicated how high one stood in God's "pecking order." This was, and is, clearly not the case in Jesus' eyes. I am sure there are many wealthy people today who believe that material possessions are the greatest, or the sole, indicator of whether their lives are worthwhile, or successful. They are materially well positioned and that is all that counts. Many boast of their wealth as contemporary indicators of their significance in life and as reminders that the rest of us ought to acknowledge that. Certainly, being materially wealthy has utilitarian value. It doesn't make one healthier or more handsome, or happier or holier. Its value depends on how one's wealth is used; hence, utilitarian. The consequences for the selfish user will differ from the consequences for the generous user…if not today, then for eternity.

The second of the two stories, or parables, in this chapter is about Lazarus and the rich man. (This is not the same Lazarus, the brother of Mary and Martha, who was raised from the dead by Jesus in John's gospel.) Lazarus is a beggar, an outcast, who sits suffering outside the rich man's house hoping for some morsels of discarded food. The rich man is oblivious to this homeless person or anyone else who doesn't share his privileged position. He doesn't commit any overt crimes against Lazarus, he simply ignores his existence. Lazarus is invisible to the rich man. It is a sin of omission.

They both die. Lazarus is taken up to heaven, a good place to spend eternity, in the arms of Abraham and the rich man arrives in Hades. It's not clear whether this is eternal damnation (Gehenna), but it is not a good scene by any stretch of the imagination. One day the rich man spies Lazarus above and begs Abraham to send Lazarus to wet his tongue, because he is suffering terribly. Abraham replies, "no can do" because there is no path between heaven and hell. They are the consequences of choices made during our earthly journey. There are no more choices. Then the rich man cries out begging Abraham to send Lazarus to his five brothers; so that they will change their ways of living and not wind up like him. Abraham's answer is, I think, what makes this story so powerful. It is not simply another story about the abuse of wealth or power. Nor is it simply a story of the lack of compassion towards the poor and suffering. It is not only a story about the idea that each of us is our sister's and brother's keeper. No, Jesus' advice is more powerful than that.

In the story that Jesus tells, "Abraham replies, (referring to the rich man's brothers and everyone else) 'They have Moses and the prophets. Let them listen to them.' The rich man replied, 'Oh no, Father Abraham, but if someone from the dead goes to them, they will repent.' Then Abraham said, 'If they will not listen to Moses and the prophets, neither will they be persuaded if someone should rise from the dead.'"

I think that the point of the story, Jesus' advice, is that each of us has, in this life, what he or she needs in order to seek happiness, what we need in order to fulfill ourselves as human persons made "in the image and likeness of God." There is no one who goes through life, whether rich or poor, theist or atheist, man or woman, who does not have available to him or her, whatever is necessary to fulfill themselves as persons created by the God Who cares. The details will differ because our situations and circumstances differ, but the God Who created us will never abandon us (remember Chapter One, God "hangs out" in the Garden with Adam and Eve) and there will always be available in our life's journey whatever we need to seek fulfillment as human persons, whether that is in the form of what we read, or what we experience, or whom we meet and, hopefully, love.

Do I believe God that in our life's journey, there are enough signposts to direct us towards fulfilling ourselves as a human person made in "the image and likeness of God?" Am I hopeful enough in my ability to reason and choose, and in my relation with others to find happiness? Am I courageous enough to accept Jesus" advice: "Love one another as I have loved you!" I do believe God has given us whatever we need to fulfill ourselves as living expressions of "being made in the image and likeness of God" and fully capable in each of our own limited ways of caring for His creation. We don't all need the same clues or have to follow the same path, but since I believe that "God is love" (1 John 4:8) then we have whatever we need.

As you know, I married a very wonderful Italian girl, and over the years I have learned a few Italian words. In getting to know Jesus, I think that one of the wonderful characteristics of Him is that He is a "scutch." (I am not quite sure if that is a correct spelling, because it is dialect.) But the word refers to someone who bothers others. I believe that Jesus bothers us to think and to act. He is a nudge. He knows that we are good. After all, with His Father and the Spirit, He created us. He knows that our humanity is subject to the need to change, because He became like us. He knows that we are afraid, because as we shall see, He experienced the Garden of Gethsemane and the Cross. He knows that at times we are fearful of walking on water even though He encourages us. He knows that we can be good because we sometimes express being a Good Samaritan to those in need, or being the Father of the Prodigal son or daughter who rejoices at their return, or being Zacchaeus who will go out on a limb simply to witness to Him, or being like Peter who answers "You are the Messiah, the Son of the living God." He knows that like His mother Mary, sometimes we are able to say "Be it done unto me according to your will." He also knows that we can walk away, but I believe we can never walk so far away that He isn't standing right next to us. We simply have to open our eyes and our ears. He does want to be known, because He already knows us.

What do we know about the historical Jesus Who becomes the Risen Christ? We know His vision is characterized by caring for everyone which He communicated with consistency. He described a priority of values to live by and the consequences that follow because actions speak louder than words. He remains a faithful friend who offers hope and advice. In the final chapter we will witness the depth of His love for us.

Where do we find Him? There is a great scene in the 1951 movie "Quo Vadis" starring Robert Taylor and Deborah Kerr as the romantic couple, a Roman centurion and a hostage Christian princess. It takes place in the early sixties in Rome during the persecutions ordered by Nero (Peter Ustinov.) It is the time around when the gospel of Mark is written. There is plenty of romance and much suffering for the beleaguered Christians. "Quo Vadis" means "Where are you going?" It refers to the voice of God directed to Saint Peter as he is trying to leave Rome which is going up in flames. Peter realizes that he is not supposed to be fleeing from the persecution of God's people, but should be there with them in their trials and tribulations. He turns around and brings God's blessing to the persecuted, assuring them of God's presence. It is in Rome around this time that Peter and Paul are martyred. We are reminded that God is with His people in times of celebration and in times of struggle.

I mentioned at the beginning of this chapter that I was part of a team who sought to focus upon teaching in Jesuit schools as a ministry, a vocation. Over a number of years, I met and shared with teachers and staff from Jesuit schools throughout the United States, Canada, Puerto Rico, Ireland and England. Other members traveled to the Philippines and to Australia. My final colloquium was held in Warsaw, Poland in 2003. The Jesuit secondary schools in Eastern Europe had reopened and our team, including my bride, traveled there to share the exercises over a three day period. There were teachers from Poland, Lithuania, Slovenia, Hungary, and even one teacher from Egypt. My colloquium experience was and continues to be a blessing that allows me to see the "face of God" in so many different people in so many different places. One of the more moving Colloquium presentations is the one on "Spirituality" which we basically approached as the practice of acting out daily our image of God, and our attempt to find God in all things. As our introduction, we presented John Dunne's "the parable of the mountain" from his book, *The Way of All the Earth*. It is about humanity's desire to find God by escaping the concerns of daily earthly living and seeking God in the quiet solitude of the mountain peak. Man discovers that God is not there because He has descended into the world, the valley, to be with His people in their hurt and in their joy of journeying with others who care for them and who don't care for them. Man's desire is to be with God apart from everyone else and God's desire is to be with us, no matter what is happening. That's why it is always possible to get to know the historical Jesus Who becomes the Risen Christ.

We don't have to discover Narnia, or climb Mount Everest to find God, even though both of those would be exciting adventures. We will find Him in the places we pass through and in the people we continually meet. Maybe a good place to start would be to become more deeply acquainted with the face we regularly see in the mirror. He or she is one of God's greatest creations. We know this because in John's gospel (15:15) He says

I call you friend…what more do we need to know?

CHAPTER SIX

The Price of Love

There are contemporary movies and songs which claim that "love means never having to say you're sorry!" *Au Contraire!* The greatest expression of love in human history is Calvary's Cross, and sorrow is certainly at the heart of that scene. Maybe the deeper question ought to be: if love is associated with joy, with happiness, with friendship, then how can sorrow, or hurt, or pain or suffering be related to love?

An old song refrains that "Love is a Many Splendered Thing!" Love is not a "thing." Love is not a "feeling" even though love is most often accompanied by deep feelings or emotions, usually positive, but unfortunately the feelings could become very negative and even self destructive, and love dies. Love is a *relationship* between people which requires both parties to contribute or the love relationship will fail to grow into the most intimate of friendships. If I cheat on my wife, or fail to acknowledge her feelings, or take her for granted, even though she remains faithful to me, our love will fail to become what it is meant to be [-] an ongoing mutual fulfilling of each other's trust and hope, which we promised at the beginning of our marital journey. If I turn my back on one of my children because I do not agree with what he is trying to accomplish in life, our parent-child relationship will never become what it has the possibility of becoming. If I lie to a friend or a neighbor, our companionship will never realize what it could and should be. If I ignore the difficulty a certain student might be having in his or her life, then I will have fallen short of serving this person as I should have. I will have failed in the Jesuit tradition of education to express the idea of "cura personalis" or the care of the whole individual person. If I refuse to accept God's care for me, our relationship will never become what it is supposed to be, even though God continues to love me and to forgive me. Without communication, coming together as one in understanding (even if there is no initial or little agreement), there will be no growth in the relationship. Subjectively, love involves a free personal choice, and objectively, love involves an interpersonal responsibility and nurturing. Oftentimes, it might be easier to love another person than to try to explain "what" love is.

For me, as a practicing Catholic, the Easter Triduum, the three days which include Jesus' suffering, death and resurrection are liturgically the most significant days in the Christian calendar because they refer to the events which clearly identify us as Christians; no matter what the varying religious practices of different Christian sects are. The Passion Narratives focus on the arrest of Jesus in the Garden of Gethsemane, His torture by the Roman soldiers, His bogus trials and unjust sentencing, and His capital (criminal) execution on Calvary's hill. I see this as part of a broader story and experience and will approach the passion narratives as more than an unjust execution which took place on a particular afternoon in time. If earthly joy is not simply the absence of sorrow, but the presence of God (and I existentially accept that), then the presence of earthly sorrow cannot be the complete picture. So what is it? What leads up to the passion narratives and what follows from the passion narratives? How do the events preceding the passion narrative and the events which follow relate to the suffering and death of Our Lord?

I began to take interest in the Passion Narratives while I was in grammar, or grade school, in the 1940's. On Friday afternoons during Lent, we would process from the school to the Church for the liturgical service called the "Stations of the Cross" or the "Way of the Cross," the *Via Dolorosa*. These are prayerful reflections on the events of Good Friday beginning with the "legal," though clearly unethical, condemnation of Jesus to His Crucifixion and Burial. I still have, and meditate upon, the little red covered book "Stations of the Cross: For Children," originally published in 1921 (which is before my time.) In 1991, Pope John Paul II reflected upon the Stations of the Cross by more closely following the Passion Narrative accounts in the gospels. He began with the scene in the Garden of Gethsemane and included Judas' betrayal and Peter's denial. This liturgical practice includes reflections upon different gospel passages, which are then associated with and related to Jesus' journeying to Golgotha, the place of His execution.

The pain and suffering inflicted upon Our Lord has always caused me to be at least, uncomfortable, probably because, as a child, I did not want to picture a suffering God. I guess that is not unlike Peter's protests when Jesus predicted His passion. Yet, I think that His willingness to suffer for us made me more sympathetic to the hurts and pains of others, even those whom I never met, but only read about or heard about in newspapers and on news broadcasts. It is not easy for many of us to gloss over or dismiss some of the sad and tragically disturbing worldly events that we read about or view on the screen. They probably give rise to the statement, a true one, I think, that "There, but for the grace of God, go I." It is tough to embrace any significance to suffering, primarily because if I am hurting there are few positive activities in which I can engage. And yet it is impossible to avoid hurt and suffering in our earthly journeying, because as we have already seen, our world is in process, is not yet completed or perfected. It has been my privilege in recent years to lead the "Stations of the Cross" devotions occasionally in my parish church. This is always a very painfully meaningful experience for me.

Television only became part of our worldly possessions after my bride and I returned from our honeymoon. Radio provided an early interest in the Passion Narratives. My family used to listen to a show called "The Catholic Hour" which, I believe, eventually became the forerunner of Bishop Fulton Sheen's television program "Life is Worth Living." Bishop Sheen was a very charismatic preacher and teacher who once thanked his four script writers, Mark, Matthew, Luke and John for the wonderful material with which they presented him. He spoke about religious and moral topics and was able to hold audiences spellbound. His eyes (when we saw him on television) were piercing and they seemed to focus only upon you as you were riveted by his words. It must have been like this with Jesus, because, in the scriptures, it refers to Him speaking "with authority." Bishop Sheen had this dramatic gift, this "authority" when he spoke. He preached about the commandments and the sacraments, Old and New Testament revelation, good and evil, the Trinity, and the suffering, death, and resurrection of Jesus. I especially remember the times he spoke about the seven words Jesus uttered while nailed to the Cross. These seven words, or phrases, or thoughts, have always been a significant part of my faith developing.

For a few years, I conducted a "pre-triduum" to the Easter Triduum in our Brooklyn parish church. On Monday through Wednesday evenings of Holy Week, I would lead a preparatory session for a deeper appreciation of the events from Holy Thursday to Easter Sunday. There would be variations, but the focus, each year, was the Passion Narratives. My foundation was always the Stations of the Cross and my primary interest were Jesus' words spoken from the Cross. One year there was an additional consideration of the passion narratives as proclaimed in the synoptic gospels. Another year featured John's passion narrative. One year contrasted the two crowds, the "Hosanna" crowd on Palm Sunday and the "Crucify Him" crowd on Good Friday. One year related the Eucharist to the Cross and the final year highlighted Jesus' travel narrative to Jerusalem in Luke's gospel account and the beginning of the Church as the apostles traveled to Rome in the Acts of the Apostles. Those were wonderful opportunities for me to share my passion for the "Passion."

In terms of more recent influences I must mention the two volume scholarly work of Father Ray Brown's "The Death of the Messiah: From Gethsemane to the Grave." Father Brown (who also wrote "The Birth of the Messiah" – see chapter four), spent ten years in putting together this insightful tome of over 1,600 pages. His purpose is to explain as clearly as possible what he, and other scholars, think is the intention of the four evangelists in writing the passion narratives. He takes a horizontal approach which involves placing all the gospel events side by side and painstakingly trying to piece together the temporal sequence of events from Holy Thursday evening to His burial on Good Friday afternoon. The evangelists wrote vertically. By this, I mean, taking into consideration the different audiences for whom they were writing, each author developed a different Christological focus, and followed through on developing that particular focus. Remember we said that Mark's focus is on Jesus as Suffering Servant, while Matthew emphasizes Jesus as the promised Messiah. Luke presents Jesus as the champion of the outcasts while John's approach is on Jesus as the Glorified Christ. Then, each of the authors presents the public ministry, passion narrative, and resurrection accounts of the historical Jesus, the Messiah promised of old, who, sacrificed on the Cross, becomes the Risen Christ. These different foci allow for varying perspectives from which each of these theologian authors viewed Jesus. Together, they give us a deeper and fuller understanding of Our Lord and Savior's purpose in embracing our humanity.

Father Brown is using the events from Gethsemane to burial as depicted in the four Gospel accounts, placed side by side. He analyzes, explores, and comments on each author's presentation in order to develop as coherent and unified a story of the suffering and death of the Messiah. His audience is more universal than the communal audiences of each of the evangelists. His approach is presented in four acts:

I   Jesus prays in the garden *and* is arrested
II   Trial and interrogation by Jewish authorities *and* the mockery and abuse of Jesus
III   Jesus before Pilate
IV   Jesus is crucified on Golgotha *and* buried nearby

There are two scenes in each of the first, second, and fourth acts, identified by the *"and."* He incorporates insights on the historical, social, religious and cultural characteristics of the times, as well as the theological concerns of the evangelists. The result is a very intense and extremely rewarding reading of a devout Christian witness to Jesus' saving action.

For a less academic, but very passionately written work, I recommend the second book in Joseph (Pope [Emeritus] Benedict XVI) Ratzinger's trilogy entitled "Jesus of Nazareth." This particular book is subtitled: "Holy Week: From the Entrance into Jerusalem to the Resurrection." His avowed reason in writing this trilogy is to try "to understand the figure of Jesus, his words and his actions..." His first book in the series focuses upon Jesus' public ministry and the last book deals with the Infancy Narratives. The trilogy is very readable, and reflects the understanding and appreciation of one of God's most faithful contemporary servants.

In the previous chapter which involved getting to know Our Lord through the gospel stories, I concluded by calling Jesus a "scutch," a nudge, someone who loves us so much that He is concerned with bothering us to be a more compassionate and caring people [-] because He knows we are good. He created us. He knows our need to change, to grow, to develop because human life is a process into which He entered intimately throughout His earthly life. He knows our fears as well as our desires and our capability of giving witness to His love through our own loving words and actions. He shows us this through His vision of life which is characterized by love especially for those who are downtrodden and poor and neglected. He expresses this through His stories, through the parables which show us how we ought to embrace and express our humanity. He reveals His expectations of us, His friends, and what we are capable of doing through our choices in life. His friendship excludes no one, except those who through their own free choices reject His love. There are no favorites and no prejudices in reaching out to others. Well, maybe there are favorites, but certainly, using a contemporary expression, there are definitely no "losers," no outcasts. He leaves no one behind. His actions confirm the universality of His ongoing concern and desire to let us know the love of His Father for each of us. This begins at His birth through the presence of the shepherds and the magi. It is made public by what he says and what He does throughout His earthly ministry. And finally it is majestically proclaimed through His body broken on the Cross, but transformed gloriously forever through His resurrection.

He knows that some of us, perhaps many of us, have refused to love because we are afraid, or selfish, or despairing of goodness in life. He is aware of those of us who have succumbed to the temptation to be less than we could be as persons created in "the image and likeness of God." He has confronted the human temptations to "look out for number one" or to place conditions on personal relationships, or simply to give up the idea that life has any goodness to it at all. He has embraced our humanity and He knows us even better than we know ourselves. Yet He has not given up on us, nor surrendered to despair. He has called some of us "hypocrites" not as some kind of lasting moral judgment, unless we freely choose it, but rather as a challenge for us to look within and begin to appreciate what Socrates and Plato proclaimed; namely, that "the unexamined life is not worth living!" For Him, actions speak louder than words, and the action that conquers everything in life, immediately and eventually and permanently, is love. In the face of those who would pass the buck with respect to being responsible for others, He is always the Good Shepherd and the Good Samaritan. Acknowledging that within families there are those who are less than appreciative, He is the loving Father of all prodigal sons and daughters. In answer to those who are in need, of anything, He multiplies the loaves and the fish that are necessary to feed the hunger of all who are starving physically and spiritually. For anyone of us, born of man and woman, He offers the same invitation that we find in Matthew 11:28-30, "Come to Me, you who are burdened, and I will give you rest. My yoke is easy and my burden is light." If I don't take Him at His word; there are consequences. If I do take Him at His word; the consequences are very different.

I am going to use Father Brown's approach and focus on the events from the Last Supper through the Ascension as revealing three aspects of "The Price of Love" [-] a joyful act, a sorrowful act, and a glorious act.

A Joyful Act

My mother and father emigrated from Galway, Ireland, in the 1920's. Our family table featured meat and potatoes, which, faithful to my cultural roots, I have never forsaken. Also in the 1920's Dona's mom and dad emigrated from the area of Bari in southern Italy. We met in the late1950's and I was introduced to the wonderful and excitingly delicious world of Italian cooking, a world which I am happy to say, has been a very rewarding experience throughout the years, for all who have shared our table, especially me. Eating together is, or should be, one of the most enjoyable expressions of people sharing the necessities, and the desserts of life, whether as couples, or family, or friends. Holiday meals should be joyful celebrations which declare that family is, at its core, the most essential life giving social unit there is. Sometimes this does not happen, but I do believe that family, whether created through blood, friendship, or community is the most essential group to enjoying life's many opportunities to share our earthly journey. The usual mealtime scenes occur in the dining room or in the kitchen area, or at the barbeque grill in the backyard, or at a quiet dimly lit table for two in a favorite restaurant, or maybe at a family gathering to celebrate a special occasion. Whatever the venue, the call is always more than the food: gather the folks, break the bread, tell the stories and share the table. Hospitality is both the purpose and the reward of a table shared by family and friends.

The Easter Triduum begins with the significance of a family meal. Jesus comes together with His friends to share a Passover Meal. The particular occasion is to remember the historical story of the passing over of their Jewish ancestors from Egyptian slavery to eventual freedom in their own land. It is a story of religious liberation which also symbolizes the spiritual passing over from sin to grace, from fear to love, from being alone to being with others. They came together to break the bread, tell the stories and share the table. The disciples had no idea that this would be the "Last (earthly) Supper" with Jesus, but they will eventually discover there will be more meaning to be understood from this particular shared meal than they [or we] could ever have imagined.

Meals have always played an important role throughout scripture. In Genesis 18, the hospitality shown by Abraham and Sarah to the visiting strangers was rewarded with the promise of Isaac in their old age. Exodus records not only the original preparation and celebration of the Passover meal, but later, in their journey of liberation, they are fed with the manna from heaven when there was nothing with which they could nourish themselves. This Passover Seder remembrance is the purpose of each weekly Sabbath meal celebrated by God's chosen people. In John's gospel, the first miracle, or sign of Jesus' divinity is at the Wedding Feast of Cana, when, at His Mother's bidding, He transforms the water into wine. By doing so, he lets the wedding celebration continue. Later on, there is the feeding of thousands of people whose response is to crown Him an earthly king, but instead He gives the "Bread of Life" discourse which many have difficulty in accepting. He offers to give them Himself as eternal nourishment, but they can only see the immediate here and now. They can only see what they touch with their hands and taste with their tongues because they are spiritually blind. Yet, on this evening, at this very same meal with His disciples, He will identify Himself as the "Bread of Life." In the synoptic gospels there is the feeding of the thousands of people with the five loaves and a pair of fish. Meals are also a part of the sharing stories with the tax collectors, Levi, or Matthew, in Matthew's gospel, chapter nine, and again with Zaccheus in Luke's gospel, chapter nineteen. The meal is front and center, even in the post Resurrection stories. After the crucifixion two disciples are fleeing from Jerusalem to Emmaus because they are afraid of being persecuted for their association with Jesus. They are joined by a stranger along the way whom they finally recognize as Jesus in the breaking of the bread as they sit down to an evening meal. The meal stories are not simply about what is being served. There are no scriptural cookbooks or recipes which indicate whether the food is organically grown or not, or how many calories are being consumed. The primary purpose of the "meal" stories is about the concept of *table fellowship*. It is more about who shares the meal than what is shared, but tonight there will be a change. There will be a deepening of the reality of *table fellowship* during the Last Supper meal when "what is shared" is identified with "Who is shared." Jesus is the "Bread of Life."

Jesus' concept of table fellowship begins with the vision of His ministry (see the previous chapter) which bars no one from companionship, or communion, with Him. His love is universal. It is neither selective nor exclusive. His table has room for everyone. There is always "open" seating at the Eucharistic table. I think that the focus on Jesus in Luke's gospel most clearly identifies the meaning of table fellowship. Jesus is the "champion of the outcasts." No one, no matter what his or her social status might be, is barred from His table. Part of the table fellowship includes telling the stories. As we saw in the previous chapter, Jesus began the Last Supper account in John's gospel with "telling" a parable in action rather than in words. Jesus washes the feet of the disciples. He is a servant and His service at this meal foreshadows His service on the Cross which will occur in less than twenty-four hours. Jesus models the purpose and significance of hospitality which is essentially to be of service to the guests who enter fully into one's life or who simply touch one while passing through our shared earthly journey.

The "last supper" scene in John's gospel (chapters 13 through 17) is very different from the same scene in the synoptic gospels. John's account, which we have already referred to as Jesus' farewell address, covers five chapters totaling one hundred and fifty-five verses. It is obvious that in John's account the focus is on telling the story because it is a key teaching section, with the emphasis on God's unconditional committing to the covenant with us. It is concerned with discipleship and Jesus' guarantee of His presence with them even beyond the crucifixion about which, at that moment, they are entirely clueless. The synoptic accounts focus more closely on the meal time actions of Jesus giving thanks, blessing and breaking the bread, and sharing Himself in communion with the disciples. Mark describes the "last supper" in eight verses, Matthew in nine, and Luke in twenty-two.

One of the wedding shower gifts Dona received was a copy of Leonardo Da Vinci's painting of the "Last Supper." It was given by a friend of my mother and it still hangs on our dining room wall today. The original painting (circa 1498) is in the Convent of Santa Maria delle Grazie in Milan, Italy. It measures fifteen feet by twenty nine feet, an amazing accomplishment for its day. Ours is much more modest in size. It is biblical art. It is an acclaimed artistic masterpiece. It captures the response of the apostles to Jesus telling the story, during the meal, that one of them will betray Him. Surprise, shock, and disbelief seem to be the apostolic expressions while Jesus remains calm, as though He has already accepted what is to happen. There are four groups of three apostles all arranged on the same side of the table as Jesus so that we can see their reactions. Da Vinci claimed that his painting tries to capture the inner sense of the apostles. They had been with Jesus for quite some time and yet still did not envision what was to happen that night. It is interesting to see that one of the groups of apostles includes the apparently angry Peter, the stunned John, and the traitor Judas who seems to be clutching a money bag (thirty pieces of silver?) and has knocked over a cup of some kind. They figure prominently in the Passion Narratives. Judas betrays Jesus while Peter denies knowing Him. John is the only apostle standing at the foot of the Cross. It is a preview of a changing scene which will shift from the joyful sharing of the ritual meal to the sorrowful fulfilling on the Cross of Jesus' words and actions during this meal.

The content of the Acts of the Apostles and the letters of Paul predate the gospels as written. We know from reading them, especially Paul's first letter to the Corinthians, chapter 11, that the Eucharistic meal was celebrated by Jesus' disciples and the early converts, using the words of Jesus, and repeating His actions from the Last Supper. Essentially in the synoptic accounts, Jesus identifies Himself with the bread and wine. He blesses the bread, breaks it and shares It=Himself with the disciples saying, **"Take, eat; this is my body."** Then He takes a cup of wine and having given thanks, He gives it to them saying, **"This is my blood of the covenant which is poured out for many..."** With these words and with this action, God does what God has been doing since the beginning of the world. He is confirming His presence with us as surely as He did with Adam and Eve, Abraham, Moses, David, the prophets, the captives in Babylon, the remnant of people who returned to Jerusalem, with Job in his suffering, and with Daniel and his companions in the lion's den where they were spared from their suffering and death. Most recently He has been with the apostles and those who followed Him. Now, today, He is with us in the Eucharistic celebration and we must explore more fully what that means to us and for us. We have replaced the apostles as His contemporary earthly guests, but He is still the gracious Host.

We must nourish ourselves in order to live; so eating and drinking are necessities of life. Meals are life giving experiences. Most of us take this for granted which is why we cannot fully appreciate the horror of starvation experienced by so many people in so many places, even today. We know that food doesn't grow in packages and liquids don't present themselves in bottles or other containers. People prepare bread by growing and harvesting and baking. Grapes must be grown on the vines, picked, crushed and allowed to ferment before being bottled and purchased by the eventual users. Any meal, therefore, acknowledges the plants of the earth, or the fruit of the earth, and the labor of people, or the work of human hands. People are involved in the preparing, presenting, and consuming of food. As Catholic Christians, we remember the significance of the Last Supper at the liturgical celebration we call the

Mass. We acknowledge the significance of people in offering food and drink to the priest in a procession, called the Offertory procession, which moves from the congregation to the altar. The priest, through the sacrament of Holy Orders, represents the main celebrant at the Last Supper, Jesus. The priest is sometimes referred to as an "Alter Christus" or "another Christ." Like the Passover meal, the Mass is a ritual remembrance, and the priest, repeating Jesus' words and actions, does with God's grace what Jesus did. Jesus becomes identified with the bread and wine.

As an aside, simply because words and phrases are often repeated, it doesn't mean they have to lose their meaning and become taken for granted, unconsciously uttered statements. I am a rabid (not literally) New York Giant football fan. I shout "Go Giants" whether we are winning or losing. When we read the psalms in the Old Testament, we know quickly whether things are going well for the people or not. Anyone watching and hearing me during a Giant game will also know whether things are going well for our team and our fans or not. The supportive meaning, however, is always present no matter how often I cheer or implore them, perhaps in unkind terms, to be "Giants." When I say "Merry Christmas" to people I hope that they, like me, will enjoy this particularly wonderful time of the year when everyone tries to be as child-like in wonderment and as joy-full in expression as possible. I don't say "Happy Holidays" because it is the Christmas season. I know what holiday is being celebrated and, even if the other person does not celebrate this day, I still want him or her to be as happy as I am; so I repeat the greeting. It has a very significant meaning for me, which I want to share with everyone I meet. It doesn't lose any meaning because I greet many people with it. No matter how often I say "I love you" to those for whom I care very closely, it expresses my ongoing concern for them. It is not an empty formula. It is a statement spoken from my heart and no matter the number of times it is uttered, it is always meaningful. If someone is suffering the loss of a loved one, or hurting from an earthly situation, I tell them that I will pray for them. I ask God to remind me to include them and their pain in my petitions to Him. Saying that I will pray for someone is a meaningful statement. It is not just simply an appropriate statement, or a nice thing to say. I believe

God answers our prayers even if the answer is not what I would like it to be. How God responds to them may not be obviously experienced by me, but I am confident that God hears "the cry of the poor" in all who pray. Praying involves communicating with God in times of struggling and in times of appreciation. Prayer is not a platitude. Prayer is a bonding. Depending on what one is repeating, repetition clearly can be significant in life's daily, or frequent, events. Repetition of words and actions need not be boring or uninteresting. Only people are boring. It is only when words or actions are repeated by people who have little or no interest in themselves or in others, do their words and actions become meaningless...or boring. Their responses reflect their care-less outlook on life. Rooting for favorite teams, and greeting people, and praying for them are also repetitious actions which reflect one's caring outlook in life.

Prayers and liturgical services which follow the same linguistic proclamation can certainly become simply repetitious expressions, if we ignore or forget the meaning of what we are doing. What is important is that we concentrate on our prayerful intentions. Why do we pray? We *thank* God for someone or something. We ask God's *forgiveness* for having neglected to love Him by the way we neglected to love those around us. We *adore* God for what He has created so that we may share life with others. We *ask* God for what we need. If we are not conscious of why we are worshipping, or why we are praying, then our words and actions can become meaningless repetitious phrases. This is sad because we lose sight of what is happening, of what we are called to celebrate, of what it should mean to us. What the priest says in the Eucharistic celebration we call the Mass is not important because he repeats certain formulae. What is important is that he is calling us to connect with what Jesus is saying and doing. This is what the priest says at Mass: *Take this, all of you, and eat of it, for this is My Body, which will be given up for you.* Jesus presents Himself as the "Bread of Life" for the apostles at the Last Supper as well as for us who celebrate this meal through the Mass. He is with us. He is feeding us. He is nourishing us, not simply physically, but spiritually as well. He enhances our meaningfulness as persons made "in the image and likeness of God."

The priest previously mixed a drop of water with the wine to symbolize the human and divine natures of Christ joined by the mystery of the Incarnation (Christmas) through which God became man – Emmanuel – God with us. Now he raises the cup and recalling Jesus' words, he says: *Take this, all of you and drink from it, for this is the chalice of My Blood, the Blood of the new and eternal covenant, which will be poured out for you and for many for the forgiveness of sins. Do this in memory of Me.* The table fellowship which the apostles shared with Jesus at the Last Supper is ours to share, as Christians, in the daily liturgical gathering. We repeat His words so that we can share Him today as intimately as Peter, James, and John and the rest of the apostles did on that holy and joyful table fellowship. Jesus continues to be with us in a very memorable and intimate way leading, we all hope, to a lasting and joyful table fellowship.

The conclusion to this part of the Eucharistic celebration is called Communion during which the assembled people receive and consume the bread of life and the cup of salvation under the appearances of the bread and wine which were previously prepared and offered at the altar. We come together as one with Our Lord. We enter into a very special union with Him, the same union that was promised in Genesis 2, Original Grace. We are graced with God's presence within us IF we accept His friendship by becoming conscious and loving caretakers of His creation. Remember, the covenant is a relationship which requires both parties to respond, to contribute. God gives Himself to us and we are called to respond. No hocus-pocus here. No magic potions. No trickery. No simply going through the motions. God has called us and we will answer with acceptance or rejection, faith or disbelief, yes or no.

It is clear that we are the guests who are being fed, who are in God's spotlight. I enjoy many of the fairytale, animated, movies. "Beauty and the Beast" is a favorite. There is a song which offers insights into the Eucharistic meal. Belle, the Beauty, finds herself in the castle of a prince, who, in the weakness of his humanity has acted uncharitably, and suffers from the ugliness of life. He is a beast. In the eyes of the people who live in the area, he is an outcast. Belle is hungry and wanders into the dining room, where she is fed by the servants of the prince/beast, led by Lumiere (light) and Cogsworth (the voice of reason.) The scene is a musical number entitled "Be Our Guest." It is the idea of being a guest that intrigues me. From creation in the Garden, we, humanity, are guests in the universe God created. Because of the suffering of the prince as a beast, all his servants are suffering as well. This is clearly a sign that we influence and are influenced by the people who touch our lives. In the song we hear, "Life is so unnerving for a servant who is not serving. He's not whole without a soul to wait on." This line captures what every Christian is called to do...to serve. Jesus has embraced our humanity, which includes the ugliness of life, the rejections and pain we inflict on ourselves and others. Table fellowship for Jesus includes both the Beautiful and the Beastly. Jesus essentially comes as servant-host. He feeds us, God's guests, in this temporal mission and we will either accept or reject His nourishment. The idea of our being guests in this earthly journey and the embracing of the beauty of grace-filled lives and the sadness of sinful lives by the Suffering Servant Messianic God is very much reflected in the passion events. It makes sense to me to look for God in the experience of life, even in some of our cinematic experiences.

What is shared, the bread and the wine, the fruit of the earth and the work of human hands, is identified with Who is shared, Emmanuel, God become man, the Messiah promised of old, the champion of the outcasts. The folks have gathered, the stories have been told, the bread has been broken and table has been shared. But there is a statement made at the Last Supper, which remains to be understood. Jesus said, "Do this is memory of Me." Do what? It can't simply be to share food. The meal is not the end. Tomorrow more of the story will unfold. It includes the suffering servant Who will carry His cross to Calvary's execution because at the Last Supper Jesus said this: "There is no greater love than this: to lay down one's life for one's friends. You are my friends if you do what I commanded you...I call you friends, since I have made known to you all that I heard from my Father. It was not you who chose me, it was I who chose you to go forth and bear fruit...the command I give you is this, *that you love one another.*" (John 15:13-16) At the Last Supper, and at every Eucharistic celebration today, He is *telling* us to do what He is doing, serving others. Tomorrow, He will *show* us what He is doing, by serving us through the sacrifice of the Cross. He is calling us to serve in the same way [-] to lay down our lives for others. This is the price of love!

The Creator God made the covenant in the Garden of Eden and renews it daily with us, identifying and maintaining His friendship with us. At Christmas He embraced our humanity. He became like us to show us how deeply significant our being human is meant to be, and how important our friendship is to Him. And that is true today, even when we fail to appreciate and express our human significance. He revealed His Father's love for us through what He said and what He did, and will show us the unconditional love He proclaims by accepting the Cross. The price of love is not only the joyful sharing of the table with friends, but may include sorrowful sacrifice. To sacrifice means to make holy. But as the beautiful hymn, "Be not Afraid, I go before you always. Come, follow Me…" reminds us, that sorrow is not the end. It is not the goal of life. No matter what we may experience, this hymn reminds us, "…know that I am with you through it all…" Maybe that is why we are called to be faith-filled people. The story is far from over, and we are never alone as our story unfolds.

A Sorrowful Act

After the meal was finished, the gospels tell us that Jesus and his disciples went out to the Garden of Gethsemane where they often went to pray, to reflect, and to sing songs of thanksgiving. But tonight will be different.

I remember when my father, then in his mid sixties, was diagnosed with cancer of the mouth. It was, unfortunately, the result of years of smoking a pipe. His was the second operation of this new kind of surgical procedure. A jawbone and part of his tongue was removed. The operation was considered medically successful and it was. He did have to relearn how to talk and how to eat which he eventually managed with varying degrees of pain, and even went back to work for a short time before retiring. You had to concentrate on what he was saying in order to understand him clearly, but you could. I remember his telling me that if he knew he would undergo that much suffering, he would not have had the operation. I mention this because in the Garden of Gethsemane Jesus knew He was going to suffer. He asked His friends to pray with Him and moving forward a bit, He fell on His knees, and in the fullness and fragileness of our humanity which He had freely embraced, He prayed that the Father would let His impending suffering simply "go away." The mental and emotional anguish was so intense that He began to sweat blood.

I mentioned in chapter five a book entitled "A Doctor at Calvary" by Pierre Barbet, a French doctor and one of the scientists who examined the Shroud of Turin, which some claim to be the linen sheet in which Jesus was wrapped for burial. The scientific documentation is interesting and persuasive, and clearly worth reading. I used his passion meditation, an appendix to the book, in my senior classes at Xavier High School, around Easter time. The description of Jesus' passion and death is medically and brutally described, with an explanation that could never be captured in any painting or sculpture no matter how cruelly portrayed. It was the first time I heard of "hematidrosa" or the sweat of blood. On the internet, I looked up the medical dictionary definition of "hematidrosis" and found the following: an extremely rare condition characterized by the "excretion of bloody sweat." It occurs in highly stressful events such as facing death, or other devastating catastrophes. The capillaries, threadlike blood vessels, surrounding the sweat glands, rupture, oozing blood into the glands which push bloody clots out the sweat ducts. Some scientists, including Dr. Barbet, describe this as an intense mentally disturbing experience indicating anxiety and agony as the struggle between Jesus' humanity and divinity is psychologically and spiritually waged within Him. In Luke 22:44, we read "In his anguish he prayed even more earnestly and his sweat fell to the ground like great drops of blood." The skin becomes bruised, very tender and very sore. In a real sense Jesus is experiencing the painful abuses he will face in the coming hours. His agony in the garden is a proximate foreshadowing of the torture and death He will undergo later this evening and tomorrow. He accepts the cup of suffering now, but He will challenge that acceptance again on the Cross. He is faithful to His Father now, and His fidelity will be challenged again as He prepares to give up His humanity. He accepts His Father's will now and will reconfirm His acceptance on the Cross. The struggle is not over.

How do the disciples respond? They slept through Jesus' agony. I wonder how often we, also His disciples, His followers, sleep through the agony of people during the course of our own lifetime. We should think about how we respond to others, but there is no time to dwell on that question now, because Judas has arrived with members of the Sanhedrin who are backed by some Roman soldiers. They are here to arrest Jesus and to "railroad" Him through the farce of legal "trials" before dragging Him away to His execution.

Words and actions have meanings. They are intended to convey "something" that is recognizable as widely or universally accepted. A kiss is essentially a sign of affection, a welcoming gesture or a thankful acknowledging for someone who has done a kindness. Judas betrays Jesus by betraying the meaning of a kiss. He kisses Jesus as a sign to the mob that this is the man to arrest. This was a "kiss of death!" This is a distortion of any sign of affection or care. Judas didn't have to betray Jesus. He made a free choice. If Judas had not betrayed Jesus, we would be reading the gospels differently. Jesus certainly had "ruffled feathers" and had bothered people to change their ways. But what Jesus did throughout His public ministry did not call for nor deserve what was about to be a terribly painful end to His earthly life.

While all of us have the possibility of changing for the better, many of us are either afraid to change or unwilling. We become satisfied with who we are and what our current situation is. We should acknowledge that hatred is not the only expression that is opposed to love. Fear is also the opposite of love. We spoke previously (chapter two) about Aristotle's "mean of virtue." Virtuous expression is the mean, or balance between excessive and defective expression. The virtue of love as consistently practiced is what allows us to accept not only ourselves, but others as well. Virtuous living should be our aim in life so that we can share our journey together. Hatred is excessive, or distorted opposition to love and is expressed by those who persecute and condemn the innocent, simply because they are trying to be caring people. Also opposed to caring, or love, is the defective or insufficient choice some people make to refuse to reach out to others. They are afraid to acknowledge virtue, or goodness. Maybe they think that they will be expected to act accordingly and choose "not to get involved." They become guarded. They build walls instead of bridges. In order to love, in order to become a virtuous person means allowing oneself to become vulnerable, able to be wounded. Without vulnerability, there is no possibility for interpersonal growth. Those who hate are trying to replace love with slavery through power, and those who fear to love are refusing to acknowledge the significance of their fellow pilgrims.

What was Judas' motive? Was he disappointed that Jesus was not a warrior Messiah who would lead the people in battle against the Romans? We can understand this position. There are those among us, even today, who think, or supposedly think that a combative or military stance is the only way to show others that we mean what we say. Was he an opportunist? He saw the possibility of making some money and took it. Was the challenge to love others as Jesus loves them not how he was willing to act? That might involve too much of a change on his part. He did try to return the thirty pieces of silver he was paid for his treachery. Was that the beginning of an apology, of being sorry? We don't know. He certainly did not follow through on confessing that He was sorry for what he did. What he did was contemptible, sinful, and wrong. Then Judas went out and hanged himself. Why? He did not think he could be forgiven. If this is so, and I am inclined to think this, then my thought is: how incredibly heartbreaking! In the time he traveled with Jesus he heard His words but obviously did not listen to them closely, and so never took them to heart. He saw what Jesus did but seemingly neither understood nor appreciated His actions. Before we leave Judas, I just want to say that I pray for him [-] not for what he did but rather because he thought he did something so terrible that he could not be forgiven. What a horrible and desperate feeling that must be! To think that any of us could do something so terrible that a freely creating and merciful God would not be willing to forgive us is the depth of despair. Injustice calls for punishment but despair calls for mercy. I pray for mercy for Judas.

I am aware that forgiveness is an act of love, and that in the Lord's Prayer we say "forgive us our trespasses as we forgive those who trespass against us." If one doesn't ask for forgiveness, one can reasonably assume that forgiveness doesn't happen, because like love, it is a relationship. If I have hurt you, and I don't say that I am sorry, then, the consequences are different than if I do ask for forgiveness, for mercy, whether you grant me this, or not. We don't know if Judas ever asked for forgiveness. Knowing that we are both powerful and fragile simultaneously, my prayer is for another human being, who like me at times, has allowed weakness rather than strength to determine a choice. And there are consequences for our choices.

The other disciples did not fare too well either. They abandoned Jesus in His hour of need. His companions, His friends, fled in fear. Rather than supporting Him, they ran away. I wonder if they hid together as a group or whether it was every man for himself. They did have reason to be afraid because they were known to be Jesus' companions. Peter followed at a distance. He was being cautious. No sense for both Jesus and he to be arrested. I guess his was a strategic maneuver; so that he would be available when needed. After all, he swore that nothing evil would befall Jesus as long as he was on the scene. Within a few hours, the gospels tell us that Peter had denied knowing Jesus three times. Like the betrayal of Judas and the abandonment of the other disciples, Peter's denial of Jesus was contemptible, sinful, and wrong. Unlike Judas, when Peter realized what he had done, "...he went outside, and wept bitterly." (Mt 26:75) His response differed dramatically from Judas. For Peter, the relationship with Jesus was more important than the terrible deed he had done. Peter remembered what Jesus had said and done and what that meant. Jesus is the Messiah promised of old and the Messiah is both loving and forgiving. In his sorrow Peter confesses his wrongdoing and is reconciled with Jesus. Time will tell whether his repentance and the willingness to change his ways will lead him to become the faithful servant he was called to be.

In the course of the evening and early morning, apparently there were two sham trials. One was initiated by the members of the Sanhedrin, the chief priest of whom was Caiaphas. The Sanhedrin was essentially the supreme court of Jewish affairs, both religious and secular. At this time, it operated with restricted or diminished authority because it was subject to Roman occupation and rule. However, it could recommend death for anyone persecuted through its court proceedings, though it could not execute that order. That belonged to the Romans under the leadership of Pontius Pilate, the Roman prefect of Judea. Like the Sanhedrin officials, he would do anything, whether legal or illegal, to hold onto his position, whether it was the ethical action to take or not. This occasioned the need for a second trial to obtain Roman approval for capital punishment.

The "religious" trial is based on the fear of the officials that Jesus was becoming too popular and people were listening to and encouraged by His message of love. Their position of "authority" was being challenged. They wanted Jesus stopped, not so much because of what He preached, but because they were threatened with the loss of imagined power and prestige. They cared primarily about their own positions, in much the same way that so many contemporary social and political leaders care more about themselves than their constituents, the people for whom they took an oath to represent lawfully and ethically. In a real sense, jealousy, and fear, is at the root of the charge concocted against Jesus. In John, chapter eleven, after Jesus had raised Lazarus from the dead, there was a meeting of the Sanhedrin. ""What are we to do with this man (Jesus) performing all sorts of signs (miracles)? If we let him go on like this, the whole world will believe in him. Then the Romans will come in and sweep away our sanctuary and our nation... Caiaphas (said)... it is better...to have one man (Jesus) die for the nation than to have the whole nation destroyed...From that day on there was a plan afoot to kill him (Jesus)..." When the selectively chosen and manipulated Sanhedrin crowd, on Friday morning, cries "Crucify Him", the Roman "leader" in the political or criminal "trial" capitulates in order to keep "peace." Pilate doesn't want the people of Judea complaining to Rome about his tenure. The cowardly Pilate doesn't want to "make waves" and so he dispenses the horribly unfair sentence of crucifixion, usually reserved for the most heinous of criminals. The Jewish leaders treasured their social and religious positions over the truth and Pilate treasured expediency over justice. Neither the religious nor the political officials discharged the leadership qualities which their offices deserved. Shame on both their houses!

What happened to Jesus before and during the trials is unspeakable. He was tortured. He was slapped and punched and kicked and spat upon and verbally abused and scourged. According to Roman law, a condemned prisoner was to be scourged prior to his crucifixion. This was done to weaken him physically. Would this hasten the dying process in the tortured person? Probably not by very much because crucifixion is designed to bring about a slow death with a maximum amount of pain and suffering. The fact that no vital organ is penetrated, guarantees that crucifixion will usually be a lengthy and extremely painful process. When Jesus is scourged, He had not yet been condemned to death [-] so much for Roman law. The prisoner is stripped of his clothing and bound by the wrists to a column. The beating is usually administered (what a terrible misuse of a word – administered) by two soldiers alternating lashes until the legal number of thirty-nine strokes have been given. I am sure that often enough, no one kept count. The whip, or flagellum, had several single or braided leather thongs which were of different lengths. They were tipped with small iron balls and/or animal bones, usually sheep bones. The leather thongs lacerated the skin ripping it apart from the victim's bones, while the lethal tips caused deep contusions, or bruises on the back that had already been seriously damaged by the shedding of blood in the Garden of Gethsemane. As the lashes are applied in synchronization, the entire back becomes one bloody oozing furrow on top of the others. Unable to stand, He slowly sinks to the ground. Did He scream much? Was He too exhausted, too tired, to cry out? Did they—we—kick Him while He was down, or spit on Him in derision?

Previously, I wrote that I believe today's world is the same biblical Garden of Eden. Its appearance has changed but it continues to be the place and the time of the covenant. We live in the Original Grace of God's creation and we share the original sin of refusing His love, His covenant. Along the same lines, I don't think Christmas is simply a night that happened at some specified time in history. I think that God, Emmanuel, continues to embrace our humanity and we continue to respond to Him. Some of us are shepherds who care for family and friends and others who are unable to care for themselves. Some of us are like the magi, seeking knowledge and entering into adventures which will help many to understand this life we share. Some of us are like the innkeeper. We are too busy making money and taking care of ourselves to bother with others. We have neither room nor time in our lives for other individuals, their families or their needs. Then there are those of us who, like Herod persecute others because we have some power, whether lawfully or unlawfully gained. It could be financial or political or military strength which we use to prevent others from making their earthly journey a peaceful one. We refuse to accept God's covenant by building fortresses to wall people out instead of bridges and tunnels to allow access between people, whether as individuals, communities, or nations. Today is Christmas. Everyday is Christmas. It is not simply a calendar event, but it is an ongoing human experience which involves our relationship with our creating God. We either appreciate the gift of life by being caretakers, or we abuse the gift of life by refusing to be appreciative guests, and instead, act as if parts of the world should belong exclusively to us. We grasp the power to abuse and enslave others in the process. Maybe we think that being home owners or business owners, or corporate management or government leaders entitles us to claim ownership of this world, or parts of this world, or the resources of this world. We hoard what nature produces and distribute nature's bounty in accordance with our own self indulgent whims. We overlook or we deny that essentially we are guests in this world, on this planet. We come into existence and we will go out of human existence, and the world will still be here...without us. There will be other guests. What will we have left for them? What will they leave for others?

I am convinced that we acknowledge the joy of the Last Supper every day through our own Eucharistic celebrations. God identifies with the fruit of the earth and the work of human hands and gives Himself to us to remind us how significant we are. He continues to nourish us on our earthly journey. He is the "bread of life." He is our reason for rejoicing. We know, only too well, that there is not simply joy, but there is sadness, and hurt and sorrow as well. There is contemporary pain that not even a call to an army of lawyers can resolve, despite what some television commercials might guarantee in their advertisements. I think that God is scourged today as He was on the evening before and the morning of His Crucifixion on Golgotha. There is simply a different cast of characters "administering" the blows. Who are they?

The first blow came from someone who raped another person, or murdered someone, or stole someone's identity on the internet causing severe loss of property and valuables. The second blow came from someone who, with vicious compatriots and mercenaries, have slaughtered and driven innocent people from their homeland, simply because they are religiously or ethnically or politically different. They have destroyed communities and ravaged the countryside in an obscene attempt to obliterate civilizations. This is followed by a blow from someone unwilling to give assistance to those who are in need of help because they are refugees. Then a blow from a CEO who took financial care of himself at the expense of hundreds or thousands of employees who lost their jobs, their pensions, their life savings, their homes and their dignity to satisfy the desire of one mean and selfish individual. Then a blow from a pedophile priest, who denied His vow to be an Alter Christus and instead became an alter Satan, denying to a child the gift of innocence. The next blow comes from an unscrupulous politician who abandons his call to serve the public, plunging so many people into despair by lining his own pockets and those of his horrible associates with ill begotten and undeserved wealth and power. Another blow is done by a safety inspector whose acceptance of a bribe overlooks a dangerous public situation which eventually causes some innocent civilians to be killed and others to be maimed. Surely he didn't mean for people to be fatally hurt; it was just a case of collateral damage. Then there is the blow from the politically connected gentleman, who, seduced by a special interest lobbyist, refuses to introduce legal proceedings which are designed for public safety or public benefit. The next blow is "administered" by the school or neighborhood bully on those shy and timid or sickly people who are defenseless. They are mocked and ridiculed by those who care only for themselves and who refuse to see "the face of God" in the downtrodden and poor. There is a blow from a drug trafficker whose aim is to intentionally and maliciously destroy God's gift of life. There, a blow from a slave trader or human trafficker who lines his pockets not only with money illicitly gotten, but also with the sweat and blood and degradation of poor innocent victims. A blow is given by a rumor monger on the internet whose lies and fabrications drive a fragile adolescent to suicide.

I could not see who dealt the next lash. Was it a police officer hiding behind his badge, inflicting violence on a perpetrator, or victim, while bringing disgrace upon all who serve faithfully to uphold the significance of the badge of lawful authority? Or was it a parent, or a teacher who was too busy with personal concerns to hear the story of his or her child or student who was crying out for help [-] "a voice crying in the wilderness." Maybe it was a bishop covering up for a pedophile priest thus becoming like so many others whose refusal to act as justice demands instead become enablers of people who continue to do terrible things to themselves and to others. Maybe it was a husband or a wife who broke the vows they took to be faithful to each other at the altar, or in the synagogue, or before the legal representative of the state. Maybe it was a doctor or a nurse who broke the vow to "do no harm." Maybe it was someone, or a couple, who decided that "pro choice" meant a human being, in his or her fetal stage of personal growth, has "no choice." Perhaps it was someone who thought that "I am my brother's and sister's keeper" was only a greeting card slogan and not a commandment to care for the downtrodden and abandoned.

I look at my hand and I am holding a whip. Did I use it when I failed to do what I should have done? Or did I use it when I performed an action that "tore someone down" instead of a loving act which is always designed to "build someone up." I am sorry and like Peter, I weep bitterly. I drop the whip and hope and pray that I will wield it no more, but that I will follow Our Lord to Calvary's hill and beyond. Only time, and prayer, and resolve will tell if my sorrow is genuine.

After more physical (the crowning with thorns) and verbal abuse, Jesus is condemned to death by crucifixion. There are two parts to the cross. The *stipes*, the vertical piece, is already planted on Calvary's hill. The other part, the *patibulum*, which is the horizontal piece, must be carried by the condemned. It weighs upwards of nearly one hundred pounds. It is the size and shape of a railroad tie or cross beam, but it is neither planed nor sanded nor in any way smooth. The jagged edges of the raw wood will cut into the bruised and bloody shoulders opening up more wounds along the way. How is Jesus to carry this about one third of a mile from the Roman seat of authority, The Fortress of Antonio, to Golgotha? It is about five or six city streets which are neither paved nor smooth, but rather strewn with rocks and pebbles and hard dirt. He hasn't eaten or slept since last evening. He has been physically beaten and battered. He has been verbally abused. He has shed much blood and clearly is extremely fatigued after His scourging. Emotionally, He has

273

been betrayed, abandoned, and denied by His friends and companions. And finally He has been unjustly sentenced to death. He must certainly be a pitiable figure, but the carrying of the Cross is about to begin. He really should be going to an emergency room for treatment, but that is not going to happen.

Probably the clearest picture we might have of Jesus' journey is that He will stagger along the way, burdened not only by the weight of the cross, or the pain which races through His body at every uneven step, but also by the realization that He alone is bearing this oppressive load. Why? Perhaps what He says on the Cross will give us some clue, but this suffering can't possibly be the primary reason that He embraced our humanity. Hopefully, we will learn more, but now let us concentrate on the scene unfolding before us. Surely He hears the scornful taunts and derisive shouts of the pitiless crowd? Does His mind wander back a few days to the Palm Sunday crowd that welcomed Him into Jerusalem with festival shouts of "Hosannah," which roughly translates as "save us, we beseech you"? Where are they? Were they the pilgrims who came long distances to the feast and have since returned home? Are some of them at home now preparing for the Passover dinner? Are they aware of what is happening? If some are, then perhaps they simply can't be bothered to come out to see Him. They are too busy with housework. Imagine the two Jerusalem walks that Jesus took within one week. One was a triumphant Messianic welcome on Palm Sunday and the other was the vicious and tragic condemnation of the "King of the Jews" on this day, which is called Good Friday.

Jesus falls three times while carrying the Cross. Does He sink slowly to the ground or is it like a vicious shove as if the burden of the cross is intentionally adding to the terrible pain of a man whose strength has been sapped by His ongoing suffering? He can't put His hands in front of Him to cushion the force of the fall. He falls flat on His face. Each time He hits the hard ground, it jars His body multiplying and magnifying the pain. Why doesn't He simply lie there and die. "It is neither the time nor the hour." The primary question for his executioners had to be whether or not He would be able to get up and move on. We can only imagine that given His physical condition, the burden of the cross, and merciless terrain that He had to travel, it was both brutal and exhausting.

Each fall triggers more pain and more hurt. Each attempt to struggle to His feet involves more agonizing movement. How will He make it?

There were three people who reached out to Him in efforts to make His journey a bit bearable. There was His mother Mary, Simon of Cyrene, and Veronica. How terribly heartbreaking it must have been for Mary to see her son treated like this, and for Jesus to know how crushed His mother's heart and spirit were as they encountered each other on His painful journey. He is stumbling along dragging the cross. She stands grief stricken, unable to comfort Him in her arms. Anyone who is a parent knows how terrible it is to lose a child and with conditions like this, how unjust, how unfair, all of this is. The loss of a child under any circumstances shakes one's faith in a caring and loving God. Part of the answer to any suffering parent's prayer and plea is how to accept what one doesn't ever want to experience. It can only begin to emerge when there is thanksgiving for the time the parents shared life with the child and when there is the realization that God will never abandon anyone He freely created and whom He loves. Do we believe God really loves us no matter what? He created us. Do we believe that makes us important to Him? If we do, then it is eventually possible for sorrow to become bearable and even eventually for joy to find its way back into one's life. When will Mary's sorrow yield once again to joy? Or will that never happen?

I often wonder what Simon's thoughts were especially in those first few moments. The soldiers were afraid that Jesus might not make it and so he is randomly chosen to help Jesus carry His cross. Was his first thought "why me?" Perhaps, much more importantly is: what are his last thoughts [-] both on that day of suffering and later on in his life? Sometimes it takes dramatic and/or spontaneous events to fracture our complacency in life and challenge us to face and embrace what is really important, what is really meaningful, in life. Too frequently we allow ourselves to fall into thoughtless routines and become blind and deaf to the world's beauty and ugliness. What meaning in life did Simon draw from his "pressed into service" experience that day? Would we be willing to help Jesus on that day? What about today? How willing are we to serve? Or do we try desperately to avoid any of today's Calvary hills?

Veronica, or Saint Veronica, is not mentioned in any of the scriptural accounts. She does appear in the liturgical devotion, the Stations of the Cross, as part of the Church's tradition. The tradition states that Veronica was a devout woman of the first century who compassionately wiped the face of Jesus as He collapsed under the cross leaving a miraculous image of Himself. (In Latin, vera means "true" and icon means "image"; hence, the true image of face of Christ on Ver-onica's veil.) It is a Christian legend which is passed along in the hopes that it would inspire Christians to be as willing as Veronica to act kindly and with pity even though all around her is a pitiless crowd. A legend usually has some link to historical events, but other than what has been passed down through the Church tradition, there is no other way to authenticate her presence as we can for Mary and for Simon of Cyrene. Perhaps, the most significant aspect of Veronica's action is the challenge to how any of us would act in situations where someone is suffering without the support of anyone else in the crowd. Do we stand up for the unjustly accused in life, or do we disappear into the merciless crowd?

Finally Jesus reaches Calvary's hill upon which there are three crosses. One is for Him while the others are for two convicted felons. Jesus is stripped of His clothing and the stripping opens up wounds on His backs and legs as more loss of blood is experienced. It is like ripping bandages that are tightly stuck on one's skin and that hurts. His arms are stretched out on the *patibulum* and long thick nails, probably five to seven inches, are driven into both wrists riveting Him to the cross. Pulling Him upwards, with no ability to shift Himself in order to avoid any bit of pain, the executioners nail the *patibulum,* or cross bar, to the *stipes,* or vertical piece of wood planted in the ground. His thumbs are tapping furiously because the median nerves, in each wrist, are being scraped by the nails and this sends burning sensations continually to the brain. Unless placed in some kind of a splint, the pain and numbness caused by aggravating the median nerves can be continuous. Carpel tunnel syndrome, with varying painful experiences, is associated with these nerve aberrations. As He is being lifted up, His head bangs repeatedly against the wood driving the crown of thorns deeper into his scalp and bleeding increases. The "procedure" is not finished yet. His right foot is placed on top of His left foot and with a few hammer blows his feet are nailed to the *stipes.* His body sags and will continue to sag for three hours hindering his breathing. In order to breathe, or in order to speak, He will have to press painfully on His feet to lift Himself up even the slightest bit. He can hold this lifted position for but a few seconds, or perhaps, at most, a minute, and then His body will drop and the breathing will become more labored. It is only a short while until tetanisation sets in causing muscle spasms throughout the body and this will last for three hours. Now, this is not simply a painful spasm in the arm, or neck, or leg. These spasms are experienced repeatedly throughout the body for the entire time He is alive on the Cross.

The sun beats down, the insects buzz around and land on His face, and the taunts of the jeering crowd continues. They are merciless. It is like a sick show. The usual responses from the crucified victims include cries to put them out of their misery, and blasphemies and curses that would incite the crowd to more venomous cries and catcalls. Jesus is trying to speak. Will He contribute to the sick spectacle? He speaks: **Father, forgive them. They do not know what it is they are doing.** (Luke 23:34) This is clearly not what anyone expected to hear. It is not a contemptuous cry or a curse. It is a prayer asking the Heavenly Father to forgive all the people responsible for this [-] Caiaphas and the "religious" officials, Pilate and the Roman executioners, the jeering crowd, the lying "witnesses" at the "trials," Peter and the rest of the disciples who abandoned Him, and everyone of us who has failed to love others as we ought. The crowd expected venom to be spewed from the mouth of the condemned, not forgiveness, which is an act of love in the midst of His own pain and suffering and sorrow. They expected that He would match their curses with His own curses, their contempt with His own contempt, but they never expected Him to intercede for them with God the Father. They never expected Jesus to pray for them. But then, some of them had probably never heard His message of love proclaimed for the past few years, or if some of them had, they did not pay any attention to it.

Shortly after, the two thieves being crucified spoke to Jesus. One asked Him to escape from his painful, but apparently legally justified, punishment and the other, acknowledging his sinfulness, asked simply to be remembered when Jesus comes into His kingdom. Jesus turns to the latter and says: **I promise you, this day you will be with Me in**

Paradise. (Luke 23:43) This is another utterance of forgiveness by the painfully dying Jesus. Did the "good" thief ever hear Jesus say: "Ask and it will be given to you; seek, and you will find; knock and the door shall be opened to you..." (Matthew 7:7)? Somehow I doubt it. Was he raised as a child to pray, but in the course of choosing a criminal career, abandoned it? None of us knows. This might even be the first prayer he ever uttered. Jesus will return to the Father with a sinner at His side. Given Jesus' track record, this shouldn't be a surprise to anyone. There is room at the banquet table of the Father for this convicted criminal. I mentioned before that there is always "open seating" when Jesus shares the table with us. Even though He just met this man today, Jesus is a welcoming host to a condemned felon.

Seeing His mother with His disciple, John, Jesus says to them: **Woman, behold thy son...**and...**Behold thy mother.** (John 19:26-27) These were certainly words of care and concern for His beloved and sorrowing Mother. He is still expressing His love for others despite the continuous physical suffering. I don't think there are any legal considerations, or conditions, involved. John is not simply accepting legal responsibility, or guardianship, nor is Mary going to "adopt" John. John is standing in our place at the foot of the Cross. He is representing all of us, all of humankind, and from this day forward Mary is our mother. She is the first of all the disciples and we pray for her maternal intercession on our behalf. When encountering difficulties in life, the majority of us will turn to Mom for help. Jesus knows this and in the midst of His own painful suffering, He continues to look out for us, giving us His "Mommy" to be our own, to care for us as lovingly and as unconditionally as He still cares for us.

The synoptic gospel authors tell us that from noon (the sixth hour of daylight) until three o'clock, darkness (an omen?) covered the whole land. At the ninth hour, Jesus cries out, "Eloi, Eloi, lama sabachthani" referring to Psalm 22 which begins **My God, My God, why have you forsaken me?** (Mark 15:34) In the Garden of Gethsemane, Jesus had prayed that His suffering might pass, but He accepted it when He said to His Father "...let your will be done, not mine." (Luke 22:42) He accepted martyrdom; so why is Jesus now crying out about His Father forsaking Him? Prior to beginning His public ministry, in the desert, He was tempted to despair, but He overcame the temptation. One despairs because he thinks God is not listening. This is not a cry of despair because He is calling out to the Father, even though He is not using the familiar "Abba, Father." If Jesus were genuinely despairing, His cry would not be to God. We have to remember that the psalms are very much part of the liturgical expressions of the Israelites. Psalms are prayers. To pray means to communicate with God; to speak to God and to listen for how God will respond. When Jesus utters these words, there must have been recognition by some, if not the majority of the crowd that the reference is indeed to Psalm 22. They would realize that it does begin with the lament that God seems far away during an individual man's or a community's sense of being alone and in some kind of distress, but it changes dramatically at the end. The psalm continues with the words *"In thee our fathers trusted...and thou didst deliver them. To thee they cried and were saved..."* The psalm confirms that their ancestors' faith was rewarded because they knew that God wouldn't abandon them. He heard them. While this reflects some initial comfort, the psalmist's lament continues until the end when sorrow turns to praise:

"...You who fear Yahweh, praise Him! All you sons of Jacob, glorify him, and stand in awe of him, all you sons of Israel! For he has not despised or abhorred the affliction of the afflicted; and he has not hid his face from him, but has heard, when he cried to him." I wonder if this led some of the crowd to reconsider what was happening, or did they simply ignore the cry, which is real, but what does it really mean? It had to make at least some of the onlookers stop and think: what are we doing? Does the same question enter into our minds?

Jesus is the innocent man who does not deserve to suffer, even more so than Job, or any innocent human being, past, present, or future. He is the most authentic image of Isaiah's Suffering Servant; so, why this cry? It has less to do with Jesus' relation to the Father, than it does with Jesus' relation to humankind, to us. Having embraced our humanity, He is experiencing what Judas experienced when he thought he could not be forgiven, but He turns to prayer instead of despair. He is experiencing what Job experienced when he thought that Yahweh was a legalistic and distant God rather than a caring and consoling God. He is experiencing what Nietzsche warned about when he said "God is dead. We have killed Him. We are His murderers. How shall we replace Him?" He is experiencing the hopelessness and hurt that any human being knows or senses when he or she cannot or will not return God's love. The prophet Isaiah, during the Babylonian Captivity, circa 587 to 539 BC, spoke of the Suffering Servant who will unjustly suffer for his people. Throughout history, many found it too difficult to relate this person with the Messiah. But in this fourth Suffering Servant song, or oracle, by Isaiah, we are looking at the Messianic Suffering Servant image of Jesus in Mark's gospel:

> *He was spurned and avoided by men, a man of suffering... Yet it was our infirmities that he bore, our sufferings that he endured...While we thought of him as stricken, as one smitten by God and afflicted. But he was pierced by our offenses, crushed for our sins; upon him was the chastisement that makes us whole, by his stripes we were healed. We had all gone astray like sheep, each following his own way; but the Lord laid upon him the guilt of us all* (From Isaiah 52:13 – 53:12)

Paul's second letter to the Corinthians further helps us to understand what is happening:

> *For our sakes God made him who did not know sin to be sin, so that in him we might become the very holiness of God* (2Cor 5:21)

Jesus embraced our humanity in its entirety. Jesus' sense of being forsaken is our sense of being forsaken when we refuse to accept God's love, for whatever reason. Is there no answer when we experience the loss of God in our lives? This must be the depth of Jesus' spiritual suffering. The depth of His physical suffering is uttered in the next words. **I thirst.** (John 19:28) There is no wonder that He is thirsty. The continuous pain, the sagging body, the tremendous effort to speak from time to time have emptied Him of His strength and dried Him up. Jesus links His physical thirst to our physical and spiritual thirst. The answer to all our thirst is God's presence in our lives. Jesus' painful experience resonates with the rich man in hell begging Lazarus to wet his tongue (see chapter five.) Jesus thirsts for everyone, for all souls, both those that are saved by His suffering and those who are lost despite His suffering. In the synoptic accounts, Jesus is offered vinegar (wine) on a stick for His thirst, but John specifies it is a hyssop stick. In the Book of Exodus the Jewish people sacrifice the Passover lamb and then using a hyssop plant stick sprinkle the blood on the doorposts of the Israelite families. This will protect them from the punishment that the Egyptians will suffer for their persecution of God's chosen people. John is obviously indicating that Jesus is the new Passover Lamb, whose sacrifice is universal, for all people. His blood is shed for our sins, for our refusal to respond to the covenant.

The Messianic Suffering Servant Who has embraced our humanity for the purpose of reclaiming all of us for the Creating Father realizes in His pain and suffering that His death may not redeem all of us. And still he suffers knowing that He has been rejected by some of us who refuse to love, who refuse to see the "face of God" in those whom they encounter, who rape the earth's resources and claim ownership over a world in which they, like us, are guests. They too, were made in the image and likeness of God, but turned away. I guess that the ultimate human pain, which Jesus embraced as fully as anyone of us has, is humanity's rejection of the goodness of creation, both spiritual and material.

The time is near and Our Lord knows it. He says **It is finished!** (John 19:30) What is finished? Is it His earthly pain and suffering? I don't think so because as long as He is breathing, no matter how shallow, He is still suffering. The muscle spasms and the pain from the median nerves being scraped by the nails are still present. The body is sagging and this is escalating the asphyxiation which will ultimately cause His earthly death. With the difficulty of breathing and the inability to raise one's body because of the pain and suffering, the crucified one eventually chokes to death. Jesus has just spoken again; so He is not yet dead. So, what is finished? The Messiah of old has come as promised to God's people to remind them of the covenant, of how precious they are to Him. The Suffering Servant has given Himself for everyone who has been and will be "made in the image and likeness of God." The

Champion of the Outcasts has raised the lowly to great places. God has embraced our humanity giving it a significance that had been lost in the Garden of Eden, replenished at the Last Supper, remembered in the Garden of Gethsemane and renewed, fulfilled, sanctified, made holy again, on the Cross on Calvary's hill. The covenant between God and humankind is once and for all fully rekindled. Salvation history is complete because the Son has identified with all humanity, past, present and future, and offered Himself through the torturous suffering of the Cross as a sacrifice for our failure to keep the covenant. Jesus is not the only innocent person who has unjustly suffered in life, but He is the only person Who could heal the broken covenant. The Creator God never abandoned the covenant, but we did. God became man so that the covenant could be renewed not as a one time temporal experience, but as an ongoing and continuously living experience. God has ransomed (redeemed) His people through His dying on the Cross, not simply for this day only, but for all time and beyond, for eternity. How do I respond to what is happening? Remember that belief, faith, goes beyond reason, not against reason. Is it reasonable for me to take God at His word, "There is no greater love than this: that one lays down his life for his friends...I call you friends.... (John 15:13-15)? These words He spoke at the Last Supper. These words are being expressed now on the Cross. If actions speak louder than words, how do I respond to His actions, to the words of forgiveness He asked of His Father, and to the words He is about to utter? My answer has consequences for me.

As if to say that He is doing this of His own will, Jesus cries out one last time, **Abba, Father, into Your hands I commit My Spirit.** (Lk 23:45) Jesus dies confirming the words He prayed in the Garden of Gethsemane, "...not my will, but yours be done..." Jesus dies trusting in the love of the Father Who sent Him to us at Christmas to reemphasize that we are made in God's image. He dies calling to each of us to accept His invitation to us to serve lovingly, and without conditions, and by doing what he is doing now [-] committing Himself to the Father. Since actions speak louder than words, Jesus knows that we can freely do this. Jesus doesn't die because of Adam and Eve's original sin, or because of our sinning. Jesus dies because He loves us. He chose to accept the Cross because in God's eyes we are "worth it." Love's fidelity trumps sorrow's suffering allowing joy to reign in life. C.S. Lewis in writing "The Chronicles of Narnia" portrays Jesus in his fantasy world of Narnia as Aslan the Lion. Aslan's universal acceptance of all creatures, human, talking beasts, and mythological characters like unicorns, centaurs, dwarfs and other beings is a reflection of Jesus' universal acceptance of all of us. Aslan also sacrifices himself for another in "The Lion, the Witch, and the Wardrobe" and rises from the altar of death. At the end of the book, the faun, Mr. Tumnus, a follower of Aslan, says to Lucy that Aslan is not a tame lion. She replies but he is good. Jesus is not a tame God, but He is good and we are the recipients of His goodness.

As Jesus dies, each of the gospel authors declare that initially it is a non-believer who acknowledges that Jesus is truly the "Son of God." The centurion or commander of the legionaries on Calvary's hill states it emphatically. (In Luke, the wording is "Certainly this man was innocent.") John again describes the scene using symbolic references as emphasis that Jesus, the Glorified Christ, is in control of His passion and death. Remember that earlier it was pointed out that a general distinction between the synoptic authors and the Johannine author is that the former focus on Jesus' humanity without ignoring His divinity, while the latter focuses upon Jesus' divinity without ignoring His humanity. John describes the centurion as thrusting his spear into Jesus' side to confirm that He is dead. "But one of the soldiers pierced His side with a spear, and there came out blood and water.' (Jn 19:34) In Jewish sacrificial law, the blood of the Paschal, or Passover Lamb must flow out onto the altar. John is identifying Jesus as the sacrificial Lamb of the New Testament, whose crucifixion offers redemption for *all* mankind, through the sacrifice of His own Blood. It symbolizes man being ransomed (redeemed) from the effects of sin to the friendship of God's grace. The covenant is renewed through the sacrifice of the Suffering Servant. The water that flows from Jesus' side symbolizes baptism, which is the sacrament of welcoming into the community of God's people, the Church.

The Jewish authorities want the crosses to be removed because it is the Passover, and they did not want any distraction from the feasting. The Roman authorities, satisfied that Jesus is dead, give His body over to His friends to be buried.

The World's Fair was held in New York City in 1964. One day, Dona and I took Pat and John, our two oldest boys to Flushing Meadows where the Fair was held. Our youngest, at the time, Marty, was in the caring company of Grandma. That day was the first time I had seen Michelangelo's sculpture "The Pieta." It is also the first time that Pat, who was five years old, and John who was three saw this incredible sculpture. I really doubt that, at that time, it affected them in the same way that it affected me. This is why experience is so important in life. Experience offers different ways of looking at reality. For some of us, experience offers a clearer way of envisioning life and for others unfortunately, it confirms a distorted view of the human condition. "The Pieta" is a magnificent work of art carved around 1498-1500. Shortly afterwards, it arrived in its permanent home which is in Saint Peter's Basilica in Rome. It depicts Jesus, after He has been taken down from the cross and placed in His mother's arms before being entombed. Chiseled from Italian Carrara marble it measures roughly five and one-half feet by six and one-half feet. Certainly it is an imposing work of art. We have seen it a number of times since on our visits to Rome and very recently an amazing bronze replica (only several inches tall, but again magnificently sculpted) at the Frick Museum in New York City. Each time I have seen it I am moved by the artistic mastery which captures this incredible image of salvation. As impressive as Michelangelo's "David" is, "The Pieta" is even more impressive because of the subject matter and the meaning it offers to all of us.

Michelangelo's masterpiece depicts Mary as sad but accepting, so it seems, of her son's death. Jesus also has an aura of peace about Him. I believe that the artist's purpose included moving the viewer's perspective from the horror of the Crucifixion to the anticipated glory of the impending Resurrection. It certainly captures that hope. And yet I can't help but think that the thirteenth station of the "Via Dolorosa" (the Stations of the Cross) would not be as comforting a picture. I envision Mary sobbing uncontrollably as she desperately holds onto the broken body of her unjustly crucified son. She held Him in her arms on Christmas morning, a tiny beautiful baby (all babies are beautiful.) She nursed Him and played with Him and watched Him as He grew, and knew He was different. But she is a mother and whether we call it "maternal instinct" or use some other phrase, there is a bond between mother and child that cannot be duplicated in any other interpersonal relationship in the world. Believe me, I am the father of five boys. It's truly wonderful. I also wonder about her parents, Joachim and Anna. Did they play with Jesus, their grandchild, in the same way we played with our grandchildren? I am sure they did. We simply don't have photographs as memories. In the "original" Pieta, as the crucified Jesus was taken down from the cross, Mary had to be devastated. Her pain came close to matching His pain, except His pain was over because He was dead. She could feel in His lifeless body the blows from the whips, the blood flowing from the crown of thorns and the nails, and the slow painful torture of His hours hanging on the cross. Her tears must have mixed with the blood still oozing from Him. I don't know if she fought to hold onto Him as His friends tried to ease His body from her grasp so as to prepare to bury Him. Did she remember what she said to Gabriel at the time of the Annunciation, "Behold, I am the handmaid of the Lord; let it be to me according to your word"(Lk 1:38)? Did she recall singing joyfully the Magnificat, "My soul magnifies the Lord, and my spirit rejoices in God, my Savior..." (Lk 2:46)? Was she able to remember her conversation with Simon when Jesus was circumcised (Lk 2:34-35)? "Behold this child is set for the fall and rising of many in Israel and for a sign that is spoken against (and a sword will pierce through your own soul also)..."

In 1815, the Church, in her wisdom, dedicated a new feast day for Mary, the Feast of Our Lady of the Seven Sorrows. When Jesus gave Mary into John's care as they stood at the foot of the Cross, Jesus knew that her sorrows would help her to be the most caring and compassionate Mother all of us could turn to in our own difficulties. As our universal Mother, she knows our hurts and she will hold us tenderly in her hands. From now on, she will be our strength in times of sorrow.

Throughout the ages, many people have wondered why this day is called "Good Friday" and not "Suffering Friday" or "Terrible Friday" or "Unjust Friday." A short answer may be that it only happened once. A deeper answer has to take into consideration all the events of the Easter Triduum [-] Holy Thursday, Good Friday, and Easter Sunday.

In the Johannine version of the Last Supper, Jesus says to His disciples, and to us, "I chose you..." He chose to represent us, all of humanity. He chose to be the one person Who could heal the covenant broken in the Garden of Eden. Just as Adam and Eve represent, or symbolize, all of us, mankind, in our choosing to sin, to break the covenant with the Creating Father; so the historical Jesus represents all of us, mankind, in healing and renewing the original covenant with the Father. The Father has always loved us and has manifested His concern through creation, through the call of the patriarchs, the prophets and the psalmists of the Old Testament, as well as through the birth, ministry and death of His beloved son, Emanuel, God become man. "God is love" John writes in his first letter. Only God could renew the covenant and only man, because we are sinners, should atone for the sinful breaking of the covenant. Jesus is God become Man and therefore the only one capable of restoring and renewing the original unconditional love of the Creator for His creation. I believe that the suffering of the Cross is endured because of the love of God for each of us. Had we not become sinners, there would be no need for Calvary. But we, personified by Adam and Eve, but not identical with them, became sinners through our own choices. So let's stop "passing the buck" and let's stop blaming Adam and Eve. Instead, let us concentrate on God's choice to love us, even when we fail to love ourselves and others, when we sin. This is what makes Good Friday [-] Good! God loves us even when we fail to return that love as we ought. Let us always remember that love is a relationship that requires both parties to contribute or the relationship will fail to become what it should. The Creating Father, the Redeeming Son, and the ever present Spirit attest to God's holding up His end of the covenant. The other end of the covenant calls for our response. Can we be appreciative by accepting what God has done (forgiven us), and become responsible for what we should do (Love one another as I have loved you)?

In one sense, I sometimes think that Good Friday should be the end of the story in which we recognize and realize God's love for us. But it is not. There is Easter Sunday and without it, perhaps we would never have appreciated the fullest extent of God's love. So the historical Jesus becomes the Risen Christ, and even that is not the end of the story.

A Glorious Act

How did the frightened band of disciples become the faithful followers, the messengers of Christ's "Good News" throughout history and the willing martyrs? They experienced the Glory of God.

When many, or most, of us worry about a real, or even possible negative experience in our lives we tend to lose focus on the "big picture" and try to zero in on what is bothering me individually and how to deal with it. Is it a financial problem? Am I being downsized at work? Am I worried about my paying for my children's educational pursuits, or perhaps some of the people with whom they associate? Are my parents' having health issues about which I should be concerned? These are clearly legitimate issues, but sometimes they become so overwhelming that I lose the ability to reasonably confront them by failing to put them into perspective. In a sense, this is understandable. I experience a fear or a sense of aloneness that can hinder any kind of constructive action. I think this is the situation facing the disciples after the Crucifixion of Jesus. The classic example of this is the story of the two disciples trying to escape from Jerusalem to Emmaus for fear that the authorities would arrest them. (Lk 24:13-35) They walked with a stranger along the way and he interpreted (the Old Testament) scripture for them. Because of their own paralyzing fears, they were blind to the presence of Jesus as the "stranger." It was only in the breaking of the (Eucharistic) bread at supper that they realized Who He is. The crucified Jesus has become the Risen Christ, the glory of God. They returned to Jerusalem, no longer afraid, to do the will of God's as Jesus had taught them. It is one of the more powerful of the post-Resurrection appearances of Jesus.

The disciples are concerned with what is going to happen to them. Jesus is gone and we're on our own. The authorities, no doubt, will hunt us down. If we are lucky, they will ignore us; so let's hide. I seriously doubt that initially they asked the question: what's going on, what does all this mean? If they prayed at all, it was probably that they wouldn't be found. They had heard what Jesus said, but did they listen closely enough? Did they understand? They saw what Jesus did. He raised Lazarus from the dead as well as Jairus' daughter and the son of the widow of Nain. Did they recall these miracles? I don't think so. They saw

Him heal the sick, feed the hungry, forgive sinners, welcome outcasts, teach with wisdom far beyond His earthly age. I think these are good men...frightened...but good. After all, they had been chosen and taught by God. They had performed good works in His name.

The apostles had been sidetracked by the ferociousness of the attack on Jesus. They had lost focus on what was important...their calling... and they got tied up in fear for themselves. Hatred, acting hostilely to others, is not the only opposite to love. Fear is also an opposite because it causes us to be paralyzed from acting towards others as we should. They cowered.

Salvation from eternal damnation has been gained for each of us by Jesus' death on the Cross. In His death, all humanity, past, present, and to come, is given the gift of eternal life because The Son has given Himself back to the Father. "Father into your hands I commend my Spirit." The covenant has been renewed for eternity.

As we saw in Chapter 4, any gift can be accepted or rejected by the one to whom the gift is offered. On the one hand, that includes the Father's gift of His Son, and we who received the gift of His Son. If His death on the Cross fulfills the ministry of Jesus, then the Resurrection and Ascension of Jesus, as well as the descent of the Holy Spirit upon the apostles are the expressions of the Father's acceptance of Jesus' sacrificial death/gift. They are also reminders to the disciples, including us, that God's love for us triumphs even death. What emphasizes that the Cross is a "glorious act" is that Jesus' embracing of our humanity proclaims that we are "worth it."

Let's be real. The apostles had to be thrilled with the post-Resurrection appearances of Jesus Whom they clearly recognized as their revered leader, their teacher. Jesus appears to them as the same person they have come to know and to love, **but** He is different. He is not simply restored to life like Lazarus or Jairus' daughter was. He is not simply resuscitated. But the difference in Jesus is a new life, a significant "fuller" life, a transformed life which expresses the glory, the splendor of God. He is the historical Jesus Who has become the Risen Christ.

The gospel authors try to give us some sense of this in describing the post-Resurrection appearances. Mary Magdalene doesn't initially recognize Him, thinking that He is the gardener (Jn 20:15.) There are the young men in white (angels?) sitting in the empty tomb directing the apostles where to go to meet with Jesus (Mk 16:5 and Lk 24:4). In John 20:19 we read "...the doors were closed in the room where the disciples were for fear of the Jews. Jesus came and stood in their midst...'Peace be to you,' and showed them his hands and his side. The disciples were filled with joy..." We read about doubting Thomas who was absent for one appearance and announces that he doesn't believe Jesus has risen. Unless I see Him, stammers Thomas, I won't believe what you are saying. Jesus returns to challenge him and call him to accept the Risen Christ, which the repentant Thomas humbly does. John's final chapter describes the presence of Jesus at the seashore of Tiberius where Jesus cooks breakfast for them after a frustrating night of fishing with no catch. Shouting from the shore, Jesus tells them what to do, and, miracle of miracles, their nets are overflowing with fish. They respond, not with "It is Jesus" but "It is the Lord." They recognize the glory of God in the transformed person they had called Rabbi, or Master.

Intuition, in the New World dictionary, is described as the "direct knowing or learning of something without the conscious use of reasoning; immediate apprehension or understanding." One looks at "something" and knows what to do or how to judge a situation. Reflection, from the Latin "to bend back with mind," involves fixing the mind on an object, contemplating it from different angles, weighing different factors and eventually reaching a conclusion as to what action to follow, or what decision to make. Sometimes we can intuit knowledge; e.g. we read that a study indicates that 62 very wealthy people in the world have as many financial assets as 3.8 billion poor people. We know, we see, immediately, we intuit this is wrong. It is an example of deep injustice. Inequality is not the problem. Exaggerated *gross* inequality is the unethical problem. However most of our learning is a result of reflection and requires time and effort to understand the meanings in life that we seek. Jesus, in the fullness of His humanity, is, I think, more intuitive than we are. Two examples come to mind: In Luke's gospel, on a trip to Jerusalem for Passover, the twelve year old Jesus remains behind and His parents don't immediately realize that He is not traveling back home with them. In a panic, they search for Him and find Him, after three days, in the temple conversing with the priests and scribes. Reasonably they are worried and question why He is here. His answer: "Did you not know that I must be busy with My Father's affairs." Even, in His youth, He grew to know, to see, to realize that He must be about His Father's work. (Lk 2:41-52) A second example is when, through His terrible pain and suffering on the cross, He asks His Father to forgive those who were crucifying Him because they do not realize what they are doing. He never reflected upon why they were doing this. He saw, He knew that they, that we, did not understand the terrible deed we were (and are) doing to Our Lord and Savior. The Sanhedrin debated that Jesus did not follow all of the 613 legal refinements of the Mosaic Law; so He's breaking the Law. For the unquestioning soldiers, orders are orders, and their orders were to crucify Jesus. His faithful followers were afraid that if they tried to defend their Teacher, they would suffer the same fate. Only Jesus realized that the suffering and death on the Cross was an act of unselfish love which would manifest the glory of God and ensure the salvation of mankind.

When we look at the post-Resurrection appearances in the gospel accounts, it is not clear exactly when Jesus ascended to the Father or even how often He ascended and then descended to be with His disciples. In the opening paragraph of the Acts of the Apostles, Luke writes, "He (Jesus) continued to appear to them and tell them (the apostles) about the Kingdom of God..." The Kingdom of God, or the reign of God, is here and now, although not yet completed. He knows that the disciples need time to reflect, to understand and to more fully appreciate what it means for them to be witnesses to the Kingdom of God on earth. The time that Jesus spent with the disciples after His resurrection was to prepare them to serve as He has served, to love one another as He has loved them. He was preparing them throughout His public ministry, but they hadn't understood what they were being called to do. This is why the crucifixion devastated them. Now they are reflecting upon their own vocations, their own calling and their own ministry. They learned the same way that we do: understanding, choice and action.

I mentioned in the last chapter that I would love to have heard what the apostles said when they realized the significance of the Transfiguration (p 160ff). Well, in one of his letters, Peter writes, "...It was not by way of cleverly concocted myths that we taught you about the coming in power of our Lord Jesus Christ for we were eyewitnesses of his sovereign majesty. He received glory and praise from God the Father when that unique declaration came to him out of the majestic splendor: 'This is my beloved Son, on whom my favor rests.' We ourselves heard this said from heaven while we were in his company on the holy mountain...." (2 Peter 1:16-18). Peter had come to understand the significance of the Transfiguration scene as a sign of hope which Jesus gave His apostles knowing that the journey to Jerusalem would bring Him to the cross. The glorified Jesus at the Transfiguration would foreshadow the glorified Christ of the Resurrection.

Referring back to the disciples on the road to Emmaus, the stranger, Jesus, interpreted the Old Testament scripture for them. It had to be understood differently because the people of God would not have made the connection between the Messiah, the anointed one, the bearer of hope and promise to His chosen people and the crucified Christ. The Messiah would come from the house of David and David, the anointed one (2Samuel 19:21-22) was the King of Israel. The Messiah was, by most people, expected to come as an anointed powerful king. Jesus rules from the Cross, not from the throne. Very few people, if any, would have identified the Messiah with the Suffering Servant from the book of the prophet, Deutero-Isaiah. They would have had difficulty seeing in the four suffering servant passages, the regal majesty of the Messianic King. But then, one of the major prophetic themes is: God's ways are not man's ways. Lucky us!

Did the Emmaus stranger interpret the meaning of the prophet Hosea when he said, "For I desire steadfast love and not sacrifice, the knowledge of God, rather than burnt offerings." (Ho 6:6). It is not the sacrificial offerings of animals or the first fruits of the harvest that God expects but rather to keep the covenant with Him by how we act towards ourselves and others. It is the Creating God Who guides the people of Israel, not the ceremonial practices or simply ritualistic expressions. They have a place in life and it is to remind us, and encourage us to "love one another." Love is an interpersonal relationship, not compliance with a set of laws. Laws can and should be valid as a means to an end (depending on the purpose of the laws) but are never ends in themselves. "To love another person is to see the face of God." The words from

"Les Miserables" are timeless, spanning the Old and New Testaments. Those fleeing disciples certainly found new meaning in the words of the stranger, Jesus, because they recognized Him in the breaking of the bread and returned to Jerusalem to do His will.

Besides the "recognition appearances" in the post-Resurrection accounts, there are also "commissioning accounts" in which Jesus calls the disciples to follow Him by continuing the ministry He began. In the last chapter of John's gospel, the disciples decide to go fishing. Throughout the night, they catch nothing. Come morning Jesus appears, tells them what to do and their nets are filled. The importance of this appearance is that He calls them to be "fishers of men" with a particular focus on Peter. Three times He asks Peter if he loves Him. Three times Peter responds insisting that since Jesus knows everything He knows that Peter's love has overcome his betrayal just as Jesus' crucifixion has overcome even death. In answering each of Peter's affirmative responses, Jesus simply says "Feed my sheep." There are no specific or detailed comments on what to do, simply "Love." I learned how to direct senior high school retreats by assisting and with the guidance of Father Jim Dineen S.J., who was both a chaplain and a teacher. He showed how this Johannine "call of the apostles" was an important exercise which we conducted towards the end of the Xavier High School senior retreat. Each young man would be asked by name if he would "feed" Jesus' sheep who included someone in their family or among their acquaintances, with whom they had either positive or negative relationships. It was a concrete and personal challenge to them, just as Jesus had challenged the disciples by the Sea of Tiberius. John ends his gospel with "There were many other things that Jesus did; if all were written down, the world itself, I suppose, would not hold all the books that would have to be written." (Jn 21:25) The time between the Resurrection and the Ascension was a time for the disciples to reflect on their individual callings to glorify God by how they lived their lives.

The end of Matthew's gospel is a particular favorite of mine because it contains all the themes found in the gospel concluding with the most important theme [-] we are never alone. He is always with us. To me, this is the most significant of the commissioning appearances of Jesus. "Meanwhile the eleven disciples set out for Galilee, to the mountain where Jesus had arranged to meet them. When they saw Him they fell before Him, though some hesitated. Jesus spoke to them: 'All *authority* in heaven and on earth has been given to Me. *Go*, therefore and *make disciples* of all the nations; *baptize* them in the name of the Father and of the Son and of the Holy Spirit, and *teach* them to observe *all* the commands I have given you. And *know* that *I am with you* always; yes, even to the *end of time.*" (Mt 28:16-20)

He commissions them to continue His ministry which comes from the Father, the author of all love. Jesus proclaims the love of the Father for everyone and tells the disciples how to share this love. Go out to everyone... baptize... teach...and don't worry, I will always be with you. You are never alone. The message is no different today. Then Jesus ascended into heaven and they returned to Jerusalem, not to hide, but to prepare to receive guidance about what to do next.

True to His promise, Jesus sent the Holy Spirit to give birth to the Church. Pentecost is the birthday of the Church and to celebrate this birthday, the apostles were true to their promise and they began the mission of bringing the "Good News" to the world. And the "Good News" is: *God loves us so much the He became like us...He shares life with us...He gives all He is – Himself on the Cross...so that we might be with Him now and forever!*

Saint Iranaeus was a bishop of Lyons, France who died around 202. He was a theologian who preached against a form of Gnosticism which basically posited two infinite sources for life. One was evil and one was good, one was material and one was spiritual. They fought for man's soul and so the human condition was viewed not as a covenantal relationship, but as a fierce struggle between opposing "divine" forces. Iranaeus knew Saint Polycarp who had known, so tradition tells us, the Beloved Apostle, John. I believe there is a connection between the belief and teachings of Iranaeus and Johannine tradition in the Catholic Church.

Iranaeus wrote: *The glory of God is man fully alive.* The truth of this statement is rooted in the "farewell address" of Jesus in the Johannine account of the Good News:

"As you, Father, have sent me into the world, I have sent them into the world, and for their sake I consecrate myself so that they too

293

may be consecrated in truth. I pray not only for these but for those [meaning us] also who through their words will believe in me. May they all be one, Father. May they be one in us, as you are in me and I am in you, so that the world may believe it was you who sent me. I have given them the glory you gave to me, that they may be one as we are one. With me in them and you in me, may they be so completely one so that the world will realize that it was you who sent me, and that I have loved them as much as you have loved me..." (Jn 17:18-23) Chapter Seventeen is often referred to as the Johannine version of Our Lord's *Our Father* prayer.

I began this chapter with a question: *if love is associated with joy, with happiness, with friendship, then how can sorrow, or hurt, or pain or suffering be related to love?* My answer is: *Love is an end-in-itself, a goal, a purpose, a fulfillment, because Love is shared...by the Lover and the One(s) Loved. Sorrow, or hurt, or pain, or suffering, are among the means to an end or purpose in life. They are not the only means to love.* Jesus did not have to die on the Cross. He chose the Cross as the means to our liberation from sin, our exodus from our failure to love as we could and ought. In Chapter Three, I wrote "The Book of Job reminds us that suffering in life is not punishment, but it will take the Crucifixion to help us to realize that suffering, while not joyful as an experience, can become an act of love and then, maybe, we will realize the significance of our creation, of our covenant... suffering could be a redeeming element..."

When we *joyfully* act with the knowledge that God is always present to us [-] and acknowledge that the *sorrow* of the Cross, which we brought about through our refusal, at times, to love, is not the end of the story [-] then we can begin to experience the *glory* of God which includes His creative covenant love, His original invitation to become the caretakers of His creation. We are never alone. He walked with His disciples on the journey to Jerusalem and He walked alone, for us, on the way to Calvary's hill. He walked with His Emmaus disciples and He walks with us today in our hurts and in our happiness. If we are able to love those with whom we walk through life, then we will always be able to see the "face of God." His final call will be for us to join Him at the banquet table of the Father and the glory of God will be ours forever!

I would like to end this book with some great borrowed advice. The advice was originally given by Mary at the wedding feast at Cana. Speaking of her Son, Jesus, to the servants, and I believe speaking to us as our heavenly Mother, she says: (Jn 2:5)

Do whatever He tells you!

POSTSCRIPT

Without life there is no activity. Without purpose there is no caring. Without Christmas there is a lesser appreciation of the significance of creation and the covenant experience. Without the Cross, there would be a lesser appreciation of how completely and unconditionally the creating God loves his creation, especially the caretakers He calls to be "wounded healers of the wounded."

Unless we come to appreciate the gift of our humanity, we will be unable to share and to care and if that becomes **the** universal condition, then we will have failed to hear the cry of the poor and refused to bear the responsibility that we are our sisters' and brothers' keepers.

Let us try to appreciate the significance not only of our own, but of all humanity, by remembering God's care, concern and compassion through

Creation – the universal and generously bestowed gift of life

Covenant – the gift of purpose, of caring for God's creation through the intimacy of friendship...through accepting, being benevolent, and committing Himself to us unconditionally

Christmas – the enhancing of the significance of our humanity through God's embracing *our* humanity

Crucifixion – the unconditional outpouring of God's love in sharing our life's journey now; so that we may participate in the glory of the Father's banquet table for all eternity

Printed in the United States
By Bookmasters